Next!

ALSO BY JOANNE LIPMAN

That's What She Said
Strings Attached

Next!

The POWER of REINVENTION in LIFE and WORK

JOANNE LIPMAN

MARINER BOOKS

New York   Boston

HarperCollins books may be purchased for educational, business, or sales promotional use. For information, please email the Special Markets Department at SPsales@harpercollins.com.

FIRST EDITION

Designed by Angie Boutin

Library of Congress Cataloging-in-Publication Data has been applied for.

ISBN 978-0-06-307348-7

22 23 24 25 26 LBC 5 4 3 2 1

With love, for Tom, Andrew, Rebecca, and Sam

Contents

Next!

THE REINVENTION ROAD MAP

Introduction:
Getting There from Here

The Stages of Reinvention

Years ago, as a newly minted *Wall Street Journal* reporter, I covered the advertising business. Every workday I would report on which ad campaigns were hits and which were flops, who was getting hired and who had been fired, and what major advertising accounts might be moving from one ad agency to another.

Which is how, way too early one morning, I found myself heading to a midtown Manhattan office building to see the guy who penned that indelible line, "I'm a Toys 'R' Us kid." He was an executive at the big ad agency J. Walter Thompson, responsible for many of its showcase accounts. He had put his stamp on Eastman Kodak's heartstrings-pulling commercials inviting us to "Picture a brand-new world." He was the man behind the burger wars battle cry, "Aren't you hungry for Burger King now?"

I stumbled into his office bleary-eyed, grumbling to myself about the early hour. The executive—soft spoken, laconic, and a bit rumpled himself—patiently endured my apologies as he waved me to a seat across from his desk. He'd been up for hours already himself, he said. In fact, before he arrived at the office he had put in almost a full day's work at home, starting before dawn. Not because he was finessing an ad campaign or typing up memos for the office. Instead, he was writing a novel.

The ad executive's real passion, it turned out, was writing fiction. Like so many of us, he harbored fantasies about another kind of life. Sure, he was a successful professional, admired in his field. He didn't have financial worries. He had already invested decades of his life in his advertising career. He was well into middle age.

Yet he had an itch that wasn't scratched by his job. He wanted to create novels, not ad copy. He squeezed in writing whenever he had a spare moment. Late at night, early in the morning, on plane flights or during lunch breaks at his desk, you'd find him scribbling his ideas and sketching out plot lines longhand, in pencil, on a yellow legal pad. In fact, he'd just gotten a novel published, he told me. Reaching across his desk, he handed me the freshly printed hardcover. I smiled politely and stashed the book in my bag. Then I got down to the business of the day, pen and reporter's notebook in hand, quizzing him on the fast-food wars.

A few weeks later, squeezed into the middle airplane seat during a business trip, I fished his book out of my bag. The novel was about evildoers scheming to blow up Wall Street. I don't recall the details, but a *Kirkus* magazine review summed up the book this way: "Abysmally dumb terrorist novel whose plot would embarrass a Superman movie. . . . Deserves drowning."

Yikes. *Good thing this guy has a day job.*

Which is why I was more than a little surprised, a few years later, when a familiar face popped up on a local television commercial. Against a plain background, there was the ad man, looking straight into the camera, holding a copy of his latest work.

"I'm James Patterson," he began.

You know the rest. James Patterson is America's single most commercially successful author. He's written or cowritten over 250 books that have sold more than 400 million copies, most famously mysteries starring his detective Alex Cross. More than

250 of his books have been *New York Times* best-sellers—including a rewritten and rereleased version of the one he gave me, with its title changed from the original *Black Market* to what is now known as *Black Friday*. He holds the Guinness world record for the most number-one titles by a single author. Multiple Patterson books have been turned into movies. His net worth is estimated by *Forbes* to be more than $800 million, making him the wealthiest author in America and second worldwide only to Harry Potter creator J. K. Rowling.

The onetime ad executive had proved the naysayers and doubters wrong. He had busted out of the confines of his old life into a new, stratospherically successful one, like some kind of scribbler superhero. "The Henry Ford of Books," *Vanity Fair* dubbed him, describing Patterson as "the advertising Mad Man turned impresario of the global thriller industry." And beyond that commercial success was something more profound: he had fulfilled the dream he spoke to me about so many years ago. He had reimagined his own future and built the life for himself that he had long hoped for.

How had he done it? How had he defied the odds to reinvent himself? And is there anything the rest of us can learn from his metamorphosis?

Three decades after that first meeting, I reached out to ask him.

WHEN YOU WERE a kid, what did you want to be when you grew up? I was going to be a spy. Starting at age seven, I carried around a black-and-white-marbled composition notebook, just like the heroine of my favorite book, *Harriet the Spy*, jotting down overheard conversations at school and secretly listening in on my big sister's phone calls with her boyfriend. After I read *Little Women*, I decided I would still be a spy, but I was also going to be a novelist like Louisa May Alcott. Then I read a delightfully gory book called

The Bog People, about the discovery of pickled Iron Age corpses in a Danish bog, and added archaeologist to my multi-hyphenate future.

I ended up, of course, being none of those things. But like me, most kids easily envision all sorts of different paths for themselves. They have no trouble flitting from dreams of rock stardom to fantasies of curing cancer. Nor does it bother them when they give up a future identity; they simply try on a new one. In a 2020 survey, when more than two thousand adults were asked what they had wanted to be as children, the most popular answer was professional athlete; other top picks were astronaut and actor. In reality, almost 80 percent of them landed in different careers than the ones they'd envisioned. (That's hardly surprising, given that, for instance, only three out of every ten thousand boys who play high school basketball will ever make it to the NBA.)

Kids easily cycle through different ideas of who they want to be. They discard and try on new identities with ease. Their envisioning of future possible selves isn't just about careers. They don't just imagine what they want to *be* when they grow up, what careers they might want, like firefighter or ballerina. They invent and discard fantasies of all the things they want to *do* and how they plan to live. When I was in grade school, on my bulletin board in my childhood bedroom I tacked up a list of twenty things I wanted to accomplish before I turned twenty. That piece of lined notebook paper is lost to the dustbin of history, but I remember a few of my top choices. Bicycle across the country. Publish a best-selling novel. Canoe through the Canadian wilderness—never mind that the only time I'd been in a canoe was during two weeks of Girl Scout camp. (And no, I didn't accomplish any of those things either.)

But somehow, along the road to adulthood, we lose the power to reimagine different futures. In college we are steered toward a major. Then, if we're lucky, we get a job. Maybe we get married, have kids, settle down, buy a home. Pretty soon it seems as if our choices have narrowed. Job, career, where we live, what we do in our free time, how we take our coffee. Changing one element means upending the others. We've gotten accustomed to a certain way of life, or income level, or professional status. It's hard to switch gears. And before you know it, without realizing it, it seems impossible to really change. We've bet on the life we have, and it's too hard to think about the life we don't have. We have invested in our current path, and we double down instead of reevaluating. "We don't let go of anything important until we have exhausted all the possible ways that we might keep holding on to it," as William Bridges wrote in his book *The Way of Transition*.

For millions of us, that sense of complacency was shattered with the Covid-19 pandemic. The crisis jolted us out of our routines and sparked a collective reckoning, one exacerbated by economic uncertainty and political unrest. We reprioritized our lives and reordered how we envisioned the future. Businesses, blindsided by events, furiously attempted to pivot. Leaders were forced to rethink their roles and recalibrate their approaches. Today almost all of us are still struggling to adapt to this quickly changing reality. "People have suffered. They've been afraid. The ground on which they stand has shifted. Many have been reviewing their lives, thinking not only of 'what's important' or 'what makes me happy' but 'what was I designed to do?'" the columnist Peggy Noonan wrote in the *Wall Street Journal* early on in the pandemic, sharing a sentiment that continues to resonate.

The pandemic changed society in many ways, but among the most consequential has been a rethinking of our relationship to our jobs. Millions quit the workforce in 2021 and 2022, and stunningly, surveys indicate that a third or more of them had no new job lined up to go to. We reevaluated how much time we want to spend at work, where and how we wanted to spend it, and our ideas about what constitutes a "good job" in the first place.

A record number of people didn't just look to switch jobs but to switch careers entirely. A 2021 Pew survey found that 66 percent of unemployed people at every income level—not just privileged high earners—seriously considered changing occupations. When Indeed, the employment site, surveyed job seekers in 2022, it found that fully 85 percent were looking for new careers outside of their industry.

It was almost unprecedented in modern history, a global reset. But in truth, even without a pandemic, almost everyone goes through this kind of reappraisal at least once in their life—and probably far more than once. The average person switches jobs a dozen times over the course of their working life. You might be fired or downsized out of a job; in my own field, journalism, 30,000 jobs have been wiped out and 2,500 US newspapers have closed amid financial challenges in the last few decades. Maybe you're no longer satisfied with your career choice and want to pivot to a new one; even before the pandemic—and before "quiet quitting" entered the lexicon—71 percent of millennials weren't engaged in their work, Gallup found. You may be facing a major personal crisis, like divorce or the death of a loved one. Or you could have been buffeted by external traumas: the pandemic, war, an accident, a natural disaster like a hurricane or earthquake.

Whatever the catalyst, it prompts in us the urgent need to pivot, to ask the question: What's next—and how do I get there?

That's a question I've been immersed in for most of my adult life. As a reporter, I covered transformations in business and society; as an editor-in-chief charged with reimagining news organizations in a digital age, I've helped lead them. As an author and advocate for gender equity, I've worked with organizations as they try to refashion their cultures. I've long been intrigued by the challenge of finding the "white space" of opportunity, where new ideas can flourish. There's no greater thrill than recognizing fresh opportunities that are right in front of your face, yet that others are too preoccupied to see. Ideas that, once you recognize them, spark that smack-the-forehead "aha!" moment. But while I've reported on, led, and lived through pivotal moments—both for better (like founding a new magazine) and for worse (seeing that magazine die)—I mostly did so by instinct, by feeling my way like a blind person. That's what most of us do. There was no guidebook to show the way.

THIS BOOK DRAWS on hundreds of personal interviews and academic research papers. It is divided into two parts. The first looks at the disparate ways in which we pivot, with chapters focused on career reinvention, gut feeling, aha moments, bouncing back from failure, trauma recovery, and navigating change when we have no choice. The second part dives into specific strategies for successful transformations, using case studies backed by the latest research. I end with a tool kit of practical steps culled from insights throughout the book. Each chapter is based in a central argument: that there is a path to meaningful change—whether wholesale reinvention or simply figuring out what comes next—if we understand the steps to take. We *can* change, for the better.

I began my reporting by seeking out people who had successfully reimagined their work or life, like Jim Patterson. They ranged from their 20s through their 90s, from a broad range of backgrounds. The types of transitions I investigated vary. Some were personal (finding purpose after a terror attack), others were professional (telephone repairman to shoe designer), and still others revived dying businesses or products. (Wait until you hear what Play-Doh and Viagra have in common.) I asked everyone I met to walk me through the process of how they reimagined what came next and then made it a reality. I've shared their wisdom here, both the strategies that worked and the pitfalls to avoid.

Then I spoke with scientists and researchers who study transformation in all its forms. This book builds on new insights in neuroscience, social psychology, cognitive science, management theory, and data science. Recent research across these fields is broadening our understanding of the mechanism of change and how to best navigate it. Advances in technology have allowed scientists to literally peer into our brains to better understand how we come up with creative new ideas and inspiration. Fields that didn't exist just a few decades ago—like post-traumatic growth among people who have survived unthinkable tragedies and yet emerged stronger—are shedding new light on some of the oldest human struggles in the world.

Through the people you'll meet and the scientists who study them, you will learn why some succeed in reinvention while others fall short. You'll find out how a stay-at-home mom used her parenting skills to transform herself into a CEO, and why sleep is the key to a famed comedian's success. You'll gain insights into how one man's "aha moment" in church led to a new multibillion-dollar business, and why a childhood memory helped an NBA player reinvent himself as a respected scholar and lawyer. You'll explore how a jazz musician transformed himself into a renowned economist, and how a Harvard-trained economist reinvented himself as a cattle farmer. Their journeys are instructive, as are the remarkable pivots of a machete attack victim who now helps her assailants' community and of a onetime fashion blogger who reemerged as an influential backer of Black-led tech start-ups. You will discover as well what separates a Blockbuster Video that fades into oblivion from a Netflix that, despite missteps, pivots and lives on.

If you're thinking of switching careers, this book is for you. If your business is at a crossroads, you'll find guidance here. If you're considering picking up a passion you dropped years ago, or want to pursue a more fulfilling opportunity, or are simply facing one of life's everyday changes—a new location, a new relationship, a way forward after a setback—you'll meet others who have successfully led the way. Whether it's today or years from now, all of us inevitably face these kinds of turning points in life, often more than once. Many of us are looking for meaningful change, seeking what's next, and yet we aren't always sure how to get there. But as you'll see, there are ways to navigate these transitions with less stress and more agency.

CURIOUSLY, AS I delved into these disparate types of transformations, I found that almost every pivot follows a similar pattern, one that can be broken down into specific steps. Scientists across multiple specialties use different nomenclature and sometimes break down the progression into a different number of stages. But essentially they are studying the same phenomenon from different angles—and coming up with almost identical conclusions. Yet these specialists don't talk to one another. They're in siloed university departments; they attend different conferences; they travel in different social circles. By pulling together their findings, backed by real-life examples, I hope to present a more holistic view here not just of how transitions work but of how to make them more successfully in our own lives.

Broadly speaking, each kind of pivot begins with a *search* to gather information. People who are switching careers, for example, may start to gravitate, sometimes without even realizing it, toward a new field. Next comes an uncomfortable, sometimes miserable, middle period of *struggle*; for career changers, this is when they have neither moved to a new role yet nor fully left their old one behind. Often taking a break—whether when you choose to *stop* or a break is forced on you—allows ideas to coalesce. Only then do you come out the other side with the *solution*, completing the transition. Taken together, these steps comprise what we might call a Reinvention Roadmap:

Search $\rightarrow$ Struggle $\rightarrow$ Stop $\rightarrow$ Solution

The process, to be sure, isn't carved in stone. A particular stage may last hours . . . or it may linger for years. You may go through the steps in a different order, or more than once. In some cases, the struggle is the catalyst rather than the search, such as for those shaken by tragedy or thrown for a sudden loop when unexpectedly fired. You may breeze through one stage only to be thrown back to repeat another one.

That said, once you become familiar with the sequence, you will recognize it in your own life—and beyond. In my interviews with scores of people who have led or experienced reinventions and in academic studies across multiple and very different disciplines, the progression remains remarkably similar. Only the terminology changes.

Career change gurus, for example, refer to the struggle phase as a "liminal" period when, as London Business School professor Herminia Ibarra says, you're "existing betwixt and between a past that is clearly gone and a future that is still uncertain." Scientists who study creativity have dubbed this the "incubation period." It's what happens when you're stumped by a problem and give up in frustration, then wake up in the middle of the night suddenly knowing the solution. For trauma survivors, meanwhile, it's the "period of struggle" that precedes personal growth after enduring war, natural disaster, violence, or disease.

Perhaps it's human nature, but we have an unfortunate tendency to focus on just the first and last steps of the pivoting process, going from search to solution. Career reinventions, for example, seem to happen overnight. Singer John Legend goes from management consultant to music superstar. *Boom.* Sara Blakely from fax saleswoman to millionaire Spanx founder. Harrison Ford from carpenter to movie star. Vera Wang from figure skater to bridal designer. Julia Child from World War II intelligence official to cooking doyenne.

Unfortunately, this kind of myth-making just makes transformations of any kind seem unattainable for us mere mortals. What's worse, the stories we tell focus on exactly the wrong things. Transitioning to a new career is not a magic metamorphosis from ugly duckling to swan. Nor can companies and organizations transform themselves with a snap of the fingers. I once worked with a company whose top executive announced a "transformation" and even named a "chief transformation officer," but he couldn't articulate what the firm was transforming to, or how to get there. He was endlessly annoyed at employees who kept questioning him, while the employees were endlessly frustrated with him. Expectations of instant transformation lead only to disappointment and disaster.

Instead, it's that middle step that is actually the most important: the struggle. It's a slog. For organizations, the struggle is focusing on the tedious *process* of getting from here to there, rather than just talking about some far-off endpoint, some great shining city on a hill. For individuals, the struggle is when you are banging your head against the wall, attempting to figure out a problem. It's when your brain hurts from thinking so hard. The struggle can be agonizing and almost unbearably frustrating. Nobody wants to go through it. Who wouldn't rather glide smoothly from one path to the next?

Too bad. The struggle isn't just necessary; in virtually every arena of transformation, it's the key to finding a solution.

Most of us, naturally enough, try to avoid unpleasantness of any sort. Nobody wants to be in distress. If you're feeling pain, isn't that a message that you should stop what you're doing? Yet recent research has found that, counterintuitively, seeking out that uncomfortable feeling can be not only productive but liberating.

When researchers asked a group of improv students at Chicago's famed Second City training center to "lean into discomfort" during a class exercise, the students took more risks and developed more skills than groups that were just told to do the exercise or to feel the exercise was working. Similarly, when study participants were asked to write about an emotional experience in their lives, those who were told that feeling uncomfortable while writing was a positive sign subsequently reported growing emotionally and developing new skills. "When people can positively spin otherwise negative cues—reappraise their discomfort as a sign of achievement—those cues become more motivating," wrote researcher Ayelet Fishbach, a professor at the University of Chicago's Booth School of Business.

Leaning into the struggle doesn't come naturally. But it is actually possible to convince yourself otherwise, to change your attitude. Social scientists Shawn Achor, Peter Salovey, and Alia Crum were called in to banking giant UBS at a particularly perilous time, when the organization was going through the twin convulsions of a banking crisis and massive restructuring. The researchers asked one group of managers to watch videos that showed stress as a debilitating condition that would hurt their performance. Another group watched videos showing that stress would actually strengthen their brains and bodies. Six weeks later, the latter group still viewed stress as a positive enhancement. What's more, they also reported a decrease in health problems and an increase in work satisfaction.

WHILE THE SCIENCE on all of this is relatively new, the sequence of steps has echoed throughout history. In literature, the progression is evident in Joseph Campbell's "hero's journey," as familiar from Shakespeare as it is from *Star Wars*. In Campbell's taxonomy, the hero leaves the ordinary world (the search); he encounters "a succession of trials" (the struggle) and is tempted to give up (the stop); and ultimately he returns in triumph (the solution). In anthropology, it's Arnold van Gennep's 1909 classic *The Rites of Passage*, in which he describes a "liminal" or transitional period (the struggle), when a person moves on from one phase of life (the search) but hasn't yet arrived at another (the solution).

In religion, Moses and the Jews wander the desert for forty years before arriving in the "promised land." Jesus wanders the desert for forty days. The Hindus have forest dwelling, Buddhists have meditation, and Muslims have Muhammed and the mountain. In folktales, "Sleeping Beauty" slumbers for one hundred years before her prince awakens her with a kiss. Little Red Riding Hood and Hansel and Gretel venture into the forest.

The importance of the struggle surfaces in contemporary works like Katherine May's *Wintering*, which she defines as "a fallow period in life when you're cut off from the world, feeling rejected, sidelined, blocked from progress, or cast into the role of an outsider." In his 2020 book *Life Is in the Transitions*, Bruce Feiler refers to this period as the "messy middle" that leads to a "new beginning." Brené Brown, in *Rising Strong*, calls it a "middle space of struggle" when you're "in the dark."

In a sense, the Covid-19 pandemic gave us all the dubious gift of a period of struggle. Consider the words that have been used to describe this era: "lost," "fallow," "limbo." We've had an epidemic of "burnout." It's "depleting," "relentless," and "messy." "It's OK to Feel Overwhelmed and Be Unproductive," *Psychology Today* assured its readers. "You're Not Lazy: Why It's Hard to Be Productive Right Now," read a CNET headline.

But if we're struggling, perhaps there's a way through and

beyond—maybe we can get to a breakthrough solution. To get to the other side, we need to embrace the struggle.

TO UNDERSTAND HOW the stages of reinvention play out, imagine for a moment that you want to switch careers. Let's say that your current job is repairing telephones. But your real dream is to be a shoe designer. Can you really get from here to there?

Recall the progression: *search→struggle→stop→solution*. The first step, the search, would suggest that you start by examining other people's shoes, studying how they're constructed, immersing yourself in the latest styles in *Vogue* magazine. In this stage, you better hang on to your day job, but perhaps you'll start sketching your own designs at home.

In fact, that's exactly what a Massachusetts telephone repairman named Chris Donovan did. Chris is a big, burly guy, with a thick Boston accent and a full gray beard. He had joined the phone company young, after stints as a bartender and a waiter, because it was a steady job. That's what his working-class parents had always stressed was most important. Finding passion in a career "wasn't the point," he told me. "It was all about finding security . . . it doesn't have anything to do with happiness." Chris took their lesson to heart: he repaired, installed, and maintained phones for the next twenty-five years.

For all of that time, though, Chris had a hobby he didn't share with anyone else. It started in high school, when a classmate showed up in impossibly high platform sandals that looked "like a piece of artwork on her foot." He began sketching women's shoes in meticulous detail, with illustrations that looked more like architectural plans than designs for practical footwear. After some kids at his Catholic school caught sight of his drawings and teased him, he hid them, first from his classmates and the nuns, and ultimately from everybody else. Yet he kept on drawing through his school years and during his decades on the job. "I drew on everything. On the back of envelopes, on napkins, on all my work orders at work," he said. At the phone company, "I had a desk drawer full of shoe drawings and *Vogue* magazines. The pole-climbing guys would come in for coffee breaks, and they'd be reading them! But they never said anything."

He never imagined he could make a living from his hobby: "Even I didn't consider it. It didn't seem like a possible career." But he began rethinking that assumption when he was already pushing forty, when he met his husband Steve. "On our first date, we were sitting at a restaurant, and I was sketching on the back of a napkin. He was like, 'That was really weird . . . but cool.'" Cautiously, Chris began opening up to Steve, sharing his notebooks and the twenty years' worth of sketches that he had shown to no one else. "The more we hung out together, the more he said, 'You really should do something with this. This is a lot more than a hobby for you.'"

Yet Chris stayed put at the phone company. It was what he knew, versus the black hole of what he wanted. He was in that liminal struggle phase, entertaining fantasies of a new career while firmly enmeshed in the old one. It was painful; he remembers a dinner with friends while vacationing on Cape Cod: "There was a store designer in Tokyo, an artist from Germany. I left really depressed. I said to Steve, 'They're all doing amazing things. I know I've got it in me. I know it's there.'" Ultimately, he signed up for continuing education courses at the Rhode Island School of Design, dipping his toes a bit deeper into the design waters.

Still, he hung on to his day job. Then, at age fifty, Chris got the break nobody asks for, the stop phase common to transitions: he was diagnosed with prostate cancer. The disease was successfully treated, but it was a wake-up call. That was when it struck him. He needed to quit the phone company. He needed to fulfill his destiny, to be a shoe designer. It was terrifying. "But when I started thinking about it, if I wound up on my deathbed thinking about 'what ifs,' it would be this massive regret for not exploring this. . . . This is what I'm here for. I didn't want to pass it up."

Chris took early retirement from the phone company. Steve volunteered the cash they'd been saving up for a new kitchen. Then, at fifty-four years old, Chris traveled to Florence, passed through the grand gates of the historic Villa Favard overlooking the Arno River, and took his place amid its frescoes and chandeliers as the oldest student by far at the Polimoda fashion school.

The adjustment wasn't easy. "This is awful. You're not fashion," one of his teachers told Chris early on after he turned in a disastrous assignment. "Look around. You see all the twenty-year-olds? *They're* fashion." Then the teacher asked what his job had been before he enrolled. When he explained that he'd been a phone repairman, it all clicked. "So you're crude," she said. "Do crude. Don't lose that." Chris ended up graduating at the top of his class.

But back home after graduation, his stellar grades didn't help. He made the rounds at leather manufacturers and handbag factories but couldn't even land a job interview. He was willing to intern for free, but nobody took him up on that either. No one wanted a middle-aged journeyman. With no prospects, he entered a long-shot contest for aspiring designers that he read about in AARP's magazine for retired people: the winner would have their work critiqued by *Project Runway*'s Tim Gunn. To his astonishment, he won. Television cameras trailed them in a bright white shoe salon as Gunn examined some of his fanciful high heels. "Have I seen this before? No!" Gunn exclaimed. "Does the world need this? Yes!"

That appearance sparked interest from potential customers and ultimately jump-started what would become Chris Donovan

Footwear. His distinctive designs look like miniature sculptures. Boots stand on bold geometric heels reminiscent of turned wood; delicate pumps evoke origami ornaments. In a nod to his roots, he has constructed shoe heels out of fiber-optic conduits. He scours salvage yards for inspiration; he has designed boots with heels made from discarded hip replacement parts and closures made with sutures. A recent collection was inspired by paper airplanes. "Anybody can find inspiration in a flower," he figures, "but what about construction and destruction that others don't find beautiful? I don't want you to see what they *are*, but what beauty you can *find* in things."

His story, to be sure, remains unfinished. He used his retirement funds to pay an Italian manufacturer for his collection, confident he would make back the money in sales from the stores interested in stocking his line. But with exquisitely bad timing, the collection launched just two months before the pandemic struck. Women retreated to bedroom slippers, not designer high heels. He has kept the business afloat by selling his shoes online and turning a spare bedroom into his design studio.

Still, he has no regrets. He has already designed his next collection; it's ready to go, as soon as it's practical to begin manufacturing again. "Even with all the obstacles, I still get to do shoes," he told me. "This is a part of me, and it's so exciting. I love it." And the junior designer is making his mark. *Boston* magazine took notice, naming him "Best Shoe Designer" in its 2020 "Best of Boston" issue. The "newest fashion superstar," as it described him, was sixty-one years old.

ON THE FACE of it, Jim Patterson has pretty much nothing in common with Chris Donovan. Yet as Patterson walked me through his career journey, there were surprising echoes of Donovan's story.

His career transition followed a similar trajectory. Experts who study transitions would find his journey familiar, perhaps even predictable.

Like Donovan, Patterson knew for years where he'd like to go but wasn't sure how to get there. His literary success didn't happen overnight; he wrote multiple books, including some flops, before he hit on his own, spectacularly marketable style. He wasn't always certain that he was on the right path. He had moments of doubt. He stayed at his ad agency for almost two decades after publishing his first book, even as he published almost a dozen more, thinking he just wasn't ready. The best-selling author of our time didn't quit his day job until he was almost fifty years old.

Born in Newburgh, New York, a fading Hudson River town surrounded by farmland, Patterson had an inauspicious start. His father scraped by driving a bread truck and then selling insurance door to door. When the family later moved to Massachusetts, young Jim earned extra cash working the overnight shift at the infamous McLean psychiatric hospital. Sometimes he would listen in as one of the patients, the not-yet-discovered singer James Taylor, performed in the coffee shop; occasionally he would watch as another patient, the poet Robert Lowell, gave recitations in his room, though "he could be a little pushy and violent."

But mostly he spent the long nights reading. He had no taste for thrillers or trashy novels. He never even picked up commercial fiction. Instead, he was drawn to serious literature, devouring James Joyce, Samuel Beckett, and Stanley Elkin. Soon he began dabbling in fiction writing himself. But he got precious little encouragement. At Manhattan College, where he enrolled on scholarship, a writing instructor told him in no uncertain terms to forget about it: "You write well enough, but stay away from fiction." *Ouch.* "At the beginning, I don't think I knew what I was doing," he told me.

After college he tried grad school for a year at Vanderbilt, but by then it was dawning on him that he "didn't want to write for that audience for serious fiction." Unfortunately, he wasn't trained to do much of anything else. He began reading more commercial books, like *The Day of the Jackal* and *The Exorcist*, and found them "pretty interesting . . . and that got me interested in the genre" of mysteries and thrillers. But how would he even think about writing popular books, the kind that were displayed in the front racks of Barnes & Noble and that made the *New York Times* best-seller lists? "I didn't know how to do mystery fiction, because I didn't read the stuff. I was a typical Vanderbilt literary snob."

Patterson ultimately landed in New York as a long-haired hippie without a job or prospects. He tried, unsuccessfully, to get hired as a cabbie, but "a guy who reminded me of Danny DeVito in 'Taxi' chased me out of his garage." He holed up in the dirt-cheap Washington Jefferson Hotel, at the time one of the city's seedier establishments, where the pendant-patterned wallpaper in his tiny high-ceilinged room was covered with ominous "X"s penned by some demented previous tenant. "My job was to get out of that room," he told me. Finally, a meeting with a friend of a friend landed him an entry-level copywriter post at J. Walter Thompson.

Patterson jumped at the job, even though "I had zero interest in advertising. I've never had any interest in advertising. I wanted to be a writer." But he needed a paycheck. He had watched his dad struggle financially for much of his life, and he listened as his father urged him to "protect, protect, be careful, be careful." The advertising job was a way to pay the bills. "Who the hell makes it as a novelist?"

He was a "shy, goofy guy" back then, he says. But he had a talent for creating ads that stuck with people. Working with the agency's showcase clients, he learned to communicate with an audience. He imagined commercials as little stories, each with a camera angle to match the storytelling in his head. His work got noticed, and promotions followed. But while he was good at it, "I didn't love it," he says. If you had met him, you'd have seen a rising ad executive. When he looked in the mirror, he saw someone else entirely.

"Maybe I was delusional, but I never thought of myself as an advertising person," he told me. "I always planned to be a writer. I hoped to be a writer. It was always in my head."

IT TURNS OUT that Patterson's vision, imagining himself in a different role, was a key part of that first stage of the *search*. His vision was similar to how Chris Donovan imagined himself as a shoe designer while he spent his days repairing phones. That kind of visualization is a hallmark of people who successfully change careers.

In 1986, social psychologists Hazel Markus and Paula Nurius coined the phrase "possible selves" to describe how we envision our future: what we may become, or want to become, or even fear becoming. Some possible selves involve changing personalities, or being happier or more confident. Others may entail physical changes, like losing weight. But imagining possible selves can be especially revelatory for people who are rethinking their lives and careers. They try on different identities. They think about themselves in new roles, far afield from the ones they are in now. And like Patterson and Donovan, they imagine those futures well before they actually embark upon them.

If you're considering switching careers or reinventing your job, management experts have found that contemplating future possible selves is a key first step. Patterson, by thinking of himself as a writer "in my head," had the right idea. It's what can help take you from daydream to a reality. When you imagine different futures for yourself, it actually becomes easier to make major changes, researchers have found. Merely by conjuring possible selves, you're more likely to stay on track and focused, to plan effectively, and to notice potential opportunities. When psychologists ask people to write down their image of themselves in the future, the exercise helps them more clearly develop goals and plan the steps needed to get there. That in turn helps separate realistic goals from fantasies.

Almost all of us consider multiple possible selves throughout our lives. When Markus and Nurius interviewed college students, 2.2 percent described their current self as a media personality, yet the majority (56.1 percent) said they had considered a possible future self as a media personality. And while only 1.4 percent were business owners, a whopping 80.3 percent imagined that career for their future self.

London Business School's Ibarra has been studying career change for more than two decades, in good times and bad, including during the 2008 financial crisis and the Covid-19 pandemic. She believes that trying on possible selves is especially important during times of disruption. "Even in happier times, career change is never a perfectly linear process," she wrote during the pandemic. "It's a necessarily messy journey of exploration—and to do it right, you have to experiment with, test, and learn about a range of possible selves."

But thinking about possible selves isn't enough on its own. The key to this first step in career reinvention, in the *search* for information, is that it often entails taking *action*. Some people unconsciously move toward their new role without even realizing it. For others, exploring possible selves is a more intentional process, as when Chris Donovan signed up for design courses at night. "Try something small. Do something differently that's manageable," said Jocelyn Nicole Johnson, who was a Charlottesville, Virginia, public school art teacher for decades before publishing her lauded first book, *My Monticello*, and garnering a fawning *New York Times* profile—at age fifty. "But start. . . . You have to start somewhere."

This first step might involve dabbling in a new hobby, or collecting information to get a sense of what you might be interested in pursuing, or shadowing someone in a different profession. Or, as in Patterson's case, getting up at dawn to write fiction. Despite the endless hours he spent at work, he sat down to write every spare moment he could. During breaks from meetings, before or after work, on airplanes and in hotel rooms during business trips, he could be found sketching outlines for his stories. "It just cleared my mind. Any stress was gone. Doing fiction, I didn't feel I had to compete with the other people there," he recalled. "I had the ability to shut everything else out."

Patterson soon finished his first novel. Excited, he sent out the manuscript to thirty-two publishers. Almost immediately, thirty-one of them rejected it. But by some stroke of luck, the final one bit. *The Thomas Berryman Number*, about a Nashville newspaper reporter trying to find a killer, was published by Little, Brown in 1976, when Patterson wasn't yet thirty years old. Even better, it won the prestigious Edgar Award for best first novel from the Mystery Writers of America. He was off and running.

Careers, of course, rarely follow a straight line. And that was especially the case for Patterson. Despite the accolades, *Berryman* wasn't a big seller. Then the unimaginable happened: tragedy hit. His longtime girlfriend, Jane Blanchard, was diagnosed with a brain tumor. For more than two years, he cared for her, refusing to travel even for big clients like Burger King. She passed away in 1982. Devastated, he buried himself in his job. "Jane was the catalyst to throw myself into advertising," he told me. He began rising quickly through the ranks and ultimately would become CEO of J. Walter Thompson North America.

In time, he also began writing again, but he had trouble finding his voice. "*Berryman* had a lot of good sentences" is the way he put it to me, but "after that, I thought there were some not very good books." He kept going, though, and by the time I met him in the late 1980s the novel he handed me was the fifth he had published. By then, he had gained renown as an advertising executive. But as an author, he was still largely unknown. He hadn't yet found his groove.

HERE AGAIN, PATTERSON'S journey is a familiar one. As he moved inexorably toward his goal of becoming a novelist, he still hung on tight to his day job. He had entered the middle stage, that liminal, in-between period. To be sure, this didn't look like a *struggle* in the conventional sense. He was a successful ad executive, and his books were being published. He was essentially holding down two full-time jobs. Yet he wasn't ready to leave the safety of one for the uncertain future of the other. "I knew I wasn't good enough yet. I didn't have the guts to just leave and do it full-time," he told me. "So I took the easy way out, to do it on the side."

Over time, as he searched for his sweet spot as a writer, he studied highly commercial books to figure out what made them successful. "At a certain point . . . I became more serious about writing books that sell. What am I good at, and what am I not good at?" Instead of tackling big subjects on sprawling topics he knew little about—like Wall Street financial systems, in the book he gave me—he narrowed his focus to subjects that he could research and write about with some authority. When he had an idea for a book with a kidnapping plot, he interviewed FBI agents who had been involved with the famed Lindbergh baby kidnapping case. He befriended police officers and military veterans. He was never at a loss for ideas; the ad man had a creative brain that cranked out potential story lines nonstop. ("I'm pretty rapid-fire in terms of ideas. I could write a novel about this conversation. It's crazy," he said to me at one point.) He was a fast writer too. Typically, before he sat down to write, he would jot down a thirty- or forty-page outline, which he would then use as a guide to complete the manuscript.

Yet even as he began his eighth novel, he hadn't quite figured out his voice. As usual, he started with an outline. This time, though, he kept adding to it. He was using all of his new research, from the FBI and beyond, informed by his growing understanding of his own strengths as a storyteller. "I was going for broke," he said. Ultimately, the outline expanded to about 350 pages. That's when he had a revelation: "This *is* the book." Spare, stripped of unnecessary detail, he turned the outline into brief chapters that move the action forward propulsively. He had found his style.

"That's the big breakthrough," he told me. "That's where the short chapters and the colloquial style of writing came from. . . . Every chapter moves the plot and characterizations forward, and turns on the movie camera in my head." He called the new book *Along Came a Spider*, the first to introduce his fictional detective Alex Cross. Not only did it become a massive best-seller, but it launched a lucrative franchise. More books quickly followed.

And yet, astonishingly, he *still* stayed at the ad agency, where he by now had risen to lead the entire North American business. "I never really liked it," he says of advertising. "In theory, creating these little movies should have been fun. But it wasn't at Thompson, because so many of the clients didn't want to make good movies." At company board meetings, the minutes ticked away in excruciatingly slow motion, torturing him. "I'd look at my watch: 7:50. And I look at my watch: 8:05. I had no interest in this stuff. . . . It just didn't appeal. It was always just a job, other than once I got to the point where I could hire people I like." His colleagues were the one saving grace for Patterson. They were smart and interesting and fit his "no-assholes" philosophy.

By 1996, he had already published ten books, more than most full-time authors manage in a lifetime. Even more remarkable, he had multiple best-sellers under his belt, including *Kiss the Girls*, his second Alex Cross book. By this point, "I was already CEO of Thompson, but the books were making a lot more money." Somehow he still wasn't ready to leave, to take that final leap.

That's when the *stop* phase kicked in for him. Experts in reinvention—whether management gurus who study career transitions or neuroscientists who are expert in eureka insights—often talk about the importance of taking a break in order to allow insights to bubble up. For Chris Donovan, the stop was forced on him when he was diagnosed with cancer. That in turn led to his insight that it was time to give up phone repair and chase his dream of designing shoes. Patterson experienced an equally transformative break, though his was admittedly not quite as dramatically life-threatening: he was sitting in traffic.

It was a hot summer Sunday, and Patterson was at a standstill as he attempted to get to his office from his beach house in Mantoloking, New Jersey. He was stuck on the New Jersey Turnpike along with all the rest of the weekenders heading back to their workday lives. That's when it hit him: *Wait a minute, this is nuts.* He watched the cars on the other side whizzing past—the ones headed *toward* the beach, not away from it. *Whoosh. Whoosh.* "I'm in this traffic, I'm cursing, it's awful, this is hideous. And on the other side a car goes by, *whoosh*. Every fifteen seconds, *whoosh*." There was no traffic heading in the opposite direction. The Jersey shore was receding behind him, but shimmering ahead for those on the other side.

"After an hour and a half, I had that 'aha' moment," he told me. "It was my job to get on the other side of the road. I'm going the wrong way. I'm going into New York to do something I don't love to do. I need to be on the other side of the road. I'm going in the wrong direction."

That moment in the traffic, he says, he had a "weird break-through." It was when he knew the time had come.

After he got back to his office in Manhattan, Jim Patterson quit.

AS PATTERSON FINISHED telling me his tale, I marveled at his whole-sale transformation from that unassuming ad guy I first met de-cades ago. "Wow, that is the ultimate reinvention story," I said.

"Actually no," he responded, sounding puzzled. To him, there was nothing transformative about it. It felt like a continuum, not a reinvention at all. As far as he is concerned, he was always the same person. He was always a novelist, just one who earned a living for a few decades doing something else. The only rein-vention, as he sees it, was his evolution as a writer. "I continually try to challenge myself to do different things," he said, pointing out that he has written not just mysteries but also kids' books and nonfiction books. He parcels out his ideas to multiple cowriters, has coauthored tomes about figures ranging from John Lennon to Muhammad Ali to Jeffrey Epstein, and has paired up with celeb-rity collaborators, including Bill Clinton and Dolly Parton. "That was reinvention to me."

That's a common sentiment that I found among others who have successfully pivoted. They aren't trying to invent a new identity; they are instead seeking a fuller expression of who they already are. Like Patterson, most of those I met took their time, taking incremental steps, often over the course of years, without trying to make over their lives in one giant leap. And they typi-cally started taking those steps long before they even realized they were pivoting.

What's more, almost all of those I spoke with said they used their previous experience in their new life, regardless of how different it seemed on the face of it. Chris Donovan's shoe designs reference his telephone repairman past; he even uses some industrial parts in his work. He never forgot his design teacher's admonition ("You're crude . . . don't lose that") to be himself, not some imaginary version of a couture designer.

In a very different field, politician and activist Stacey Abrams has said she regularly calls on skills she learned in her earlier incarnation: writing steamy romance and mystery novels under the pen name Selena Montgomery. "Leadership requires the ability to engage and to create empathy for communities with disparate needs and ideas. Telling an effective story—especially in romantic suspense—demands a similar skill set," Abrams said. "Good romantic suspense can never underestimate the audience, and the best political leaders know how to shape a compelling narrative that respects voters and paints a picture of what is to come."

Previous experiences, however unsatisfying, can prove to be valuable, even if they ended in failure. Vera Wang was a competitive figure skater who just missed a spot on the Olympic team before becoming a fashion journalist and then, at age forty, transitioning to a career as a fashion designer. She went on to become renowned for her iconic wedding gowns. Figure skating, she said, "teaches you discipline. It gives you the joy of self-expression. There's speed; there's movement; and when you fall down, you pick yourself up and try again. It's a good metaphor for life."

Jim Patterson took especially full advantage of the skills he learned along the way from his advertising career. His breakout hit came after he began advertising *Along Came a Spider* on television—an unheard-of move in book publishing at the time— using a commercial he created (and paid for) himself. He is still intensively involved in every aspect of book marketing: covers, titles, typography, promotions. His career as an author, he says, is informed by years of creating ads: "The biggest thing I got from advertising is understanding the audience." As an ad man, he imagined commercials as "turn[ing] on a movie camera in my head." Now he does the same with his books. "That's the carryover from the advertising. That's what I try to do."

Patterson is still a font of ideas, just as he was when he was churning out ads for Burger King and Toys "R" Us. He is still always thinking about what's next. As we spoke, he was in his Florida home cooking up plans for his next round of books—he had about a dozen in the works, just for 2022. And as always, he was in the market for a new story. As we brought our conversation to a close, he turned one last question on me: "What is *your* next reinvention?"

1

Is It Time to Jump?

Knowing When to Trust Your Gut

The only real valuable thing is intuition.
—ALBERT EINSTEIN

As a kid, I was a serious musician. I practiced my viola for hours every day. My parents drove me from New Jersey into Manhattan on weekends to study with Juilliard teacher Paul Doktor, a renowned violist with a mellifluous Viennese accent who was one of the very few artists of our eccentric instrument—bigger than a violin, smaller than a cello, more awkward to play than either—to make a living as a soloist. As an adult, I stopped playing, but music remains an important part of my life. My first book was a music memoir, and I've occasionally written articles about world-class performers.

One of the musicians I came across had an especially interesting journey. In some ways, Alan reminded me of my son Andrew. Like my son, Alan grew up in Manhattan as a baseball fanatic and diehard Yankees fan who could recite every starting lineup and final score in a given game. Like my son, Alan was obsessive about box scores. He taught himself fractions by calculating batting averages—3-for-11 was .273, 7-for-22 was .318. And like me, Alan's mom—much to her son's embarrassment—showed off his uncanny ability by having him calculate big numbers in his head to entertain party guests. Both boys started music lessons after becoming inspired by a cousin who began studying an instrument first.

Unlike my son, though, Alan quickly became as obsessive about music as he was about baseball. He started clarinet lessons at age twelve and before long was practicing four, five, even six hours a day. He loved classical music but found that he was even more drawn to jazz. He was especially transfixed by recordings of some of the old jazz greats, like Benny Goodman. Soon he also took up tenor sax, so that he could learn how to play those bluesy jazz riffs too.

Alan's family wasn't wealthy; his divorced mom worked at a furniture store. At the big public high school he attended, he was a strong math student but did "just okay in courses that didn't interest me," he later recalled. He didn't have time to devote to schoolwork anyway, given all the hours he spent on music and baseball practice. In any case, as indifferent as he was as a student, he was a superb musician. In his teens, he was good enough to make a bit of money playing gigs on weekends. After he graduated, he enrolled at the prestigious Juilliard School, one of only a handful of clarinet students in the country chosen to study at the conservatory that has trained everyone from cellist Yo-Yo Ma and violinist Itzhak Perlman to jazz great Miles Davis.

At Juilliard, Alan set himself to studying piano and composition, in addition to clarinet. But he felt vaguely dissatisfied. Classical music, the focus of his classes, just didn't move him the way jazz did. And so, when his tenor sax teacher told him about an opening in a professional jazz ensemble, he jumped at the chance to audition. He was elated when he was accepted. "It was not quite like making the major leagues, more like AAA ball," as he put it later, combining references to both of his favorite pastimes, "but it was still a full-fledged professional job."

The group performed up and down the East Coast. Playing with fellow musicians was exhilarating. As any musician will tell you, there's a thrill, an almost physical sensation, when connecting with like-minded performers. "The experience of playing in a good band is utterly different from what you hear simply standing in front," as Alan put it. "Voices and overtones come to you from all directions; you feel the rhythm section in your bones; and all the people in the band dynamically interact."

As passionate as he was about performing with his fellow musicians, Alan had less in common with them when the music stopped. Not to put too fine a point on it, but he was the group's resident nerd. While his bandmates spent their off hours partying, he spent his preparing their tax returns. During performances, when the band took its union-mandated twenty-minute breaks, his colleagues would disappear into the greenroom to get high—while he stayed behind and read. He didn't care much for novels, but he devoured nonfiction. Given his affinity for math, perhaps it isn't surprising that he was transfixed by books about the stock market and biographies of financiers. Slowly, it dawned on Alan. "I started looking forward to the twenty minutes" of break time, he told me, "and I realized that I found that more interesting than music."

That's when Alan decided it was time to go back to school. As much as he loved music, he now envisioned a new career for himself—on Wall Street. He was ready to take a leap.

And so the professional musician gathered his courage, left the band, and enrolled in New York University, intending to study finance. The transition was uncomfortable. By this point, Alan had been out of high school for several years. "I was apprehensive about how I'd do," he said. Academia was foreign to him, while music was familiar. He bought his course books the summer before classes started to get a jump on his assignments, just in case. When he arrived on campus, he still kept a foot in the music world, performing with the school orchestra and singing in the glee club. His social life revolved around music. "People tend to do what they excel at because it enhances their self-esteem. So if you're particularly good at a certain thing, you spend an awful lot of time at it, and it's self-reinforcing," he told me. Music was his strength, the thing he spent his time on.

Alan still wasn't sure he was on the right path. Plenty of other students were interested in Wall Street, and they were singularly focused, with the courses, grades, and experience to vie for those coveted posts. Who was he to think he could join them? "I wasn't confident that I would succeed in finance," he conceded.

DID ALAN MAKE the right choice by turning his life upside down and heading down an unknown road? When I speak with people who are thinking of changing course, switching careers, or otherwise upending their lives, it's the number-one dilemma I hear. You may feel in your gut that making the change is the right thing to do. But how do you know if you're making the right choice, and if so, whether now is the right time to jump?

Perhaps the most difficult step in any transition is the first one: deciding whether to make a major pivot at all. Even if we want to switch gears—because our skills have become outdated, or our lives are no longer fulfilling, or we've lost a job—there are powerful cultural forces arrayed on all sides to stifle us. Reinvention seems impossibly daunting. Books and magazine articles are full of muscular advice about what it takes to blow up old ways and master new ones. It often seems like it's just for the swaggering, bold few, those who dare to lead. Self-help guru Tony Robbins commands his followers to "destroy" their fear, berates them for being "weak," and at least one time insisted that an audience member roar like a lion to show strength. We need "to take on the status quo with reckless abandon," as Josh Linkner puts it in his book *The Road to Reinvention*.

Yet few if any of the people I've met in the course of reporting this book hew to that swashbuckling stereotype. Alan certainly didn't. That kind of macho flame-throwing isn't available to most of us anyway. The rules are different for men who don't fit the alpha-male machismo mold, and even more so for women and people of color. Researchers have found that those groups tend to be penalized if they step out of line.

Meaningful change seems out of reach, and so we shrink away from it. "Power through." "Suck it up." "Move on." "Get back on track." We've all said it at one time or another, probably to ourselves. To an extent it's human nature. When everything around us is in flux, our instinct is to look for solid ground, not for new shores. We scramble for certainty. Whether we intend to or not, we've internalized that we are supposed to snap out of it and get back to what we were doing, to keep moving straight ahead, without veering.

And yet if we cling to what *is*, as opposed to opening ourselves up to what *could be*, we stifle creativity, innovation, and fulfillment. Australian palliative care nurse Bronnie Ware spent years caring for people in the last weeks of their lives, and she collected their final thoughts in her book *The Top Five Regrets of the Dying*. The most frequent regret that her elderly patients shared: "I wish I'd had the courage to live a life true to myself, not the life others expected of me."

THE KIND OF transformation that Alan was contemplating is confusing at best, and at worst it can be terrifying. For those who already have a stable job or lifestyle, as he did, there's an enormous risk in giving it all up for the unknown. It's like a looming black hole, with no way to see to the other side. The upside shimmers distantly in the future; the downside might swallow you whole at any moment.

It's even worse for those without a backstop. Perhaps you've been fired or downsized, or your employer has gone out of business.

Or you've been dealt a sudden personal blow—a death in the family or a divorce. Perhaps family circumstances have changed and you need more flexibility, or you've moved to a new location where your skills don't transfer. Maybe, like millions during the Covid-19 pandemic, you've simply become burned out and need to quit. For those who don't have a safety net, or who don't have a choice, taking the leap is one of the most petrifying moves they can make.

As we've seen, people who make major transitions, whether in life or at work, often follow a similar trajectory. At the start, they *search*, collecting information as they think about possible futures. Then comes that uncomfortable middle period, the *struggle*, which may last moments or may stretch out for years. Often it requires them to *stop* and take a break, before they can get the clarity they need to come up with a *solution*.

But that begs the question: How do you even know if it's time to start? There are so many variables to consider, all with the potential to derail your transition. How can you judge the risks and rewards? Logically, it seems that when you're turning your life upside down, there should be a methodical way to calculate all of this. You should be able to weigh every factor carefully and rationally. It seems like there should be some sort of decision tree. Or an Excel spreadsheet. If ever there was a time to think things through slowly, with extra intentionality, now should be it.

Yet when I asked scores of people who had successfully navigated these waters, I was surprised by how many didn't mention any such thing. Instead, they talked about "gut feel." The pros and cons written on a piece of paper didn't compare to what they felt was the right decision. What's more, a surprising number of those who looked back on their pivots realized that they had begun transitioning long before they actually made the conscious decision to jump. They were reinventing themselves before they even realized it.

Frankly, it seemed nuts. It made no sense that they'd make a significant life change without scrutinizing the data. That's especially true now, when the quantity and quality of information at our fingertips is beyond anything our forebears could have imagined. Today more than ever, we have the capacity to get granular when it comes to weighing such a major decision. If you're making a personal move, you can google all you need to know about a new career, a new city, a new workplace, and more. Businesses are awash with information about their customers: how old they are, where they live, whether they're married or single, what brand of mayonnaise they buy. Digital platforms like Facebook and Google spit out thousands of data points about us; in many ways they know more about us than we know about ourselves.

But it turns out that too much information can actually end up sending us in the wrong direction. There's a reason why it's often easier to shop in a boutique, with a heavily edited selection of clothing, rather than in a department store with way too many choices. Rather than spinning yourself into a frenzy, sometimes you just have to forget all of the endless variables and listen to your gut.

Intriguingly, management experts have found that successful executives often intentionally block out much of the data flying at them and rely on intuition instead to make significant and even transformative decisions. When John R. Graham, a professor at Duke University's Fuqua School of Business, surveyed one thousand chief executive officers and chief financial officers, he found that almost half of them allocated spending based on "gut feel." They had plenty of other information and consulted traditional financial measures as well, but at the end of the day they relied on their intuition and on other nonfinancial factors—like the reputation of division managers—not simply on hard data, to decide how to allocate investments among divisions.

"In the textbook world, professors teach and students learn certain formulas on how to make investment decisions," Graham told me. "In reality, what is surprising is that they also use a lot of informal and/or simple decision rules."

It seems a dangerous game, especially at a time when Wall Street is breathing down the necks of top executives to improve financial results and company boards are demanding that CEOs meet precise metrics. Graham's findings puzzled me. I wanted to understand what was going on inside the heads of these CEOs, what motivated them to ignore data. So I reached out to Shabnam Mousavi, a fellow at Berlin's Max Planck Institute for Human Development, who studies such things. Why, I asked her, would executives rely on gut feeling?

"Because it works," she said flatly. "Deliberate ignorance of information has led to successful outcomes."

We all like to believe that we make rational decisions, and that we can weigh every imaginable risk factor before making a decision. In corporate life I've seen an insistence on it before a project is green-lit. I've spent hours putting together presentations that list every imaginable variable in order to convince higher-ups that a project that we *know* is right will deliver exactly the results that executives demand, on exactly the timetable they insist upon. But life is far more complex than that. Mousavi argues that simple rules of thumb can outperform complex algorithms because it's unrealistic to nail down every possible eventuality.

Academics cite the popular metaphor of a dog catching a Frisbee. Rover instinctively follows the flying disc with his eyes in order to position himself to catch it. If you watch carefully, you'll note that the pooch keeps his gaze at a steady angle on the airborne target as he runs. Nobody teaches a dog to do that. Rover doesn't need a class in physics in order to catch the Frisbee. It's easier, and certainly a lot quicker, than attempting to calculate trajectory, spin, wind speed, humidity, and every other factor involved while the Frisbee is aloft. *Not to mention, the dog can't do math.* By the same analogy, financial systems are so complicated that experts who attempt to analyze every factor to make predictions are doomed to get them wrong. The "calculations can provide illusory certainty," Mousavi and her colleague Gerd Gigerenzer wrote in a 2013 paper.

Yet most of us simply don't want to cop to the fact that we go by intuition. "Gut feel was suppressed forever because it was considered unscientific," Mousavi says. "People are hesitant to say they are using their gut feeling because historically, the idea of going by your gut feeling is inferior." So executives who use gut feeling for a decision may end up asking subordinates to come up with a rationale to justify it—or, in a move I've seen more than once, they resort to the smokescreen of hiring pricey consultants to recommend the path that they know they already plan to take.

PEOPLE WHO SUCCESSFULLY switch careers, or who make other major transitions, often cite the power of gut instinct. Consider Clea Shearer, who had no ready career prospects when she moved from Los Angeles to Nashville for her husband's new job. She was at a loss as to what to do with herself. She remembers thinking, *Okay, I'm a thirty-three-year-old woman in a brand-new city and know zero people. We moved our family here for my husband's career, but NOW WHAT??!* Clea had to reimagine her life. She just wasn't sure how.

Not long after, she met another recent Nashville transplant. Joanna Teplin, a film major with an artistic bent who had once created a line of greeting cards, had also moved from the West Coast with her family. Like Clea, she too needed to start over. Both young moms felt out of their element in their new city. Introduced by a mutual friend, they met for lunch one day . . . and four hours later had hatched a business partnership. "It was obvious from the minute we met that we would be starting a business together," they later wrote. It was pure "gut instinct."

By later that night, in between bathing their kids at their respective homes, they had solidified their plan to launch a home organizing company and come up with the name: The Home Edit. Within five years that brainstorm would balloon into a phenomenon, spawning a nationwide business, a TV series, three best-selling books, and a licensing deal with the Container Store. Along the way they attracted clients like Reese Witherspoon, Kim Kardashian, and Gwyneth Paltrow, along with more than 5 million Instagram followers who oohed and aahed over the pair's trademark rainbow-colored organizing strategy, with pantry shelves full of cereal in sparkling clear containers and Legos arranged in perfect ROYGBIV symmetry in playroom cubbies.

"Of course, years later we're both like, 'I can't believe I went into business with someone I knew for only a few hours and didn't do a background check or even a thorough Google search,'" they wrote in their book, *The Home Edit*. "Not the most advisable course of action, but . . . we figured we might as well continue down the path of following our gut instinct."

Many factors go into any successful venture, of course, just as many mistakes result in failures. The women had complementary skills and a knack for creating envy-inducing Instagram posts. They took advantage of their West Coast contacts early on to nab a celebrity client—actress Christina Applegate, a fellow mom in Teplin's child's preschool—which led to other famous clients. They also created a clever twist on home organization, which typically focuses on getting rid of stuff and paring down your life. Instead, they specialized in reorganizing the stuff you already have, to create the mouth-watering pantry or gorgeous garage. What they were selling was a rainbow-hued lifestyle, along with their BFF personalities.

While Clea and Joanna's story is specific to them, their insight about not overthinking things is worth considering. "We both have the ability to tap in to our instincts and just do. We don't mess around with analyzing things until we're blue in the face. We just go for it and make it happen," they wrote.

The two women likely didn't realize that their intuitive approach has been validated by organizational psychologists. In a 2002 experiment, for example, Max Planck researchers Daniel Goldstein and Gerd Gigerenzer asked a random sampling of Germans and Americans this simple question: "Which city has a larger population: San Diego or San Antonio?" You'd understandably expect that Americans would be more knowledgeable and thus more likely to know the correct answer: San Diego. Surprisingly, though, 100 percent of the Germans answered correctly, yet only two-thirds of the Americans knew the right answer.

The reason, the researchers concluded, is that the Americans knew too much about American cities. They overthought their answers. They considered all of the data they had collected over the years—geography, industry, demographics, and more—before carefully, analytically weighing their decision. The Germans, though, had no such ostensible advantage. They only knew that they had heard of San Diego, which is more famous than San Antonio. For them, there was no extraneous information to muck up their thought process.

In a similar experiment, when British and Turkish students were asked to predict the winner in a British soccer match, the Turks—who knew virtually nothing about the teams—were almost as accurate as the Brits. The Brits simply were too knowledgeable about the details of their own teams—such as which players choked under pressure, or who was injured—while their Turkish counterparts had only a passing familiarity with the names of the most successful teams. "Can a lack of recognition be informative?" the researchers asked provocatively.

Apparently the answer is yes. In other experiments, amateurs equaled or bested experts in picking the winner of 127 Wimbledon men's tennis matches, the outcome of political elections, the size of record sales, and the quality of colleges. Newfoundland students could even pick which National Hockey League players were more successful. And in one unintentionally hilarious experiment, random people interviewed on the street picked stock portfolios that outperformed those put together by finance grad students. Researchers concluded that the finance experts simply knew too much about individual stocks and performance variables. They overthought their choices, while the amateurs mostly went by name recognition.

There's ample evidence that overthinking derails all sorts of decisions. In one experiment, researchers asked people to choose one of five posters, including Impressionist paintings and funny animal pictures, like a cat perched on a rope with the caption "Gimme a Break." One group simply chose the poster they liked, without giving the decision much thought; they overwhelmingly chose the Impressionists. The other group was instructed to first describe exactly what they liked or didn't like about each poster. They had to think through carefully what choice they made and why. Most of them ultimately chose the animal poster, but when they were contacted three weeks later, they said they regretted their choice. They should have gone with the Impressionists.

Overthinking does that to us: it can make us change our minds—and to make a worse decision as a result. That's true not just for choosing a poster, which is a matter of personal taste. When we overanalyze a situation, we may come to an *objectively* wrong conclusion. Researchers asked people to do a blind taste test to rate five kinds of strawberry jam. In a previous ranking by *Consumer Reports*, one of the options came in first and several of the others were ranked at the bottom of the list, one as low as forty-fourth place. One group of testers was asked to taste the jams and immediately rate them; their results followed the *Consumer Reports* rankings closely. A second group was asked to think carefully about why they liked or disliked each jam. Their rankings were a disaster—they didn't come even close to the *Consumer Reports* rankings. Overthinking "changed people's minds about how they felt," the researchers found—and actually made their conclusions less accurate.

Too much information is especially problematic when it comes to creating something new—a breakthrough idea, a new invention, or a reinvention of an existing product. The poster child for information overload gone disastrously wrong is the famed New Coke fiasco. In 1985, the Coca-Cola Company had embarked on what, at the time, was considered the most extensive market research in history in order to reformulate its classic drink. The company was on the defensive after rival PepsiCo's introduction of the "Pepsi Challenge," which showed that consumers preferred Pepsi in a blind taste test. (It later turned out that Pepsi won mostly because it was sweeter and so tasted better with a single sip, rather than a full glass.)

New Coke was formulated specifically to win the sipping competition. Yet after it was introduced, irate consumers rejected it almost immediately. Despite spending $4 million on research and conducting almost 200,000 taste tests, then-president Don Keough later acknowledged, all the market data in the world couldn't measure Coke drinkers' "deep and abiding emotional attachment" to the original product. Coke had overanalyzed itself into the most embarrassing product flop in history.

Today even companies that collect massive amounts of data will willfully ignore it when attempting to create breakthrough products. Amazon is famously reliant on data and market research for almost everything. It has said it collects more than 2,000 data points for every order. A BBC reporter who retrieved his Amazon profile found out that the company had tracked more than 115,000 interactions, including every time he tapped his Kindle and the 48 times his young daughter requested the *Frozen* anthem "Let It Go."

And yet, when it comes to creating something new, Amazon looks beyond the data. "No customer was asking for Echo," as Amazon founder Jeff Bezos has said. "This was definitely us wandering. Market research doesn't help. If you had gone to a customer in 2013 and said, 'Would you like a black, always-on cylinder in your kitchen about the size of a Pringles can that you could talk to and ask questions, that also turns on your lights and plays music?' I guarantee you they'd have looked at you strangely and said, 'No, thank you.'"

In that, he calls to mind Apple's Steve Jobs, who famously said, "People don't know what they want until you show it to them. That's why I never rely on market research. Our task is to read things that are not yet on the page." He was being more than a little disingenuous, considering that Apple collects and analyzes plenty of data. But despite his, shall we say, poetic license, Jobs's broader point is correct: if you want to invent something new, by definition no one is asking for it. As Jobs also said, "It isn't the consumer's job to know what they want."

Similarly, James Patterson ignored decades of book publishing expertise when he insisted, against the advice of his publisher, on making a television commercial for his breakout hit *Along Came a Spider*. "There's always skepticism," he told the *Harvard Business Review*. "But my gut is right a lot. And people who work with me come to realize that reluctantly."

THERE IS A difference, though, in what separates the successful gut decisions from those that are ill informed and lazy, the "I don't feel like doing my homework" types. When you dig into the genesis of truly breakthrough ideas, it turns out that the common denominator is a bountiful well of experience and knowledge.

We may think a friend has "great instincts," or a leader has extraordinary intuition. But what we're seeing is actually the culmination of deep expertise. Indeed, researchers have found that what may seem to the outside world like a lightning strike out of the blue is actually more prosaic pattern recognition: these innovators recognize patterns from past experience, even in something that may seem completely new. Paradoxically, their gut is correct precisely because they have analyzed so many previous situations. Jeff Bezos and Steve Jobs didn't invent devices out of thin air; they and their colleagues were bolstered by decades of innovation, research, and understanding of their audiences. For his part, James Patterson had decades of advertising experience to inform his understanding of how to appeal to consumers.

In almost all cases, acting on intuition is a matter of extrapolating familiar patterns into something new. Chess masters, for example, seem to glance for just a moment at a board and then know the right move, no analysis necessary, but researchers have found that they can do this because of their reservoir of 50,000 to 100,000 patterns. In one intriguing experiment, Japanese researchers spent several months training a group of novices to become expert players at shogi, a Japanese game similar to chess. The researchers used imaging equipment to examine participants' brain activity while they played. At first, the players struggled with the game. They spent time carefully analyzing each move. Yet sure enough, as they became experienced and began making quick and apparently intuitive winning moves, their brains showed increased activity in the area associated with nonconscious thoughts and automatic behavior. The players, in lay terms, had actually *developed* intuition—they'd created a "gut feeling" where none had been before.

Erik Dane, a management professor at Washington University's Olin Business School, noted a similar phenomenon in an experiment in which people who already owned a designer handbag could instantly spot fake Louis Vuitton and Coach pocketbooks. They didn't need to examine the stitching or color. They couldn't necessarily explain why they knew. They just *knew*. The same went for basketball experts: Dane found that those who had played at least three years of high school ball could accurately rate the difficulty of basketball shots without having to break down the play in order to analyze every move. When they watched a video of basketball players, they didn't have to think about the shots they took; the degree of difficulty was immediately apparent to them.

In one well-documented case a few years back, a fire commander made what seemed to be a miraculous gut call that saved the lives of his entire crew. While fighting an apparently routine house fire, the group trained their hoses on the flame, yet puzzlingly, their efforts had no effect. Meanwhile, the home was intensely hot, even hotter than the fire would suggest. It was also bizarrely quiet. The commander had no idea why this was happening, yet suddenly he found himself shouting to his crew: "*Evacuate!*" The men fled the home. Within a minute, the floor where they had been standing collapsed. The source of the fire, unknown to them all, was beneath their feet, in the basement.

The commander didn't know that was where the fire had started. He simply had a "sixth sense," as he later explained it, that his men were in danger. But when cognitive psychologist Gary Klein and his colleagues analyzed the case, they concluded otherwise. "We would be less poetic and infer that the mismatch was the cue. The pattern of cues deviated from the prototypical patterns in which heat, sound, and water are correlated," they wrote. The fire commander's deep expertise was what enabled him to understand that the pattern was wrong. That deviation was what set off his "sixth sense" and gave him that urgent gut feeling that disaster was imminent.

Neuroscientist Antonio Damasio defines this kind of intuition as rapidly coming "to a particular conclusion without being aware of all the immediate logical steps" preceding it. Damasio demonstrated the effect in a study using a card game called the Iowa Gambling Task, in which players chose from four different decks, with each card either adding or subtracting small amounts of cash. Players needed up to fifty turns before they consciously realized that two of the decks were "winners" and two were "losers"—yet after just ten turns they began showing physical signs of stress when considering the "losing" decks. Their bodies were leading them in the right direction before their brains had caught up. Damasio, who leads the University of Southern California's Brain and Creativity Institute, stresses that gut feeling isn't superior to reasoning, but that the two systems, the body and the mind, work together. As he writes, "It is not only the interaction between mind and brain that is mythical: the separation between mind and body is probably just as fictional."

ACTING ON GUT feelings unsupported by prior experience, on the other hand, can be deadly. Consider the early-twentieth-century New York physician known for his "golden gut": he seemed to have remarkable intuition about which patients would develop typhoid fever. His diagnostic method almost never failed him: he would examine patients' tongues, feeling them with his fingers for shape and texture. Of course, considering that he didn't wash his hands between exams, his "intuitive" power to predict who would fall ill hardly seems miraculous today. "He was a more effective carrier, using only his hands, than Typhoid Mary," notes scholar Robin Hogarth.

For a modern-day object lesson in gut gone wrong, look no further than Hollywood veteran Jeffrey Katzenberg. A wunderkind who ascended to the chairmanship of Walt Disney Studios while still in his early thirties, he was a hyperkinetic schmoozer who scheduled three business breakfasts every morning and seemed to have every reporter worth knowing on speed dial. What Jeffrey wanted, Jeffrey seemed to find a way to get. Once, he tracked me down at home on my unlisted phone number as I was putting my kids to bed, to try (unsuccessfully) to harangue me into pulling an upcoming article about his business partner David Geffen.

Equal parts obsessive, bullying, and charming, Katzenberg quickly gained attention and—unusual for an executive—a measure of mainstream fame. He reinvented Disney's aging animation unit, producing new classics like *The Little Mermaid* and *Beauty and the Beast*, and he later cofounded DreamWorks Animation, which produced hits like *Shrek*. And so, when Katzenberg teamed up with storied tech executive Meg Whitman, a former CEO of Hewlett-Packard and eBay, to create a new streaming service, expectations were high. Quibi—short for "quick bites"—would offer short mobile content with big-studio production values. It would showcase A-list Hollywood talent, from Jennifer Lopez to Steven Spielberg. It quickly raised $1.75 billion from investors, "largely because they trusted the gut instincts and vision" of the founders, the *Wall Street Journal* reported.

Six months after it launched, Quibi was dead.

How had gut gone so wrong? One of the perils of having previous success with your intuitions is that it leads to overconfidence. Katzenberg and Whitman had plenty of experience in their respective fields, but they didn't grasp how different their fields were from the world of social media. The key to social media relevance is viral content, yet Quibi didn't allow users to easily share videos with friends. The cofounders also initially ignored advice that viewers needed to be able to stream videos on their televisions, not just on their phones. Nor could Quibi explain why people should buy a subscription when it seemed to be replicating services that could already be had for free, like YouTube and TikTok. The final indignity, and one over which they had no control, was Quibi's launch date of April 2020—the month after the Covid-19 shutdown began.

At heart, the problem was the "cult of the visionary entrepreneur," as business writer James Surowiecki put it: the visionary believes that "if everyone thinks something is a crazy idea, but you think it's brilliant, you should trust yourself and place the bet." Ultimately, Quibi was a colossal, humiliating failure. Investors rushed to fund Quibi because they "trusted the gut instincts" of the founders, as the *Wall Street Journal* reported. "Instead, they witnessed one of the fastest collapses in the entertainment business."

To be fair, none of us ever have perfect intuition. Not even Steve Jobs. Remember the revolutionary Apple Lisa personal computer? If not, you aren't alone. It was introduced with great fanfare in 1983, but potential customers recoiled at its price tag of almost $10,000 and its sluggish performance. It flopped almost immediately.

A SIGNATURE FEATURE of a gut reaction is that your body tells you what to do even before your mind catches up. That points up another common thread we've seen among people who successfully navigate major transitions. They almost all start to pivot before they even realize they're doing so. Chris Donovan was creating detailed drawings of shoes years before he ever thought of becoming a designer. Queen guitarist Brian May recorded the band's first three albums while he was still a doctoral student in astrophysics. The same is true not just for people who undergo professional transitions but also for those going through personal ones: they often set themselves on a new path long before they realize it. Sociologist Diane Vaughan even found that couples who split up and divorce sometimes begin the process of "uncoupling" well before they're aware of what they're doing.

From today's vantage point, we would consider Jim Patterson's writing and Brian May's performing while still working in their day jobs as a "side hustle"—not their "real" job but a passion pursued in their spare time. When you examine the journey of others who have undergone career makeovers, you often find the same pattern. Google's two founders were still Stanford University graduate students when they created the company. "We almost didn't start Google because my co-founder Sergey [Brin] and I were too worried about dropping out of our PhD program," cofounder Larry Page has said. Companies as diverse as Under Armour, Yankee Candle, and the Skimm newsletter all started out as side projects.

Perhaps the most audacious example of a side hustle that I came across was some years ago, when I was the editor in chief of the business magazine Condé Nast *Portfolio*. An investment firm had invited me to its annual conference. Walking into the evening reception at Manhattan's Metropolitan Club that November, I felt lost in a sea of middle-aged men in suits. They were gathered in clusters, deep in conversation with each other as their eyes darted around the room in search of somebody more important to buttonhole. Women were few, and apparently invisible. Nobody seemed to notice me. Self-consciously clutching my glass of white wine, I scanned the room and saw someone who looked just as awkward. Standing by himself was a young guy in blue jeans and Adidas flip-flops instead of a suit. I felt badly that no one had clued him in on the dress code. He looked like one of my daughter's high school friends. Nobody was paying any attention to him either, so I walked over to introduce myself.

He shook my hand and smiled politely. "Hi, I'm Mark Zuckerberg."

It was 2006, and Facebook was already well on its way to becoming a behemoth. Rumor had it that Yahoo wanted to buy it for the gargantuan sum of $1 billion. (As of this writing, Facebook, now called Meta, is valued at more than $360 billion.) But this young Harvard dropout wasn't drawing as much attention as the establishment CEOs—or the one other tech wunderkind in the room, Chad Hurley, co-creator of YouTube, which Google had just bought for $1.65 billion. What struck me most about our conversation, though, was when I asked Zuckerberg about his decision to quit Harvard. He hadn't actually dropped out, he clarified. He was still on a leave of absence. He still could go back.

It seemed so counterintuitive. Zuckerberg had already built a billion-dollar company, but he was hanging on to his college affiliation "just in case." It made no more sense than Jim Patterson still churning out Kodak ads at his ad agency desk even after his books started climbing the *New York Times* best-seller lists. For Mark Zuckerberg, Facebook was still a "side hustle."

BACK AT NEW York University, Alan similarly was preparing himself for a career change without realizing it. His early fascination with math, his prodigious reading about finance and Wall Street, even the free time he spent calculating his bandmates' income taxes, all had served him well. Despite his jitters about returning to school, he surprised himself by managing to get two B's and the rest A's during his first semester. Every semester after that, he got straight A's. The indifferent high school student became a college standout. "I loaded up on courses in advanced math. Economics appealed to me right from the start: I was enthralled by supply and demand curves, the idea of market equilibrium, and the evolution of international trade," he said. He stayed on at NYU to earn his master's degree and, ultimately, a PhD in economics.

"The most important economic decision I ever made," he told me years later, "was to decide to leave music and go back to college."

That is an extraordinary statement—especially coming from him. Because the onetime professional jazz saxophonist didn't just become an ordinary economist. He turned out to be the five-term chairman of the Federal Reserve Board, overseeing America's financial health. Over the course of his more than half-century career, Alan Greenspan made a greater number of "important economic decisions" than perhaps any other person on the planet.

His gutsy career change paid off after all. And by the way, he didn't leave music completely behind either. He played the grand piano at home to relax, he told me. His wife, broadcaster Andrea Mitchell, was a violinist herself in her youth. When I left the *Wall Street Journal* after twenty-two years to launch a new magazine, Dr. Greenspan, then at the Fed, wrote me a lovely if slightly tongue-in-cheek note, recalling his reaction to one of the first front-page pieces I had written as a cub reporter at the *Journal* two decades earlier, when I played my viola on the street to experience the life of a street musician.

"With that story, you magically combined three subjects dear to me: the warmth of classical music performance, the kaleidoscope of humanity traveling the streets of the city, as well as the sheer joy of engaging first hand in comparative wage analysis," he wrote. "Despite my strong conviction that Manhattan could never have too much Bach in the air, I can only wish you the best of luck with your latest endeavor, even though I expect it will keep you off the streets and away from your viola."

The framed letter still hangs in my office.

Learning to Love the Struggle

So You've Failed. Now What?

Success consists of going from failure to failure
without loss of enthusiasm.

—WINSTON CHURCHILL

If you've ever watched the TV series *La Femme Nikita* or *Highlander*, you're familiar with Marla Ginsburg's work. A longtime American television executive, she made a splash in Paris by bringing those popular series and others to an international audience. For decades she was a force to be reckoned with. One of the most powerful women in television. A staple at Parisian fashion shows. A woman about town in Chanel and Chloé, paired chicly with a white T-shirt and jeans.

In 2003, lured by a cushy production deal, she moved back to Los Angeles. She easily managed the million-dollar-plus mortgage on her new home, along with the gardener, the pool cleaner, and the nanny for her two kids. Life was good.

Until it all fell apart.

First, a writers' strike hit, shutting down the town. Her work evaporated overnight. Suddenly no money was coming through the door. No sooner had the strike ended when the 2008 financial crisis erupted. Her savings, most of it invested in the stock market, plunged in value. Her home's value crashed as well. In an attempt to stay afloat until things turned around, she drained the pool, fired the help, and gave up the lease on her car. It wasn't nearly enough. Soon she had emptied her bank account and sold her stock at a loss. With no cash to feed her family, she took in a boarder and used the rent money for groceries. She became an expert in stretching Monday's hamburgers into Friday's meatloaf. Her financial adviser told her it was time to declare bankruptcy. She was done.

Ginsburg was over fifty in a town that prizes youth, and a woman in an industry run overwhelmingly by white men. She would have to start again, from scratch. But what was she good for? And how would she make a change anyway? She had no financial resources. Her credit was shot. *Girlfriend, this may be over for you,* she remembers saying to herself. *If it is, what's next?* She laughs sardonically as she recalls her thinking at the time: "I had two really realistic dreams. One was to have my own talk show. The other was, I always had a dream of becoming a clothing designer. In retrospect, both of these goals were highly ridiculous."

But she was desperate. So she bought herself a sewing machine at Sears and googled how to thread a bobbin. She spent hours trying to figure out how to use it—more googling—and then hours more crafting creations that she would show to her still-wealthy friends, who had no idea how dire her financial situation was. She bent over her sewing machine for days on end. "I was in the throes of menopause in the Valley and it was steaming hot. My kids thought I'd lost my mind."

For a fleeting moment, it looked as if her hard work might pay off. Through a chance meeting—she overheard two strangers arguing about their son's bar mitzvah menu, and the man turned out to be a clothing manufacturer—she snared an investor who offered to finance a clothing line. Her agent lined up a spot on HSN for her to hawk it, and Nordstrom carried more upscale pieces. But when the real estate market crashed, the investor disappeared. A subsequent deal with another manufacturer didn't work out. Her options dwindled . . . and then disappeared. As her financial situation deteriorated, her last facade of normalcy crumbled.

Reluctantly, she unloaded her house for less than the value of the mortgage and retreated with her sewing machine to Montreal, trying again with yet another clothing company. In search of potential new business partners, she began making regular trips to Manhattan. The trouble was, she had no cash to get there. So she would board the overnight Greyhound bus in Montreal, ride all night, then freshen up in a Starbucks bathroom after arriving at the Port Authority bus terminal the next morning. She'd couch-surf with a friend before heading back home on the bus. It was all she could afford. "I was flat-out, on-my-ass broke. I was taken down to my knees," she told me. "A lifetime of experience doesn't count. All of a sudden, you're nothing."

Her bad luck seemed only to keep multiplying. Just as she felt like she was finally climbing out of her financial hole, her eighteen-year-old son was stricken with Hodgkin's lymphoma. He was treated in Holland, where his father lived. Marla followed, camping out for months in a borrowed apartment. "When you lose your money and your house and have a kid going through cancer . . . I must have been f-ing Mengele in a past life. I just kept getting knocked on my ass."

THERE ARE BOOKSHELVES of tomes promising that failure is the best thing that will ever happen to you. It's a theme of commencement speakers everywhere. "I wish you bad luck," Supreme Court chief justice John Roberts told students at his son's ninth-grade graduation in 2017. "If you don't fail, you're not even trying," Denzel Washington told University of Pennsylvania students in 2011. Stories of soaring success often start with an "origin story" of failure, whether it's J. K. Rowling writing her Harry Potter series while on welfare or Mark Cuban getting fired from his first computer software job and flaming out with a powdered-milk start-up.

But when you inevitably fail, those stories can only make you feel worse. Maybe Mark Cuban can pull himself up and become a billionaire, but what relevance does that have for the rest of us? The "failure is good" refrain seems to be something that only successful people talk about. And only safely *after* they've succeeded. Does failure really lead to success? Maybe that's just something successful people tell us to flatter themselves, or to make us poor schlubs feel better. Maybe these folks are exaggerating. Maybe they're outliers.

There's the added complication that in this Instagram filter age, even when you're doing well, it's too easy to look at others' perfectly curated lives and feel like you're coming up short. Everybody else seems impossibly better looking, smarter, more glamorous, and more successful than we are. Anxiety and depression have soared as a result, especially among teens. The search for perfection has reached such crazy heights that some of the students I teach at Yale feel they've failed if they get an A- grade. Even objectively successful people too often feel like they're just not cutting it.

Making a transition in any circumstance is never easy. But when you feel like you've failed at something, it's an even steeper hill to climb. As we've seen, transformations of all sorts share common elements. You *search* for clues about how to transform, you *struggle* through the process of transitioning, you may find yourself at an impasse and *stop* before finally landing on a *solu-*

tion. But trying to reset yourself after failure adds another level of complexity. To be sure, failing at something—a class, a career, a marriage—doesn't make *you* a failure. Even under the best of circumstances, career coach Orville Pierson has calculated, the average job seeker is rejected by twenty-four decision makers before landing a job. But that's hard to remember in the midst of a downfall. Failure seems much more personal. It can rob you of self-esteem and confidence. And most troubling, it can instill fear that prevents you from reimagining a better future. It hobbles you from taking the risks that may be necessary to take that next step.

This is especially true in the case of career flameouts like Marla's. Many of us, especially college-educated Americans, have fallen into the misguided tendency to equate ourselves with our work. *Atlantic* writer Derek Thompson describes it as "workism," a philosophy he defines as "a kind of religion, promising identity, transcendence, and community." But if your identity is tied to your job title, and the job suddenly vanishes, who are you? How do you think of yourself? How do you answer that first question everyone you meet asks: "What do you do?" Suddenly, you're falling into an existential black hole.

Psychologists call this "enmeshment": when there is no boundary between you and your job, you lose your self-worth and your very sense of who you are if you lose your position. More viscerally, Marla describes it as conflating your identity with your office chair. "And when that chair is pulled out from under you, all the people who you thought were part of your circle? No. They're surrounding the person who's now sitting in that chair."

What's more, we're conditioned from childhood to see failure as inherently bad. In a study of fifth-graders, Stanford psychology professor Carol Dweck found that those praised for being "smart" became less confident if they struggled. They felt like failures and figured that, since they were having trouble, they must not actually be smart. But kids told that they were "hard workers" became more confident, more motivated to tackle a challenge, and ultimately better performers. "The whole point of intelligence praise is to boost confidence and motivation, but both were gone in a flash," Dweck wrote in her 2007 article "The Perils and Promise of Praise." "If success meant they were smart, then struggling meant they were not."

Yet when failure is explained as part of the process of learning, it has the opposite effect: it can actually increase motivation and help students do better in school. When low-income high school students in one study read stories about how Albert Einstein and Marie Curie encountered failures before their successes, the students' grades improved. They related to the trials and tribulations of famous people who failed before they succeeded, and they became more motivated to learn. But when the students learned only about the scientists' great achievements, the grades of some of them declined instead. "Failure is information," says cognitive scientist Xiaodong Lin-Siegler, the Columbia Teachers College professor who led the study. The key is to analyze failure, understand why it happened, and figure out how to correct it for the next time around.

Failure, done right, can actually be a counterintuitive predictor of success. Dashun Wang, a Northwestern University computational social scientist, has found that competitive athletes who fall just short of the podium early on—finishing fourth, below the three medalists—often end up leapfrogging the competition later. They can "overcorrect" to become champions. Jamaican sprinter Asafa Powell, for example, who came in fourth at a championship event as a high schooler, subsequently bested his competitors to become a four-time Olympian who once set a world record for the 100-meter dash.

The same dynamic holds true in arenas beyond athletics. In

academia, scientists who have early career setbacks end up out-performing their ostensibly more accomplished peers, Wang found. He compared junior scientists who just missed winning a prestigious National Institutes of Health grant with those who just managed to snag the award. Conventional wisdom—or the Matthew Effect, the theory of cumulative advantage better known by the old adage "The rich get richer and the poor get poorer"—suggested that the winners would remain on top, reaping more financial rewards and opportunities.

In reality, though, the "failure group" ended up on top a decade later. They published just as many papers, their breakthroughs were more original, and their research had more impact than that published by the winners. They embodied philosopher Friedrich Nietzsche's famous remark, "What does not kill me makes me stronger." Their success reminds me of Tomas Lindahl, the Nobel Laureate in chemistry, who upon winning the prize recalled the one high school class he failed: "The ironic thing is that the topic was chemistry. I have the distinction of being the only Chemistry Laureate who failed the topic in high school!"

"What these results begin to establish is, failure can be a counterintuitive predictor of success. It makes me feel better whenever I fail, which occurs on a daily basis," Wang told me cheerfully. "It makes me feel much better and hopeful."

TO BE SURE, only some failures lead to transformative success. The key question is, why? And more importantly, what can we do to boost our odds of success after failure? Research to date suggests that the answer comes down to *how* we fail. Indeed, there's one element that almost all successful failures have in common: those who ultimately succeed are those who tweak, adjust, and fiddle after every flameout. They don't give up the whole endeavor and start from scratch. Instead, they embark on the iterative and sometimes painful process of isolating one component at a time. For them, it's all about the process and the journey, not the outcome. They *search* for the right elements, then endure an often protracted *struggle*, before finally figuring out a new path forward, the *solution*.

This winning strategy requires something that most of us want to avoid: leaning in to discomfort and embracing the struggle. It requires the patience to make tiny tweaks instead of grand, sweeping gestures. Those who turn failure into success "engage in 'intelligent improvement,' yielding incrementally better attempts and, ultimately, victory," Wang and his colleagues have found. "The key is to think of every failure as a wonderful experience . . . to make sure you're learning enough so that you aren't starting from scratch" every time, he told me. That means throwing out elements that don't work while keeping those that do, then trying again and repeating. "You are learning over and over, and failing faster and faster. You're trying to learn from the past, eyes on the prize, to figure out the components that need to be updated and changed while retaining the parts that do well," Wang explains.

In a recent study, Wang and his colleagues analyzed scientists, entrepreneurs, and—disturbingly—terrorist groups to understand which failures lead to success. They defined success for scientists as snaring funding and, for the entrepreneurs, either selling their business or taking it public. For the terrorist groups, they tracked more than 170,000 attacks in the Global Terrorism Database. "Failure" for the terrorists was conducting an attack in which no one was killed; "success" was defined, gruesomely, as causing at least one fatality. Eerily, the same strategy of incremental improvement held true for members of all three groups who ultimately succeeded after a failure.

Lin-Siegler has seen a similar phenomenon in an ongoing study of high achievers, including Olympic gymnast Simone Biles and soccer star Julie Foudy. Although her research is still preliminary, she told me that "I can say without hesitation, failure is one of the major forces of invention." Lin-Siegler, too, has found that the key to successful failure is to focus on the iterative process—what we've termed the *struggle*—rather than the endpoint. Those who are motivated only by the end-game reward, whether that be a reinvented career or an Olympic gold medal, are almost inevitably setting themselves up to fail.

"For people to be really inventive, to be successful and always come up with new things, they cannot focus on outcome," she told me. "If you focus on outcome you are going to be repeatedly disappointed to the point you are disgusted. You have to love the process." That process, the *struggle*, involves repetition and making small refinements on the road to improvement. It's almost inevitably "boring" ("you're repeatedly doing the same motion all the time"), so the key to innovation, Lin-Siegler explained, is finding ways to make the journey enjoyable.

Human nature, though, works against seeing this process as fun. Nobody wants to hear about a boring, repetitive process, much less to sign up for one. We all want instant gratification. That whole struggle stage sounds just too darn tedious. As a result, we tend to omit this step when we tell the great reinvention stories.

We don't often hear details, for example, about the many miserable years when J. K. Rowling struggled, when she contemplated suicide and was turned down by a dozen publishers before one took a flyer on Harry Potter. Henry Ford is famous for the Model T, but few realize that he drove two automakers into bankruptcy before founding his eponymous car company. Before he found fame as an animator, Walt Disney was fired as an illustrator for the *Kansas City Star* by an editor who told him he "lacked imagination and had no good ideas." Thomas Edison was fired from two jobs for lack of productivity, and he flamed out with multiple inventions, including a super-creepy-looking early "talking doll." As he famously said, "I have not failed 10,000 times—I've successfully found 10,000 ways that will not work." Basketball great Michael Jordan echoed Edison when he said, "I've missed more than 9,000 shots in my career. . . . I've failed over and over again in my life. And that is why I succeed."

Figure skating champion Nathan Chen, who placed fifth in the 2018 Olympics before returning to win gold in 2022, spoke openly about the importance of that decidedly unglamorous process. His singular obsession in 2018 was with winning gold, an unhealthy fixation reinforced by breathless media coverage, his face on a Corn Flakes box, and his image on a Times Square billboard. That focus proved to be his "demise," he said. The key to his record-breaking comeback was switching his focus away from the end point—the gold medal—and toward the process of getting there. He spent the next four years broadening his scope as he attended college and continued to train. "I think it took him focusing on school and working every part of his brain to finally realize that skating was not life or death, and that perspective took some of the pressure off," said Adam Rippon, another 2018 Olympian who helped coach him. As Chen told the *New York Times*, "Ultimately, I think within my career I've learned that you learn the most from your failures, and that's how you can grow the best."

THE KEY TO all this tweaking and fine-tuning is that eventually, if you are going to succeed, you reach a tipping point. You may fail and fail, over and over again. But then comes the magical moment when things start to fall into place.

Wang compares this to melting an ice cube. Imagine your job is to melt the cube. The room temperature is 20 degrees Fahrenheit, so you raise it by one degree. Nothing happens. You raise it by another degree, but once more nothing happens. Then you try again, one more degree, and another, and another. Finally, you reach 30 degrees, then 31. You might be tempted to quit. If you do, all your incremental changes, all of your work and experimentation, will have been for naught. But then you turn up the heat one more time, to 32 degrees—and suddenly the ice is melting.

You take exactly the same, iterative step that you have been taking all along, but suddenly it unlocks the answer. That's the tipping point.

Just as with ice cubes, sometimes the problem is that we simply give up too soon when we fail. The difference between failure and success isn't in the amount of work we do. It's in understanding that so much of the work happens beneath the surface and is invisible until we reach that final step. As Edison also said, "Many of life's failures are people who did not realize how close they were to success when they gave up."

Wang's insights suggest that we don't have to be the cleverest or luckiest person in the world to go from failure to success. Indeed, when 143 creativity researchers were asked to name the single most important factor in creative achievement, they didn't mention innate intelligence or ability; instead, they cited the ability "to learn from experience."

That's a comforting thought. But there is one quality we do need: persistence. It takes a strong constitution to pick yourself up again and keep trying even after you've fallen—especially if you've already washed out multiple times.

Being urged to constantly tweak and iterate sounds a lot like the "fail fast, fail often" mantra that's been ubiquitous in Silicon Valley. That approach has been given credit for innovations like Elon Musk's SpaceX rockets and Tesla cars. But it has also been twisted and contorted to the point that at times it's almost meaningless. "Fail fast, fail often" has given birth to a culture that moves with reckless speed and launches half-baked products that aren't ready—or that never should have been launched at all. Sometimes "fail fast" is paired—with disastrous results—with another well-worn tech maxim: "Fake it till you make it." Elizabeth Holmes, the CEO of Theranos, was convicted of defrauding investors after conflating the two, by pushing to market a supposedly revolutionary blood-testing technology that didn't work.

The "fail fast" doctrine has been so bastardized that the *Globe and Mail* dubbed it "the stupidest business mantra of all time." Yet that's missing the point of what *does* work: patience, and the ability to learn from previous mistakes. "We say fail *faster*," Wang told me. "The interval between two consecutive failures should be shorter. That seems to be the signature we are seeing from the data. . . . If you want to fail fast, you have to make incremental changes." Success won't come from recklessly abandoning one project for the next, or flailing about for a shortcut. "Failing fast" can take years.

THAT WAS CERTAINLY the case for Katalin Kariko. The Hungarian-born biochemist, the daughter of a butcher, grew up in a home without running water, immigrated to the United States after her lab lost its funding, and was subsequently threatened with deportation by an early supervisor. Ultimately she landed at the University of Pennsylvania, where she spent years studying something called "messenger ribonucleic acid." She hoped that these molecules could be harnessed to cure rare diseases or to mend damaged tissue after a heart attack or brain injury. Unfortunately, she couldn't convince anybody else that her esoteric work had a future. Year after year, she applied for research grants; year after year, she was rejected. Her career was nothing but a series of failures.

Things got so bad that Penn pulled her off the professorship track and demoted her to a researcher. It was a humiliating come-down. "I was up for promotion, and then they just demoted me and expected that I would walk out the door," she said. The experience prompted a bout of soul searching and doubt as Kariko wondered, "Maybe I'm not good enough, not smart enough."

Instead, she dug in her heels ("I just have to do better experiments") and continued plugging away as a low-paid, low-status researcher. For the next decade, through the 1990s and then into the 2000s, Kariko kept going, with little to show for it. Injecting the molecules into mice kept causing immune flare-ups, a vexing problem that stood in the way of using them for vaccines or other treatments. Finally, after iterating endlessly on her experiments, she and colleague Drew Weissman figured out a solution. Nobody much noticed their breakthrough at first. But undeterred, they quietly kept chipping away, ultimately helping pave the way for clinical trials.

It's hard to imagine what the world would look like now if Kariko had abandoned her obsession during the many years people doubted, degraded, or just plain ignored her. If she and others hadn't continued trying, and failing, and trying again to perfect their experiments, we would almost certainly be in a much darker place.

Today just about everyone knows about Kariko's ground-breaking research on what is known as mRNA, even if they still don't know her name. Her obsession led directly to the Covid-19 vaccine developed by Pfizer and other pharmaceutical companies. It was, wrote Damian Garde and Jonathan Saltzman, "the starter pistol for the vaccine sprint to come."

I was fortunate enough to meet Kariko in 2022 at *Time* magazine's Time 100 Gala, where she was honored alongside luminaries like Apple CEO, Tim Cook, and actress Zendaya. Sporting no-nonsense short dark hair, glasses, and a modest black gown, she surveyed the glittering scene around her. Every "negative (event) actually had to happen, because always something positive" resulted, she told me. "I wouldn't be here if I would not be terminated in Hungary, wouldn't lose my job, wouldn't have gone through many difficulties." As fellow honoree Mary J. Blige took to the stage to entertain the audience, Kariko joined her daughter, herself a two-time gold-medal winning Olympic rower, to dance. "I always come up with solutions," Kariko told me before taking her leave. "I focus always on what I can do. That is the mantra."

WHAT IF THE problem isn't quitting too soon, but *not* quitting when you really should? In other words, how do we know if the correct course of action is to give up? That's one of the thorniest challenges when it comes to making a major pivot. We know that in the march toward reinvention, people move from the struggle to the stop to the solution. But sometimes, when they reach the stop, they actually *should* quit. They're staring not at a temporary barrier but at a bright red light. They should just pack it in. How do you know whether you should forge ahead or stop chasing an impossible dream?

Certainly, there are obvious cases. It's pretty clear that if I decided to reinvent myself as a ballerina despite being uncoordinated, flat-footed, and several decades too old, I would quickly see the error of my ways. But for less obvious situations, we are badly in need of a method for self-diagnosis.

There are no easy answers, but as it turns out, medical researcher Melanie Stefan has stumbled onto one useful strategy. Her approach is one that can give you a much-needed dose of reality. It can help you set—or reset—your course when you're considering your future.

Counterintuitively, the strategy is to catalog your failures.

When I reached out to Stefan, an Austrian native now living in Scotland, she gave me the thumbnail version of her eye-popping CV: Double major in mathematics and biology. Two master's degrees. A PhD from Cambridge. Fellowship in Tokyo. Postdoc at Caltech. Teaching fellowship at Harvard Medical School. Senior lecturer at Edinburgh Medical School. Computational neurobiochemist.

"Wow," I said. "That is some gold-plated résumé."

"Now I'll tell you the story again," she said.

The undergrad and master's degrees took thirteen years instead of five. Stefan's biology master's supervisor thought she was hopeless and "told me I should look for jobs outside of science." She was rejected by all but one PhD program. Her Caltech lab experiments went awry, and her supervisor warned her that the teaching fellowship at Harvard would be the nail in the coffin because teaching was for losers, a death knell for serious academic researchers.

"Looking back, it all *sounds* so great," she told me. "But when you are in the middle of it, it doesn't look like that. Every step, you don't know if it's going to work out or not. There was a lot of failure. And also, a lot of anxiety and uncertainty on the way."

During one particularly fraught period, while she was in Japan with no idea what she'd do next, her insecurities boiled over. "I started thinking, what is this shit?" she recalls. "Being in this highly insecure position as a recent PhD graduate, I just didn't know what would come next." But the more she mulled, the more she realized she wasn't alone; this was all part of the punishing process in her highly competitive academic field, where statistically those looking for a job need to apply to dozens of positions before being offered one. So she sat down and began cataloging her many misses.

She ultimately created a new kind of résumé for herself: a CV of failures. She included every professional flameout. And then, taking a gulp, she made it public. She wrote about her project in a 2015 *Nature* magazine article. In it, she calculated that for every hour she spent working on a successful proposal, she spent *six hours* on failed ones. Her official CV, she pointed out, "does not reflect the bulk of my academic efforts. . . . At conferences, I talk about the one project that worked, not about the many that failed," she wrote. "As scientists, we construct a narrative of success that renders our setbacks invisible both to ourselves and to others. . . . Therefore, whenever we experience an individual failure, we feel alone and dejected."

When the article landed, you could almost hear the sigh of relief. Stefan was airing the dirty secret that everybody fails, and now everybody knew it. Simply admitting it out loud opened up the floodgates among her colleagues and peers. "People are just so relieved that somebody is talking about failure," Stefan told me. She now occasionally speaks to graduate student groups and others about failure. (Her Twitter bio describes her as "Poster Child of Failure.") Every time she projects her CV of failures up on the screen, students eagerly offer up their own:

> "Rejected (and not wait-listed) from all 9 PhD programs I
>   applied to."
> "[Dissertation] rejected by five journals and remains
>   unpublished seven years later."
> "Failed driver license exam, twice."

But there was a side benefit to constructing a CV of failures—one Stefan hadn't counted on. Her CV of failures, it turned out, helped her determine her next step.

A CV detailing all of your failures can signal whether you've reached the kind of impasse you should power through or whether you've reached a solid wall and need to quit. It can tell you, when you reach the struggle and stop phases, whether you should soldier on or pack it in. In short, as Stefan said, a CV of failures "may actually tell you something about yourself."

Her own CV of failures was revelatory; it signaled to her that it was time to pivot in her own career. When her biology supervisor told her to get the heck out of science, "it was absolutely gutting," she said. But as she reviewed her CV of failures, she realized that she had been focusing on the wrong kind of science. In his lab, she was doing hands-on experiments with zephyr fish, when her actual comfort level was in computational biology, manipulating data rather than fish eggs. That realization prompted her to change her focus entirely. She pivoted to specializing in biomedical sciences, using computers and her computational skills to understand learning and memory.

"Failure is an opportunity for reflection," Stefan told me. What's more, realizing that we *all* fail helps take the sting out of failure and makes it easier to give up on truly fruitless pursuits. When she was applying for university appointments, she and her mother made a game of it: "My mum said, 'When you have thirty rejections, we'll open a bottle of Champagne.'" Each rejection was just one more step toward their glorious Champagne moment, making it more of a contest and less of an existential crisis. She scored an appointment before they hit the magic number for bubbly, but one of her suggestions to students is to similarly gamify the process when odds are they'll be facing plenty of failure before success finally comes.

Stefan encourages fellow scientists to compile their own CVs of failure. She is quick, though, to add one caveat: not everybody should *publish* their litany of failures, the way she did. "It's very useful if successful people are open about their failures, but for a lot of people being open about your failures relies on a certain amount of privilege and power," she says. "You can only do it if you're in a secure position and your next job doesn't depend on it."

Others have adopted the practice too. Inspired by Stefan's article, economist Johannes Haushofer, then at Princeton University, published his own CV of failures online, listing jobs, funding, and awards he didn't get, as well as the multiple rejections of his research papers from academic journals. "Most of what I try fails, but these failures are often invisible, while the successes are visible," he wrote. His goal was to take the sting out of failure for his colleagues and students. "I have noticed that this sometimes gives others the impression that most things work out for me. As a result, they are more likely to attribute their own failures to themselves, rather than the fact that the world is stochastic, applications are crapshoots, and selection committees and referees have bad days."

He ended his CV with a "meta failure": "This darn CV of Failures has received way more attention than my entire body of academic work."

The odds are long not just for academic appointments but for almost any other kind of job. Taking stock of our failures can be therapeutic. When I graduated from college into the teeth of a recession, my college roommates and I made a game of papering our entire communal bathroom with rejection letters from the dozens of firms that we had interviewed with on campus. I don't think we realized at the time that we were the living embodiment of Winston Churchill's adage: "Success consists of going from failure to failure without loss of enthusiasm."

There's an added benefit to owning up to failures. Those who boast about their successes are often the target of "malicious envy," a condition that psychologists say motivates others to try to undermine and tear down the perceived braggart. As Harvard Business School researchers have found, though, sharing failures as well as successes inspires "benign envy," which encourages others to build themselves up instead.

Copping to failure can also inoculate you somewhat against further failures, by freeing you up to take more risks, which in turn can lead to great payoffs. If you've failed enough times, you start to realize that failure isn't the end of the world. You become less fearful about failing again, and you're more likely to take the calculated risks that lead to a breakthrough. Business school professor Jeffrey Kudisch actually assigns his students to ask questions designed to fail ten times—everything from asking for free food at a restaurant to asking a police officer for a joy ride. The idea, he wrote in the *Washington Post*, is "to get them comfortable with 'no' and the excitement of finally getting a 'yes.'"

When Nobel Prize winner Shinya Yamanaka, the first scientist to create stem cells from normal body cells, was asked to describe his process, he laid it out like this: "Usually it's just failure. Failure, failure, failure, success." He had gotten used to failing regularly, not only as a scientist but as a marathon runner, he explained. That helped him continue on despite every obstacle. In fact, he soldiered on in his stem cell research after many setbacks only because he felt like he had nothing to lose. "Now I can see any failure as a chance. That result will teach you something else, something new."

When you stop berating yourself about failure, you also are able to see paths forward that otherwise might go unexplored. That was the case with one of the greatest medical breakthroughs in history. Alexander Fleming, a Scottish researcher, was experimenting with the influenza virus at St. Mary's Hospital in London in 1928 when he went on a two-week vacation. Upon his return, he noticed that a petri dish he'd left out near an open window had become contaminated with mold, a "fluffy white mass which rapidly increases in size." After a few days, the mold changed color from green to black to yellow.

Rather than beat himself up about his carelessness, he investigated this curious phenomenon. He soon realized that what he called "mould juice," the stuff secreted by the growth, was killing off the staphylococcal bacteria in the dish. It was an extraordinary revelation. Fleming's sloppiness had created something that could obliterate the pathogens that caused fatal diseases like scarlet fever, pneumonia, and diphtheria. Ultimately, his mistake would lead to the discovery of penicillin. "One sometimes finds what one is not looking for," he later said. "When I woke up just after dawn on September 28, 1928, I certainly didn't plan to revolutionize all medicine by discovering the world's first antibiotic, or bacteria killer. But I guess that was exactly what I did."

FLEMING MADE REMARKABLY good use of a mistake that could have been a career-ending debacle. He didn't see his failure as a detour to get past or to bury; instead, it was a key contributor to his later triumph. Others who succeeded after flaming out embraced this same philosophy: never let a good failure go to waste. Many of them used failures in one career to supercharge another. Indeed, failure can be the best preparation for a career change, and even a catalyst for total reinvention.

One who learned that lesson well was Harland David Sanders, who washed out as a lawyer, was fired from a dozen jobs, started a restaurant that failed, and was broke by the age of sixty-five—and credited all of those failures to finding his life's work. Born in 1890 in Indiana, he had had a hardscrabble childhood, leaving home at thirteen. He worked on a railroad for a few years, stoking the coal-powered steam engines, but was fired for insubordination. He lost another railroad job for brawling with a colleague. He studied law through a correspondence course, but his legal career ended after yet another fight—this time with his own client, in the courtroom. Other failed ventures included selling life insurance (fired for insubordination), manufacturing acetylene lamps (failed), selling Michelin tires (laid off), running a service station (closed in the Great Depression), and owning a North Carolina motel and restaurant (destroyed in a fire).

By the time he reached retirement age, he seemed to have well and truly failed at almost everything. He was living off of his $105 a month in Social Security benefits and his savings. That's when he finally came up with a new idea that ultimately proved successful: selling franchise rights to his now-closed eatery's popular fried chicken recipe. It wasn't a sure thing. To sign up franchisees, he traveled around the country, asking restaurant owners to let him cook his chicken in their kitchens, hoping to convince them to sign on. At night, he'd sometimes sleep in his car. Restaurant owners who agreed paid him a mere four cents for each chicken meal they sold. Legend has it that he was turned down 1,009 times before signing up his first franchisee.

Ultimately, though, word spread about his recipe. Hundreds of restaurateurs signed on. His wife mixed the spices and sent them to the franchisees. Taking full advantage of an honorary military title that he'd gotten years before back in Kentucky, Colonel Sanders became the face of the brand, in his familiar white suit with matching white goatee. He stayed on in that role even after selling the chain in 1964. When he died, at age ninety, there were more than six thousand Kentucky Fried Chicken outlets in forty-eight countries.

Looking back, Sanders found that his life's biggest failures had planted the seeds of his greatest success. He had learned to cook by necessity after his father died when he was six and his mother was away peeling tomatoes at a canning factory. He got into the restaurant business accidentally: he had been running a gas station and needed to bring in extra cash on the side. He stumbled onto his fried chicken recipe only because pan-frying was too slow for his customers, so he switched to the then-newfangled pressure fryer, which was faster. His road to riches was the ultimate meandering path, full of iterations and stumbles and falls on his face. Even though he had nailed down his "secret recipe" of herbs and spices by 1940, it took more than a decade before he was able to sign up his first franchisee, and almost twenty years before he could start the company in earnest. Colonel Sanders never set out to become the face of fried chicken. But he got there because he spent his life focused on the journey, not the destination.

ALL OF THOSE elements—the *search* for a new career, iterating and focusing on the process rather than the result, immersing oneself fully in the *struggle*—would play important roles for Marla Ginsburg. She had hit bottom, but she was determined not to stay there. "If you let the loss overwhelm you, it isn't even palatable," she says. "It isn't doable to say, 'I used to fly on private planes, and now I'm on a Greyhound.'" As the experts would have recommended, she attempted to reinvent herself as a designer by focusing on getting through each day, not on some seemingly impossible end point. "It was about not looking back, and not looking way too forward. It's, *what can I accomplish today.* If I spent time looking backwards, I would kill myself, and if I looked too far forward, I felt so far from the finish line."

After losing her money and her home and moving to Canada, she put all her energy into building her design label, which she called MarlaWynne, using her middle name. ("Would you want to say, '*I'm wearing a Ginsburg*'?") Her designs were moderately priced, with simple silhouettes, tailored to women who knew what it was to "turn forty or forty-five and you become invisible" and "your bodies are shifting and changing and you're suddenly, 'Do

I want this arm showing? Does it jiggle?'" She sold the clothing herself, becoming the face of the brand on HSN.

Every step she took seemed to trigger the proverbial two steps back, sometimes more. "I remember calling my dad a million times, saying, 'I can't, I can't, I can't.'" She willed herself to at least not slide backward: "Even if it was a baby step, my job every day was to not lose ground." Marla was struggling, but her clothes were finding an audience. Her designs were easy to wear for women of all shapes—neither too sexy nor frumpy, neither trendy nor geriatric. They came in multiple sizes, from extra small to 3X. And as her business grew, her Greyhound trips began to pay off. She found a new manufacturer in Manhattan and moved back to the United States.

Then came the dreaded *stop*—the one no one asks for: her son fell ill. She was rocked to the core. After she followed him to Amsterdam for his cancer treatment, her world narrowed to taking him to chemotherapy and school. She didn't have friends in the Netherlands, nor the usual distractions of home. Her life had a singular focus—ensuring her son's survival. With nothing else to fill her days, she found herself sketching clothes when he wasn't at home. "I dug into my creativity. I just threw myself into work, and my work saved me," she says. "I felt like a shark, like if I stop moving, I'll die. The pain was so huge."

She didn't quite understand why, but her creativity blossomed. Modern-day science would suggest that was because she had that *stop* that took her out of her normal routine and triggered creative breakthroughs. Ironically, her harrowing move across the ocean also enabled her to ease into a new identity. In a 2016 study of eight hundred households, researchers found that people who had recently moved to a new home were more easily able to make major life changes. Simply swapping out their environment enabled them to break old habits and embrace new ones.

As London Business School's Ibarra has noted, "Change always starts with separation."

Marla didn't know anything about the science, but she saw the results. She honed her vision for her designs and began thinking more expansively about what she wanted the brand to become and where it could go. "That was a long, lonely period, but one of the most creative times of my life . . . my work was the only thing I could control."

Thankfully, her son recovered. After Marla got back to New York and regained her footing, she pivoted again by diversifying into a new line that was geared to younger women and featured layered clothing that could be mixed and matched. When she launched WynneLayers in 2017, she finally felt like her business was on solid ground. It had been a decade since she began her path to reinvention. Marla had been iterating, with plenty of setbacks, every step along the way. Now, for the first time, "I finally got the business to a place where I could breathe again. I didn't breathe for ten years."

Marla is fully aware that even in her worst moments she was more privileged than many. She was educated, white, and she had a circle of friends and professional contacts. At the same time, like others who have reinvented themselves—including those with none of her privileges—she pursued a process that was long, arduous, often miserable, at times humiliating, and above all iterative. "I think many people can do this. There's nothing special about me except an indomitable will. I just work hard," she says. "Reinvention is a battle. You have to keep working at it and working at it."

What's more, like others who have successfully pivoted, she found that she used almost all of the skills from her old life in her new one. "Producing television is exactly like making clothes," Marla told me. A television series starts with an idea for a story; a clothing line starts with "an idea, I do a sketch, and I tell the story of a collection." In television, the next step is producing and testing a pilot before ordering a full series; in apparel that next step is producing and testing samples before ordering a full collection. And in both, "it's a team sport" that involves multiple people with different roles and talents.

She counts herself fortunate as well to have the support of multiple others, ranging from her parents to almost total strangers. There was the acquaintance who lent her the apartment in Amsterdam, and the friend with whom she couch-surfed after getting off the Greyhound in New York. She tears up as she tells me about the clerk at the fancy Los Angeles cosmetics store she used to frequent back when she had money. For her first appearance on HSN, penniless, she went to the shop to ask whether they had any marked-down sale items. "Ms. Ginsburg, you've been shopping here a long time and never asked me that question," the clerk said. Then he handed her a bag, saying, "Whatever you want in the store is my gift." She didn't even know his name.

"Help will come from the most unexpected people, not from the people you think," she told me. "It literally comes from the kindness of strangers."

TODAY, MARLAWYNNE IS a multimillion-dollar global brand sold in Europe and Asia as well as in the United States. You may catch a glimpse of Marla when you tune in to HSN, her short blond hair slicked back, sporting items like the WynneLayers Everywhere Drawstring Vest while breezily cracking jokes, just like the talk-show host she once dreamed of becoming. During a recent hour, when the program's host tried to direct the camera to Marla to show off the next outfit, she yelped, "I'm still getting dressed! . . . I'm a hot mess, girl. I just want you to know it's liiiive TV . . . my life is ridiculous!" At sixty-six years old, she is self-deprecating, sometimes profane, and hilariously but also brutally honest, qualities that have helped propel sales of her HSN line and led to her being named to *Forbes* magazine's "50 over 50" list of accomplished older women, alongside Kamala Harris and Nancy Pelosi.

Still, she appreciates that it could all go away in an instant. "I feel like I'm always living on the precipice of losing it. Once you've lost everything, you know it can happen to you," she told me. Yet she also believes that having endured trauma and failure before, she will be more prepared the next time around.

"Reinvention makes you live in the damn moment," she says. "You have to get up every morning and do the work."

The first time she failed it almost crushed her. Not anymore. "My entrepreneurial journey has been born out of adversity." The difference now, she says, is that when adversity inevitably strikes, she knows how to use it.

3

Eureka!

What Your "Aha" Moments Are Telling You

A moment's insight is sometimes worth a life's experience.
—OLIVER WENDELL HOLMES SR.

Spencer Silver was a young Minneapolis chemist, fresh out of grad school, when he ran into a problem. He was attempting to invent a new adhesive, searching for the holy grail of glue: a supremely powerful adhesive that would come off easily in water. He envisioned Band-Aids you could pull off under water without tearing the hair off of your skin in the process, or picture frames whose labels would peel off effortlessly under the tap without leaving a residue. The possibilities were endless!

Unfortunately, the substance Silver mixed up that day was a flop. Not only did it not dissolve in water; it didn't dissolve at all. When he studied it on a slide under a microscope, he could see that it was made up of tiny spheres, less than the width of a hair. The spheres "had fabulous properties. They could stick and remove without any loss of tack or adhesion," he recalled. To his chemist eyes, the mixture was actually quite beautiful. But it was devilishly tricky to control, the spheres sometimes sticking to one surface and sometimes rubbing off on another. It was finicky stuff. For the life of him, he had no idea what to do with it.

Silver showed his invention to his colleagues, but they couldn't figure out a use for it either. They told him to forget about it and move on. It was reasonable advice. His company, 3M, was in the business of Scotch tape and industrial-strength glues. This adhesive was different, sure, but it apparently wasn't actually good for anything.

Silver stubbornly kept hoping. He gave presentations about the new adhesive at internal talks for fellow 3M scientists. He made bulletin boards coated with the stuff—*Look! You can attach papers without thumbtacks!*—and gave them to the office secretaries, hoping to catch the eyes of their bosses. Still no luck. "It was my baby, and it was unique, and I was fresh out of graduate school, and I wasn't going to give up on it," he told me. "I had other things to do. My bosses would tell me, you can't give up on all your other projects. . . . A lot of people said, 'Don't bother with this!' or 'Do something else!' But I pretty much ignored that." His beleaguered colleagues nicknamed him "Mr. Persistent" for his annoying refusal to get over it already.

That might have been the end of it. In fact, it almost was. Except that six long years after Spencer Silver first mixed the concoction in a flask in his lab, a 3M scientist named Arthur Fry got frustrated one day while singing in his church choir. At his regular Wednesday practice, he had carefully marked the pages of that week's chosen hymns with scraps of paper. But when Sunday services rolled around, his makeshift bookmarks kept slipping out, sending him scrambling. He furiously paged through the sheets in embarrassment, trying to keep up with his fellow choir members. "Everybody else is singing, and I'm trying to find which page I'm on," he recalled of that day.

That's when Art Fry had an "aha" moment that would change

the course of his life. That particular Sunday there happened to be "an especially dull sermon, my mind was wandering." His thoughts drifted to Silver's adhesive. He only vaguely knew the young chemist, but he had heard about his mystery concoction from a colleague on the company golf course, and he had attended one of Silver's presentations. If the adhesive was applied right, Fry mused, he could make a bookmark that would stick to his sheet music but wouldn't tear the pages when he pulled it off. The first thing the next morning he rushed into Silver's lab, retrieved a sample of the stuff, and got to work, applying it to scraps of paper. Sure enough, he could stick the scraps to a page and pull them off without leaving so much as a smudge. Fry had invented the perfect bookmark.

Not long after, compiling a report on a different project, Fry had a question about some data. So he slapped one of his bookmarks on the report, drew an arrow pointing to the data in question, and sent it off to his supervisor, who used the same bookmark to write a note in return. That's when it hit Fry. "Holy cow, this isn't just a bookmark. It's a whole new way to communicate!"

That realization, thanks to a somnolent clergyman and a wayward chemistry experiment, would lead to one of the most profitable reinventions in history: from a failed adhesive into Post-it notes. When 3M finally began selling Art Fry's Post-its in 1980—a dozen years after Spencer Silver first mixed the concoction in his lab, after several fits and false starts—the sticky notes became an instant success. The company reportedly now sells more than 50 billion Post-it notes every year, in 3,000 varieties in more than 150 countries.

More than half a century after that day in church, when I asked ninety-year-old Art Fry about that moment, he lit up with excitement, as if it had just happened yesterday. "That was the 'aha moment,' that flush feeling you have and so forth, when you have a discovery of a new principle," he told me. "When you have a creative idea, a moment of seeing things that you haven't seen before." It's "a physical feeling," he told me. "It's sort of a flush, a flash—a flush and a feeling of excitement."

IF YOU'VE EVER woken up in the middle of the night with a great idea or suddenly come up with a brilliant insight in the shower, you've had an "aha!" moment too. Perhaps you've been stuck on a problem, or you're searching for a new direction in life or work. Suddenly you miraculously know the solution. There's hardly a better feeling. A great, revelatory idea pops into your brain, seemingly out of nowhere. It's a smack-the-forehead, "eureka!" feeling. A "bolt of lightning." A "stroke of genius." It comes to you "out of the blue."

There are many ways to say it, but all describe the same phenomenon: you've conjured a vision that is absolutely unique, and you are absolutely certain it's correct. It pops into your head in its entirety. It's completely original and yet so obvious that it seems inconceivable that nobody has thought of it before. You can't wait to test-drive your new brainwave. For those who make major transitions in life or work, the "eureka!" moment can be the catalyst for change.

In some ways these flashes of "insight"—the technical term for the phenomenon—are similar to a gut feeling, as when Alan Greenspan moved away from music and toward economics, or when two Nashville moms who had just met over lunch decided they should be partners in The Home Edit. Your decision just feels right, even if you don't know why. But unlike a gut feeling, an "aha" moment isn't about making a decision, like choosing between one job and another. Instead, it's a moment of insight—a new concept that comes to you unbidden, in a flash.

Some of history's most notable breakthroughs and creations

have emerged from these moments. Film director James Cameron has said that the "Terminator" appeared to him in a fever dream. J. K. Rowling has claimed that Harry Potter popped into her brain "fully formed" while she was on a train ride in 1990; the idea emerged "out of nowhere, it just fell from above, . . . Really, it was weird." Nobel Prize–winning poet Louise Glück was working on a book that had "tormented" her for four years, when she "suddenly saw how I could shape this manuscript and finish it. It was a miracle." Carole King said of composing her iconic song, "You've Got a Friend," that it was simply there, as a finished work, when she sat down to play the piano one day: "It purely came *through* me."

Scholars, philosophers, and scientists have been trying to figure out how this happens for thousands of years. Homer in the *Iliad* and Virgil with the *Aeneid* invoked the Muses for inspiration. The phrase "eureka moment" itself dates back to the third century BC, when, legend has it, the Greek mathematician Archimedes was challenged to determine whether a crown was made of pure gold or mixed with cheaper metal. He was stumped, until he lowered himself into a bath—and as the bath water rose he suddenly realized that he could calculate the crown's density using water displacement. According to lore, he leapt up from the bath and ran through the streets, buck naked, crying "Eureka!," which loosely translates to "I have found it!" That origin story is almost certainly apocryphal, but the phrase stuck.

For centuries afterward, the eureka moment was viewed as divine inspiration. Inventors, artists, and scientists believed they were simply receptacles for a higher power, not responsible for their own works. Michelangelo considered himself and his tools to be God's instruments. Milton asked God to "instruct me, for thou knowest," in his 1674 *Paradise Lost*. Harriet Beecher Stowe supposedly claimed that a vision in church led her to write *Uncle*

Tom's Cabin. The word "creativity"—as in something original that is hatched in the brain—didn't even come into popular usage until the 1920s.

But only in recent decades have scientists been able to understand how the process works. And while the science behind eureka moments is neither as romantic nor as mythical as those past geniuses would have us believe, it is eminently more useful for the rest of us. Using tools like functional magnetic resonance imaging (fMRI), which maps the brain's blood flow, and electroencephalogram (EEG), which measures its electrical activity, scientists can actually see what happens in our brains as we are having an "aha" moment. And their new revelations shed light not just on those sudden insights but also on the process by which we come up with completely original ideas, inventions, and even new pathways. Understanding how the process works can help lead us to be more creative, whether we're solving a difficult problem or reimagining a new path in life.

WHEN YOU'RE FACED with any challenge, there are of course multiple ways of searching for a solution. You might try to solve the problem analytically, in a rational, step-by-step way. If you're considering a career change, for example, you might make a list of your strengths and weaknesses, research different types of jobs, and interview people in different fields. You might even shadow someone to learn about other careers, or perhaps you'd volunteer to get a tentative taste of something new.

For some people, though, the solution appears much more suddenly. It comes in a flash, in a eureka moment, seemingly without any effort on their part at all. Out of the blue they have a rush of clarity about what it is that they really want to pursue.

A few years ago, Olin Business School's Erik Dane asked five hundred people if they'd ever had an epiphany, which he defined as "a sudden and abrupt insight and/or change in perspective that transforms the individual's concept of self and identity" and that creates "new meaning in the individual's life." About half of the participants reported having had one. Some had epiphanies that led them to abandon toxic relationships. Others were motivated to break a bad habit. But to Dane's surprise, a sizable number of participants, about 20 percent, were inspired to reinvent their careers. A common thread throughout their responses was that the epiphanies had gone beyond a thought or a realization—they had served as a spark that literally prompted them to *take action*, to make meaningful changes.

One man, an engineer, suddenly decided he wanted to quit his job and go back to school to become a management consultant. A woman in the US Air Force realized that she no longer saw her future in the military, and she set her sights on a new path. "They go from zero to sixty, from life in a state of confusion to suddenly having this epiphany," said Dane.

The participants couldn't predict when or where a sudden insight might strike. But they could point to the exact moment one came on. One participant had a sudden realization while driving to work. Another was sitting in a school assembly. A third was in a nursing home, where "my dad had just passed away. I realized that I didn't want to end up going out feeling remorseful for not having done what I wanted because I was too scared. I decided that I will change my life by enjoying it more and work on getting a job that I love instead of living in the bad dead end job I have."

Conventional wisdom dictates that you need to devote a lot of thought and analysis to making a change so profound, so life altering. You wouldn't simply abandon years of mastering a profession because you had a jolt out of the blue, right? We'd all like to think that we would carefully weigh our options and deeply probe all of the factors involved before coming to any kind of rash conclusion.

But that's not what Dane found. Instead, participants reported that this sudden clarity came to them as if delivered by an outside voice. They didn't feel responsible for their own insights. The participants were grateful for this sudden wisdom, but they didn't consider themselves to be the authors of their own epiphanies. Instead, they felt that these revelations were "bestowed as gifts upon them," he told me. One woman reported, "It was kind of weird, because it was almost physical to a certain extent. I kind of felt like I could see colors better." Dane's research also suggests that those who experienced these epiphanies were open to them—and that overthinking might have led them to shut down these insightful moments, or to trivialize or ignore potentially breakthrough ideas.

There was one other peculiar characteristic of epiphanies that participants reported. They said that it was as if their brain had gone AWOL in order to work behind their back to knit together unrelated bits and pieces of information on the sly. Disparate ideas suddenly "came together" without any conscious effort from them, they said. They couldn't explain how it happened. "I think that all of the pieces were there and floating around and swimming in my head for a very long time," as one woman said. Another explained, "You kind of stumble across a connection," one for which "you weren't specifically looking." A third described her thoughts as "noodling around in an inarticulate way and then suddenly it all just comes together," sparking her realization that she needed to look for a new job because she was being asked to carry out orders she felt were unethical.

As it turns out, the study participants had unwittingly described the classic stages of creativity and creative problem solving. In 1939, an advertising executive named James Webb Young laid out a step-by-step formula in a little booklet called *A Technique for Producing Ideas*. Webb explained that inventing a fresh new concept starts with collecting disparate threads of information—what we might consider the *search*. Next you call on all of the flotsam and jetsam floating around inside your skull to try to put together the pieces in some new way, "like a jigsaw puzzle." You *struggle* to create this fresh idea, and inevitably you fail: "You will reach the hopeless stage. Everything is a jumble in your mind, with no clear insight anywhere." That's when you *stop*: "In this third stage you make absolutely no effort of a direct nature. You drop the whole subject, . . . What you have to do at this time, apparently, is to turn the problem over to your unconscious mind and let it work while you sleep." It's only after that, he wrote, that "out of nowhere the Idea will appear"—the *solution*. In other words, put Webb's steps together and you get:

Search→Struggle→Stop→Solution

The nineteenth-century mathematician Henri Poincaré was one of the first to notice this progression. In his 1908 essay "Mathematical Creation," he described how, while puzzling over a new theory, he suddenly saw the solution when he boarded a bus: "At the moment when I put my foot on the step the idea came to me, without anything in my former thoughts seeming to have paved the way for it." Even though he hadn't verified the idea, "I felt a perfect certainty." He theorized that to come up with that kind of breakthrough, you first must *search* for the right elements and *struggle* to put them together, immersing yourself in the problem until it's "absolutely fruitless and whence nothing good seems to have come." When you reach an impasse, you *stop* to take "a rest, longer or shorter." During that break, the subconscious brain churns out "a great number of combinations," and the correct *solution* ultimately rises to the top. That's when "a sudden illumination seizes upon the mind of the mathematician." Eureka!

Search → Struggle → Stop → Solution

Poincaré's description was prescient. Neuroscientists have literally seen the same progression in their laboratories. The phenomenon that both Webb and Poincaré explained—and that Dane's subjects described as thoughts "noodling around in an inarticulate way" and suddenly coalescing—isn't just a curious quirk. It's neurologically correct. And it's key to the entire "aha" phenomenon.

Cognitive neuroscientists John Kounios and Mark Beeman found as much when they scanned the brains of people as they solved word puzzles designed to elicit "aha" solutions. At the precise moment participants had a eureka moment, an area of the brain that connects disparate pieces of information lit up. In other words, the brain was making connections between unrelated, or very remotely related, concepts to come up with a solution. For the study participants, as for Dane's career changers, "suddenly it all just comes together." In brain scans, you can actually see the moment it happens, Kounios and Beeman write in their book, *The Eureka Factor*. "Almost literally, this is the spark of insight."

The word puzzle the scientists used in their study is known as the Compound Remote Associates (CRA) test. It gives participants sets of three unrelated words and asks them to come up with a fourth that completes all of them. For example, what fourth word fits with "pine," "crab," and "sauce" to create a compound word? You might puzzle out the answer analytically. Perhaps you'll think "cone" goes with "pine," but then, sounding it out with the other words, you realize it doesn't make sense when paired up with "crab" ("crabcone?") or "sauce" ("conesauce?"). You'll keep trying different word combinations and almost certainly fail.

Alternatively, if you're lucky, the answer pops into your head in a flash, almost without thinking, and you have an aha moment: the word is "apple"! "Pineapple," "crabapple," and "apple sauce."

Try a few more:

Shock/shave/taste
Line/fruit/drunk
Bump/egg/step

In a series of studies, the scientists measured the brain activity of participants as they tried to solve these puzzles. In some cases, the participants wore what looked like a bathing cap covered with electrodes, each wired to an EEG machine that charted their brain waves in real time. As the participants tackled each word set, the electrodes detected changes in their brains' electrical activity. Other participants tried solving the puzzles while an fMRI scanner measured changes in their brain blood flow. Participants were given thirty seconds to come up with each answer; after each word group, they were asked whether they came up with the solution by insight or analytically.

Analyzing the brain activity of their subjects, Kounios and Beeman were able to see that when participants solved one of the word puzzles with a flash of insight, both imaging techniques clearly showed a burst of activity in the right hemisphere of their brains, in an area of the right temporal lobe known as the anterior superior temporal gyrus, which is associated with understanding language and linking disparate pieces of information. "It has connections to lots of other parts of the brain," Kounios explains. "It seems to integrate different types of information from other parts of the brain," bringing those seemingly unrelated tidbits together in a novel way that then suddenly erupts, fully formed, into our consciousness.

What's more, in the milliseconds before the insight appeared, participants had what the scientists call a "brain blink": the part of the brain that processes vision shut off, as if the brain were screening out all distractions. It's similar to what happens when you are asked a difficult question: as you think about it, you stare off into space or you even squeeze your eyes shut. Without realizing it, you're blocking out excess stimuli in order to come up with a solution. The brain, when preparing for an insight, does just the same thing.

In the interest of science, I tried the word game myself, using the same test as Kounios's study participants. For some three-word combinations, the answer was a puzzlement. I took a stab at different answers in my head, mentally adding and discarding possibilities, but came up empty handed. It was clunky and frustrating. Nothing worked. The words seemed to bear no relation to one another at all. But sometimes it was as if I barely read the three words—I didn't even have the time to say them silently to myself—when the answer popped into my head. The three words seemed to appear as a single group rather than as individual elements, and almost immediately the answer was right in front of my face. I didn't have any conscious thought, yet somehow I just *knew*. It was completely self-evident, almost embarrassingly obvious.

Alas, the word sets above weren't among the ones I solved. If you've had a eureka moment yourself, you're one up on me. You already know that the answer to the first is "after" ("aftershock," "aftershave," "aftertaste"); the second is "punch" ("punch line," "fruit punch," "punch-drunk"); and the third is "goose" ("goose bump," "goose egg," "goose step").

How could I not have seen that?!

PEOPLE WHO HAVE had major creative breakthroughs, who know nothing of the science or psychology, nevertheless often describe an almost identical progression of steps. Legendary advertising executive Keith Reinhard credits one of these "aha" moments for his greatest reinvention. In 1980, when his ad agency was competing for the coveted McDonald's account, he was given the unenviable task of trying to reimagine Ronald McDonald. This was perilous territory. At the time, Ronald was a dud. A competing ad agency suggested getting rid of him. In truth, Ronald hardly seemed worth saving. But his fate was a delicate question, considering that the clown's creator was a member of the McDonald's team responsible for choosing the winning ad agency. So instead, Reinhard's group diplomatically suggested that Ronald McDonald had "great potential," but his character needed "to be strengthened." That approach did the trick—his agency won the account.

Now came the hard part: How do you make wimpy Ronald into a hero? Just as the creativity experts would have predicted, Reinhard immersed himself in that question. Searching for inspiration, he flew to Los Angeles to visit the legendary animator Chuck Jones, creator of Road Runner and Wile E. Coyote. Jones listened carefully, then offered this advice: what Ronald McDonald really needed was a nemesis. An enemy to fight against would make this rather weak cartoon character *appear* stronger. Reinhard loved the idea and immediately brought it back to his creative team. They spitballed about various villains they might conjure up as a potential foil to Ronald. Pirates. Monsters. Aliens. But as much as they tried, they couldn't come up with a credible villain. None of them made any sense. They had hit a wall—an impasse. They were defeated. Reinhard had passed through the *search* stage, endured the *struggle*, and now was at a dead *stop*.

A few nights later, Reinhard was sound asleep—distracted from his problem—when he jolted awake at 4:00 AM with a single thought in his head: "'Burger' sounded like 'burglar.'" Instantly, he knew the *solution*. "And voila! The Hamburglar was born." Just like that, Reinhard had solved a seemingly intractable problem: he had invented a villain, a cartoon bad guy intent on stealing hamburgers, who could transform Ronald McDonald into a dashing hero who saves the day. Within hours, his art director partner sketched out the now-familiar villain, in mask and prison stripes, while on the train commuting to work. The Hamburglar not only delighted the client but led to a character universe (remember Mayor McCheese?), a clothing line, games and toys, playgrounds, and more.

Years later, Reinhard was named to the Advertising Hall of Fame for coming up with slogans like "You Deserve a Break Today" and "Just Like a Good Neighbor, State Farm Is There." But looking back, he counts that "aha" moment—when the Hamburglar popped into his head in the middle of the night—as one of his proudest accomplishments. It inspired a "marketing concept that transcended advertising," he says.

For Marie Kondo, an "aha" moment proved personally transformative. Growing up in Japan, she spent five years as a Shinto "shrine maiden," assisting priests with rituals, selling trinkets, and helping to clean the shrine grounds. With her straight black hair cut as sharp as a sheet of glass, her perfectly tailored clothing, and her immaculate home, she was the picture of orderly discipline. But she had no idea what she actually wanted to do with her life. When people asked her about her career aspirations, "I would hesitate and then finally say in desperation, 'Read books,' all the while wondering, 'What do I like to do?'"

It wasn't until she had "a sudden flashback while tidying my room"—a memory of how she loved being the classroom cleaner as a school child—that she realized her destiny was organizing. At one point, she said, she fainted. "When I came to, I heard a mysterious voice, like some god of tidying telling me to look at my things more closely. And I realized my mistake: I was only looking for things to throw out. What I should be doing is finding the things I want to keep." Less than a decade later, the "KonMari" method of organizing, based on retaining only items that "spark joy," had spawned four best-selling books (including *The Life-Changing Magic of Tidying Up*), a Netflix series, and a global consulting business.

It would be lovely if we could will transformative "aha" moments into existence. Sadly, we can't. In fact, trying too hard to come up with a breakthrough idea can actually shut down your brain's creative process. Some people are wired for eureka moments and seem to have creative brainstorms with ease. Not so much for the rest of us. The good news, though, is that we can create the conditions under which we're more likely to have them. Scientists have pinpointed three especially key factors: distraction, relaxation, and a positive mood.

DISTRACTION

Most of us have been conditioned to power through a problem: come up with that solution, keep going until you figure it out, work until you burn out. But research has shown that this is exactly the wrong approach. Exhausting your brain, wearing it down and becoming more and more uptight, is the emotional equivalent of folding yourself into a defensive crouch; you find that any spigot of freewheeling thought is shut off. Instead, stopping and distracting yourself is often the only way to come to a solution. That's when your subconscious allows crazy, unrelated whiffs of ideas to float together to form a novel new thought. Taking your mind off the problem at hand so your brain can let loose, whether by sleeping, eating, watching TV, or singing in church—almost any distraction will do—is essential.

Consider how Keith Reinhard and Marie Kondo came up with their "aha" moments. They immersed themselves in a problem, *searched* for a solution, and then, after a period of *struggle*, reached an impasse and pretty much gave up. Reinhard was flummoxed about how to turn Ronald McDonald into a hero. Kondo was stumped when asked what she wanted to do with her life. Both were at a point reminiscent of where the archetypical Archimedes found himself—defeated in his attempt to figure out the composition of a crown. For each of them, it was only after the *stop*—when they were distracted, by sleep or a fainting spell or a bath—that the solution suddenly made itself known.

Similarly, when Art Fry came up with the idea of Post-it notes, his mind was wandering during a boring sermon. It so happens that this is an ideal condition for creative breakthroughs. Jonathan Schooler, a professor of psychological and brain sciences at the University of California–Santa Barbara, calls it mind *wandering*. That's when you're daydreaming while in a curious state, thinking about an interesting new idea or some other productive outcome—as opposed to the often frantic kind of mind wandering we do when we're worried.

In a study that Schooler led about a decade ago, participants were asked to come up with novel uses for everyday objects like a brick, a bucket, or a pair of shoes. The test was designed to measure whether participants were thinking analytically about a well-defined solution or whether they were thinking more creatively, staying open to less obvious solutions. All participants were given a twelve-minute break in the middle of the test. During the break, some participants were given a challenging memory task, while others were given an undemanding task meant to prompt mind wandering. When the participants returned to the test, the daydreamers' creativity levels soared by 40 percent, while that of the other group barely budged. The latter group offered pedestrian responses (a brick to build a house), while the daydreamers came up with wild and crazy ideas (a brick as a coffin for a Barbie funeral).

"That wandering mind can stumble onto insights. If you always have those blinders on like a horse, you're only looking straight ahead. It's those peripheral thoughts that trigger insights," Kounios says.

There's a reason why Aaron Sorkin, the prolific screenwriter who created *The West Wing* and penned *The Social Network*, among other films and TV series, has said that when he has writer's block, he takes a shower—up to eight times a day! That technique was perhaps best crystallized in the words of a character he didn't create: Alec Baldwin's blowhard boss Jack Donaghy in *30 Rock*. In a 2012 episode called "The Shower Principle," Donaghy yells at Tina Fey's Liz Lemon for interrupting him while he putts a golf ball in his office: "I don't have time for your nonsense, Lemon. I'm working. I know this doesn't look like work, but are you familiar with the Shower Principle?"

He goes on to explain:

The Shower Principle is a term scientists use to describe moments of inspiration that occur when the brain is distracted from the problem at hand. For example, when you're showering. . . . If the cerebral cortex is distracted, by showering or putting, then another part of the brain, the anterior superior temporal gyrus, is activated. This is the site of sudden cognitive inspiration.

Exactly. What he said.

RELAXATION

There's another reason why insights are more likely to pop up in the shower—or, for that matter, while you're golfing, or sleeping, or otherwise giving your brain a rest. Insights are most likely to emerge when your brain is relaxed—specifically, when the part of the brain that controls executive decision-making is offline.

Our brains have an unfortunate tendency to be control freaks. They are like overbearing parents telling us to stop daydreaming and start doing our homework. The prefrontal cortex, essentially the control center of the brain, keeps us on track, but it also can stifle the free-flowing thoughts that lead to new ideas. Sometimes you need to tell that inner parent to stand down. You need to remove the guardrails in your brain and allow disconnected thoughts to swim together unimpeded, so that they can coalesce into something brand-new.

For financial executive Sallie Krawcheck, the key is "thinking and thinking and thinking and then relaxing." One of the most prominent women on Wall Street, she is among the few who have run a major bank. She's also been publicly fired twice—as CEO of Citigroup's wealth management division and as president of a Bank of America division. Her biggest and best ideas, she says, have often come during a break, either when she was between jobs or "when I was standing or sitting, and sort of thinking or playing, and all of a sudden, things shook." One of those moments led her to create Ellevest, an investment platform for women. The firm, of which she is CEO, now boasts a portfolio of more than $1 billion—all from an idea that literally popped into her brain when she was "putting on mascara one morning."

Krawcheck has found that insights suddenly appear during "relaxed, more tired states, and you don't put a governor on your thinking." Neuroscientists have documented this exact process by studying the brains of jazz guitarists in real time. In 2020, researchers asked the musicians, who ranged from novices to professionals, to improvise while hooked up to an EEG machine that measured brain activity. Jazz experts then evaluated their compositions. Sure enough, when the experienced improvisers generated highly original riffs, the part of their brains linked to self-censoring and inhibition was deactivated; by contrast, the beginners had to amp up their analytical thinking to come up with tunes. The scientists could see that in the experienced musicians the prefrontal cortex—the inner parent—had stood down. At the same time, the part of the brain associated with motivation, language, and emotion lit up with activity. That meant the musicians' thoughts could mix and flow, without guardrails.

Researchers who used brain imaging techniques to study poets while they composed stanzas, illustrators while creating book covers, and rappers improvising freestyle verses came up with similar results. Expert poets, for example, were better able than novices to "suspend cognitive control" while in the midst of creation, while rappers' brains were "freed from the conventional constraints." Famed jazz trumpeter Miles Davis described the process in more accessible terms. "I'll play it first, and tell you about it later," he once said.

The musicians and artists illustrated another essential point. We may think these "aha" moments pop into our brains unbidden, and that they are strokes of genius. But in fact they are more likely to be the product of all the knowledge we already have swimming around in our heads. The most experienced jazz guitarists in the study had as many as 1,500 live performances under their belts. They had innumerable combinations and a vast knowledge of patterns stored inside their brains. They had already gone through the *search* phase of collecting massive amounts of information. When they relaxed their "inner parent," those elements could swirl together in novel new ways.

Those experiments bring to mind another musician's experience. In 1964, not long before the Beatles burst onto the international stage, Paul McCartney was living in the London attic of his girlfriend's parents. His room was tiny, barely big enough to fit a bed with a piano wedged against it. One morning, as he recalled later,

> I woke up with a lovely tune in my head. I thought, "That's great, I wonder what that is?" . . .
>
> I liked the melody a lot but because I'd dreamed it I couldn't believe I'd written it. I thought, "No, I've never written like this before." But I had the tune, which was the most magic thing. And you have to ask yourself, "Where did it come from?"

For months, McCartney sat on the tune, so certain was he that somebody else must have composed it. He didn't even write lyrics for it; he and his bandmates called it "Scrambled Eggs." They made up funny lyrics for it: "Scrambled eggs, oh my baby how I love your legs. . . ."

The song, of course, was the now-classic "Yesterday." But it took quite a while before McCartney could convince himself that he had actually composed it. "It came too easy," he said. "I couldn't believe it. I didn't believe that I had written it. I thought that maybe I had heard it somewhere before, it was some other tune. I went around for weeks playing the chords of the song for people, asking them, 'Is this like something? I think I've written it.' And people would say, 'No. It's not like anything else, but it's good.'"

McCartney by that time had already spent years composing and performing music. The individual notes and patterns were in his head. It may have seemed miraculous to him, but scientists would posit that it wasn't surprising that in his sleep those patterns rearranged themselves inside his brain into what would become one of the world's best-known songs.

There's a reason that Richard Branson's mantra is A-B-C-D: "Always Be Connecting the Dots." The Virgin founder has made waves in travel, outer space, music, and the culture at large, but he doesn't pretend that his ideas come out of thin air. You need to have those "dots" of knowledge before you can connect them into something new. Similarly, Steve Jobs famously said, "Creativity is just connecting things." In that way, the entrepreneurs share something in common with Picasso. In a famous, though likely apocryphal, story, a woman approached the painter in a café and asked him to sketch something on a napkin. He did so, handed the napkin back to her, and asked for $10,000. "But you did that in thirty seconds!" she protested.

"No, madam," Picasso responded. "It has taken me my whole life."

POSITIVE MOOD

There's one final way to coax an "aha" moment: you're more likely to have one if you are in a positive mood. In a 2009 study, when Kounios and Beeman and their colleagues scanned the brains of seventy-nine people trying to solve the three-word remote associates test, they found that those who were in a better mood were more likely to come up with the solutions using insight. Anxiety, on the other hand, led to analytic solutions. Being in a positive, relaxed mood "expands the scope of thought," Kounios says. "You're more able to see the remote associations, the alternative possibilities and different perspectives. When you're in a negative mood, particularly when you have anxiety, you have the blinders on."

In a negative mood, your brain is more likely to be on the defensive, to shoot down novel ideas that may emerge rather than welcome them. Conversely, in study after study, being in a frame of mind to "welcome" new ideas creates an upward spiral—the more open you are, the more likely you are to be gifted with an insight. Recall that in Erik Dane's research, participants who had life-changing eureka moments told him that they had been open to the experience. "Readiness," as he calls it, was a crucial factor in whether they experienced the transformative moments in the first place.

That was certainly the case for thirty-two-year-old tech entrepreneur Sheena Allen. She told me how a new business idea had "clicked" for her when she opened her mind to reconciling two seemingly unrelated parts of her life. Growing up in tiny Terry, Mississippi, a majority-Black town outside of Jackson, she always had an inventive, curious personality, but "my view of entrepreneurship was my uncle who owned the florist shop, or cousins who are barbers or hairdressers." It was only after she enrolled in college and learned about Mark Zuckerberg founding Facebook that she realized there were other ways to feed her entrepreneurial appetite.

"Freshman year, it was in my head to create a competitor to Facebook. I drew it out on printer paper in my dorm room. All the freshmen were partying, but I was like, 'No, I want to work on this website.'" By the time Sheena graduated from the University of Southern Mississippi, she had developed two mobile apps. Soon after, she headed to San Jose ("When I went to Silicon Valley, it was me googling, 'Where do you go to build tech companies?'"), but "when I got there, I was super-shocked that I didn't see any Black people. Literally, no Black people." A few months later, she moved on to Austin, where she joined a tech accelerator and worked with a mentor.

Her head was filled with the details of her new world—pitch decks, coding, marketing, fundraising—when she went back home to visit. Suddenly seeing her town through fresh eyes, she was struck by a gaping, unfilled need in her community that she could never have noticed while growing up. In Austin nobody used cash; back home everybody did. Her hometown was essentially a banking desert; many of her friends and neighbors didn't have bank accounts or credit cards. Her great-grandmother kept her savings in the cushions of her recliner. At the grocery store, people lined up at the cashier to get their checks cashed. The world of direct deposit and cashless payments didn't exist for many in her community. Theirs was a world instead of payday loans and check-cashing stores. "We're far behind here, and we aren't the only ones," she realized.

"What clicked to me, eventually, was this whole cashless economy is going to impact the Jackson, Mississippis, the Birmingham, Alabamas," Sheena told me. "No one else [in tech] is going to understand what it's like growing up in a banking desert. . . . They might have the best degrees from the Harvards and Stanfords, but they wouldn't make the connection between what it's like growing up in a low-income, underbanked community and also understanding the tech community."

Combining her intimate knowledge of both of her worlds, Sheena came up with a new venture: a mobile banking platform geared to underserved communities. Once the idea hit her, she recalls, "I had to ask myself, 'Am I crazy? There's no way there's an opportunity that's that big, that nobody has tapped into.'" She wasn't crazy. Today she is the founder and CEO of CapWay, a fintech company that offers mobile banking and financial literacy. Its user-friendly app, in soothing tones of teal and blue, uses intuitive language ("move money," "send money") and offers articles on topics like applying for student loans, investing, and filing taxes. Just as she imagined in college, it also takes a page from social media by allowing users to request help from the community.

"It was definitely me coming home and seeing the people I grew up with pull out the wad of cash. . . . And then I'd go back to Austin and it would be, no cash allowed," Sheena explains. "All those little things were adding up."

SHEENA HIT ON one other essential feature of an "aha" moment. It just feels *right*. When she describes how she came up with the idea, she talks about how obvious it felt to her, like it was written in neon lights. Why had no one else come up with it?

"Aha" moments feel right, apparently, because they often are. In a 2016 study, researcher Carola Salvi, now at the University of Texas at Austin, teamed up with colleagues to test the accuracy of those eureka feelings. They asked people to solve four types of problems, a mix of word and visual puzzles. One was the remote associates test—requiring participants to come up with a fourth word to match a group of three words. Another was an anagram quiz, with participants trying to unscramble four- and five-letter words. A third test was deciphering a rebus, in which a word is rendered in a mix of symbols and letters. The fourth was a visual test, in which participants had to figure out what a partial picture depicted. Participants were given fifteen seconds to answer each problem and then asked to report whether they solved it through insight—that is, with a sudden "aha!" feeling—or through conscious analysis of the problem.

Overwhelmingly, the problems solved with an "aha" moment won, by a significant measure. In the word problems, a stunning 94 percent of the answers solved with "aha" moments were correct, compared with 78 percent of those solved analytically. When puzzle solvers were given visual puzzles, requiring them to identify the image in a partial picture, their "eureka" answers again were far more likely to be correct. The answers felt right because they were in fact right. As Salvi put it, "It's as if it's Mother Nature's trick to attach a bunch of emotions" to an "aha" feeling—to signal, "That idea has a higher quality."

There was a catch, though. When puzzlers ran up against the time limit in the last five seconds, their brains clenched up and froze. Searching for the right answer, they quickly tried to analyze the problem, but trying too hard had the opposite result. They often came up with a Hail-Mary pass of an answer that was wrong. "In order to have insight you have to be more relaxed, be in a state of mind that facilitates insights," Salvi found.

THAT CERTAINTY, THE rush of good feeling that comes with a eureka moment, can be discombobulating. It can be tempting to ignore it, to shrug it off as a bit of nonsense. Doing so, though, may be ill advised. Some of the greatest scientific advancements in history were sparked by "aha" moments that puzzled even their creators.

"At times I feel certain I am right while not knowing the reason," Albert Einstein wrote in 1931. One of the most notable of those times came when, as a young man, Einstein was a clerk in the patent office in Bern, Switzerland. During his off hours, he had been puzzling over a seemingly impossible physics problem: how to reconcile two seemingly incompatible theories about space and time. He turned the problem over and over again in his mind. No matter how hard he tried, he couldn't work it out. Month after month he returned to the problem, with no luck.

"I had wasted time almost a year in fruitless considerations," Einstein later recalled. Finally, all but ready to give up, he confided his frustration to his friend Michele Besso, who worked with him in the patent office. That day in May 1905, he talked through every element of his analysis, laying it out in detail. And by quitting time . . . he had gotten absolutely nowhere. He hit a brick wall.

He had passed through the *search* phase, endured the *struggle*, and now was at a *stop*. Einstein was utterly defeated. He was done, he told his friend. He had failed.

On the streetcar on the way home, he put the whole sorry mess out of his mind and stared up aimlessly at the clock tower that dominated the skyline. That's when the answer suddenly came to him. "A storm broke loose in my mind," as he put it. All the pieces fell into place. He had the *solution*, one that would lead to his theory of special relativity. The next day he showed up on Besso's doorstep. "Thank you," he said, without even a hello. "I've completely solved the problem."

Over the years Einstein recounted having had other flashes of insight while bike riding or playing his violin. He supposedly once said of his most famous equation, $E = mc^2$, "I thought of it on my bicycle." To be clear, most of his theories were backed by years of constant contemplation and hard work. As with others who had transformative breakthroughs, Einstein's discoveries were the result of a long search and struggle, an iterative process of relentless trial and error. "Every step is devilishly difficult," he wrote to Besso in 1912. Yet the breakthroughs often presented themselves only after he stopped and took a breather. "Music helps him when he is thinking about his theories," said Elsa Einstein, his first cousin, who became his second wife in 1919. "He goes to his study, comes back, strikes a few chords on the piano, jots something down, returns to his study."

Einstein's greatest ideas, as he once said, came about by making "a great speculative leap"—and only then working backward to figure out why the heck he was right.

Most of us aren't Einstein, and few of us are wrestling with theoretical physics problems as challenging as the ones he took on. Fortunately, another key feature of "aha" moments is that you don't necessarily have to be struggling with a problem at all. An insight may spring on you seemingly out of the blue. In such cases you get to skip the *stop* stage—the painful impasse—altogether. You go right to the *solution* before you even knew you were looking for one.

Kounios and Beeman tell a delightful story about Richard James, a Navy engineer during World War II. One day James was trying to stabilize instruments aboard his ship, so they would be easier to read as the vessel rolled and bobbed in the water. He was using springs as shock absorbers when one "popped out and bounced around the room as if it had a life of its own." James watched in wonder, took it home to show his wife . . . and within a few years the couple introduced it as a kids' toy, the Slinky, which by 2012 was estimated to be a $3 billion business. Sometimes, the authors concluded, a eureka moment can "trigger the solution to a problem that you didn't even know you had."

ALL OF THIS sheds new light on how Art Fry and Spencer Silver were able to take a useless adhesive and turn it into the Post-it juggernaut. Scientists have found that some people are more likely to attack problems analytically, while others, the ones prone to "aha" moments, are what they call "insightfuls." Art was the latter. Growing up in small-town Iowa and in Kansas City, Missouri, he attended a one-room schoolhouse, listened in on the older kids' lessons, and amused himself by bringing things home from the dump, tearing them apart to see how they worked, and refashioning them into something new. "Curiosity has always been a huge part of my psyche. How do things work? I look for problems and how can we solve those in unexpected ways. Not just taking the same old puzzle pieces and putting them together in expected ways, but how do I find new pieces."

After graduating from the University of Minnesota with a

degree in chemical engineering, Fry went to work at 3M, which he chose largely because it offered scientists the chance to spend 15 percent of their time working on projects of their own choosing. Blue-sky creative time has become fashionable at tech companies like Google, but 3M has been doing it for more than seven decades.

At 3M, Fry focused on new products, vacuuming up information anywhere he could find it. He read the patents filed by his fellow scientists and debriefed his colleagues about the projects they were working on. He attended the technical presentations that scientists hosted two or three times a week and chatted up engineers on the company's twenty-seven-hole golf course. It was on the golf course, which 3M owned until 2016, where he first heard about "Mr. Persistent" and his funky adhesive. "On the second hole of the Red nine, I asked the guy what was happening in Central Research, and he says, 'This guy, Spence Silver, has this adhesive, and it's interesting, but nobody knows what to do with it.'"

Fry filed that tidbit away, along with all the other random intelligence he picked up along the way, until that fateful day when it popped out of his subconscious in church. Yet even then, Post-it notes weren't inevitable. In classic creativity theory, there's one final step that comes after the "aha" moment: verification of the revealed solution. That is, figuring out if the idea actually works. As it turned out, that process would take years in the case of Post-it notes.

There were technical challenges like formulating the right adhesive coating mixture, a tedious process of trial and error. Then there was the problem of manufacturing, since no machinery could make a pad with a sticky strip on each sheet. "We talked to people all over the world about how to make them in a pad format, and nobody really knew." Fry ended up building a pad-making machine in his basement. Then, when the notes were finally tested in a handful of markets under the generic name "Press 'n' Peel," the product flopped. "Everybody thought it was a dumb idea," he said. "There were people trying to kill the program in marketing, saying, 'Who needs a sticky note? It's ten times the cost of scratch paper.' That's what they were comparing it to."

The project almost died multiple times. But Fry wouldn't let it go. He used his 15 percent time to work on it and leaned on colleagues in other departments to spend their blue-sky time with him as well. "If it had been a regular project, it would have been killed. But because it is that 15 percent, you can keep it alive."

The company gave it one more try in Boise, where it blitzed the town with free samples, allowing people to figure out how to use the darn things. The notes flew off the shelves. The product was finally introduced in 1980, with its name changed to the familiar Post-it brand, though Fry objected. ("I thought 'Fry Paper' would be nice," he laughs.) From the moment when Spencer Silver first mixed his mystery adhesive in a flask in 1968, a dozen years had passed. Finally, Art Fry's insight at church, which felt absolutely right at the time, was proven correct. Post-its were an immediate hit.

Today the sale of sticky notes, led by Post-its, is a multibillion-dollar global business. Post-its are sold around the world, in every conceivable shape and size and in dozens of colors. They've become cultural icons themselves. The dreaded "Post-it Note Breakup" was immortalized in a *Sex and the City* episode. Post-it notes are incorporated into artworks in the collection of the Museum of Modern Art and into couture clothing, and they appear as a plot point in the comedy *Romy and Michele's High School Reunion*.

More than half a century after Spencer Silver first mixed up his concoction in the lab, I tracked him down in St. Paul, where at age eighty he was fully immersed in a new career—as a painter. I admired his creations; they were dreamy abstracts, pointillistic visions in greens, blues, browns . . . and in vivid, Post-it note yellow. As I gazed more closely at those paintings, I could see they were made up of tiny dots, reminiscent of the adhesive microspheres that he viewed through his microscope lens years ago as a freshly minted young chemist.

The resemblance was no accident. "The two careers are related," Silver told me. "I'm trying to translate some things from chemistry into art. . . . I'm a very visual person. That was what was cool about the Post-it note development. It was a visual thing. I saw something under a microscope and said, 'This has got to be useful.'" He added happily, "I'm reinventing myself as a painter." Sadly, just a few weeks after our conversation, Silver passed away.

As for Art Fry, at age ninety he is still working on new inventions. The license plate on his Prius reads POSTIT. His greatest eureka moment came decades before neuroscientists began probing human brains with imaging machines to unravel the secrets of creativity and reinvention. Yet when I asked him to describe his own process—how he had an "aha" moment in church about a failed adhesive and turned that into a multibillion-dollar product—he outlined almost word for word what neuroscientists have found in their labs and what psychologists describe in classic creativity theory.

"Our lives are governed by patterns," he told me. "Most good innovators have a whole bunch of balls in the air at once," as they *search* for a fresh new invention. But the process becomes a *struggle*: "So you work on something, you're getting fatigued on that. You haven't gotten the answer right. Solving it is a problem." You get frustrated, reach an impasse, and you *stop*. You distract yourself with something else: "Then you start working on another project,

and then another, and your brain compares different patterns"—
and suddenly the answer appears: "So often, you discover the answer for project A lies in project C, and, aha!" The *solution*.

    Search→Struggle→Stop→Solution

    Art Fry didn't need any scientists to tell him how the "aha"
moment works. He has spent almost a century as living proof of it.

4

Bouncing Forward

Growth after Trauma

*The world breaks every one and afterward many are
strong at the broken places.*
—ERNEST HEMINGWAY, *A Farewell to Arms*

It was a gorgeous Saturday afternoon, perfect for a hike in the woods near Jerusalem. The sky was clear, the sun high in the sky. Near the trail entrance, families picnicked in the shade of pine trees. Men hovered over grills. A child's party was in full swing, with blue and white balloons bobbing in the air.

As she maneuvered her car into the Matta Forest's parking area, tour guide Kay Wilson was already rattling off the history of the place to a new client and friend. Kay, a British-born jazz pianist and painter with tousled brown hair and an easy smile, had immigrated to Israel as a young woman. She had spent two years of intense training in her adopted country to become a guide, a job she loved. Today she was showing off one of her favorite spots to Kristine Luken, a Christian American tourist whom she had befriended when they met on a previous tour in Poland.

The women gathered their provisions of water, apples, and a

penknife for peeling. With Kay's dog Peanut yapping at their feet, they set off for Caesar's Path, a onetime Roman road that is part of the Israel National Trail—Israel's answer to the Appalachian Trail. They stopped to marvel at the ruins of a Byzantine-era church, its mosaic floors still intact beneath a layer of sand. Then they picked up the trail, a peaceful path that left the nearby road behind. Wending their way through the woods, the women stopped at an overlook to enjoy the view. They sat down on a rock outcropping and shared a snack of sunflower seeds.

That's when they were ambushed by two men bearing machetes.

In the grisly attack that followed, Kay was bound, gagged, and stabbed thirteen times with a machete that tore open her lungs and diaphragm. One of the attackers broke her sternum in two places, her ribs in six places, dislocated a shoulder, broke a shoulder blade, and beat her with such force that her rib bones splintered into her lungs. Just a few feet away, the other man brutally hacked Kristine, stabbing her over and over again as she writhed on the ground. Desperately hoping to stop the slaughter, Kay played dead. She willed herself to keep her eyes open and unblinking, an excruciating exercise made more so as she watched her new friend draw her last breath just a few feet away. Finally, the attackers left—only to return moments later to ensure the women were truly dead. One of the assailants plunged his machete into Kay's chest one more time, just for good measure. Then the men fled.

Barely conscious and hardly able to breathe, Kay managed to pull herself up, still bound. One foot in front of the other, she attempted to get back to the trail head. One lung was collapsed and she was still gagged; each agonizing breath was like desperately trying to suck oxygen through a straw. She was certain she would die. She just wanted to get as close to the parking area as she could so that someone would find their bodies. For a mile, in bare feet—

the attackers had taken her shoes and used the laces to bind her wrists—she stumbled through the woods. To focus on staying conscious, she imagined herself playing "Somewhere over the Rainbow" on the piano. It was from her favorite film, *The Wizard of Oz*, and the last song she had heard on her car stereo, a jazz rendition by Oscar Peterson. "I was thinking about the harmony around chords. 'Let's put it in C, but what would sound nice is a flat nine,'" she recalled later. "I never dreamt I would survive." The life ebbing out of her, splintered bones poking out from her skin, she pushed on, focusing hard on the notes with each stumbling step. Finally, in sight of a family of picnickers, she collapsed.

It was a miracle that Kay survived. Doctors later determined that the machete stab wound to her chest missed her aorta by just four millimeters, barely the width of a piece of string. It would take almost three years before Kay's physical wounds healed enough for her to care for herself. The psychic wounds would last far longer. She couldn't sleep. She was haunted by flashbacks. She heard Kristine's last cries all day and night, as real to Kay as if the murder were happening in front of her all over again. She would plug up her ears to try to block out the sound, digging her fingers in so deep that they emerged bloody, to no avail. Unable to focus, she drifted off in the middle of conversations and struggled to place even the most familiar faces. She couldn't bear to think about the attack, yet couldn't think of anything else. She hated herself and was convinced that her friends hated her too.

As her wounds slowly healed, she began therapy. She was terrified of being alone, and even more terrified of leaving the house. She vowed she would never go back into the woods. Her therapist instructed her to venture out to look at a tree for five seconds, then stay a bit longer the next week, then ultimately go out to look at a clump of trees. As part of her treatment, she also had to write down her memories of that day, in minute detail, noting every sight, sound, and smell. It was an excruciating, interminable process. She was stuck living and reliving her own personal hell.

In the first moments of the attack, Kay had tried to fight off her assailant with her pocket knife, jabbing him in the leg before he disarmed her. By a stroke of luck, the police were able to extract his DNA from some drops of his blood on her sleeve. Ultimately, those few drops helped them catch both attackers, two Palestinian men who, it turned out, had previously murdered another woman. In an Israeli documentary about the case, police footage shows officers leading one of the attackers back to the crime scene. With a close-shaven beard, handcuffed, and wearing an orange prison jumpsuit, he remains chillingly emotionless, as unmoved as if reciting from a grocery list, as the police question him (as translated from Arabic):

Police officer: Why did you choose this location?
Attacker: *We wanted to kill.*
Officer: Kill who?
Attacker: *Jews.*
Officer: Why?
Attacker: *Just because. We wanted to kill.*
Officer: For what reason?
Attacker: *No reason.*

Kay was forced to relive her trauma yet again as she testified against the murderers in court; they were given life sentences. After the trial, Kay fled to the desert. For three full years, she stayed there, living alone, not talking to anyone, silent, not so much as listening to the radio. She still couldn't sleep. She couldn't tolerate noise. Even the sound of her own breath was unbearable; she wished she could stop breathing altogether. She poured her memories and heartache into her therapeutic writing, ultimately publishing a beautiful, searing book, *The Rage Less Traveled*.

Today, more than a decade later, Kay is still haunted by the attack. Her symptoms are unabated. Her nights are sleepless. She still can't abide noise. She is hypervigilant. She lives with survivor's guilt, for leading Kristine into the forest that day. Her fight-or-flight instincts seem to be permanently on high alert. Anxiety and apprehension are constant companions. Her life as a tour guide, the job she once loved, is long over.

Her rage at her attackers is as raw as ever. Yet incongruously, she has funneled her energy, not into revenge against her Palestinian assailants, but into helping Palestinian children. With a young Palestinian friend, Kay founded an after-school program for kids in his refugee camp named, in a tribute to the song that helped save her, the Yellow Brick Road Project. She has reached out to other traditional enemies, growing a circle of friends that includes Israeli Arabs as well as Palestinians. A few years ago, she made headlines when she hid an Arab teen in her home after he received death threats for criticizing the kidnapping of Israeli teens by Hamas, the militant Palestinian group.

On a Zoom call, sitting in her brightly lit kitchen in a sweatshirt and cheerful multicolored scarf, her dogs Sheba and Munchkin barking in the background, she tells me that she has started painting again. She shows me her latest work for a friend's young child, a riotously colorful parade of animals marching happily along in primary colors. "I love color, I love cartoons, I like making people happy. There's been a rebirth of that," she told me. She plays piano again too, mostly for herself now, though she performed a soulful jazz arrangement of "Somewhere over the Rainbow," inspired by her trek that terrible day, during a Washington, DC, appearance a few years ago. Her sense of humor is intact as well, as when she tells me she has figured out a way of putting her chronic insomnia to use. "I love bird watching and I don't like noise. I had this eureka moment: I'll take people bird watching. The birds are up early—and you can tell people to shut up and listen."

I try to make sense of these two sides of her personality, seemingly at odds with one another, yet living at once inside of her: the survivor still suffering daily from the brutal trauma of surviving attempted murder; the painter of cheerful pictures who has befriended the children of her sworn enemies.

"I think I've had enough darkness in the last ten years," she explains. "It's like behind all this darkness and the messy society we live in, there is a lot of beauty there. We just have to look for it."

SINCE THE BEGINNING of recorded history, there have been tales of the horrendous aftereffects of trauma. Like Kay, battle-scarred heroes of old suffered anxiety, insomnia, and depression. Mesopotamian cuneiform tablets dating as far back as 3200 BC, unearthed in what is now Iraq, describe warriors felled by horrific visions and nightmares after battles. They were paralyzed with fear, unable to focus; their symptoms, the Mesopotamians believed, were inflicted by the spirits of the enemies they killed. One soldier acted as if cursed by "rancid oil, his mouth is seized so that he is unable to cry out to one who sleeps next to him." In ancient Greece, too, returning warriors were felled by visions and immobilized with fear. Herodotus in 440 BCE recounted how a soldier named Epizelus, who fought in the Battle of Marathon, went blind "without blow of sword or dart"—he was unable to see, though nothing was physically wrong with him—after a vision in which a "ghostly semblance" of "a gigantic warrior, with a huge beard," killed the man next to him.

The ancient scriveners seemed remarkably unconcerned about the psychic wounds of the women who were raped and pillaged during those same battles. In their texts, these women simply went "mad." Unlike the men, the traumatized women were deemed at fault, either because they angered the gods or because they had a "wandering womb" that traveled all over their insides and made them act crazy. That pesky uterus (*hystera* in Greek), incidentally, would also be the genesis of the later diagnosis of "hysteria." Yet madness in women often looked an awful lot like battle scars in men; Shakespeare described it pretty well in his Lady Macbeth, who wandered in a sleepwalking daze and washed nonexistent blood from her hands.

Over the centuries, the same affliction has gone by many names. In the Civil War, veterans returned from the front with "soldier's heart." After World War I, returning warriors crazed by fears, nightmares, and intrusive memories were said to be "shell shocked" by the bombings. World War II veterans suffered from "battle fatigue." More than 1 million soldiers from the Greatest Generation were treated for the malady, and it was responsible for 40 percent of all discharges from the Army.

It wasn't until 1980, after psychiatrists documented the same symptoms in soldiers returning from the war in Vietnam, that the syndrome was finally formalized in the medical literature and given a now-familiar name: post-traumatic stress disorder, or PTSD. Sufferers learned, to their relief, that they weren't crazy, nor were their symptoms imaginary. Instead, psychologists theorized that our brains are incapable of making sense of the most awful events. We're unable to process them. Unfiltered memories of the trauma rear up unpredictably, intruding at any moment. Our brains play tricks on us to avoid these unthinkable thoughts— thus the symptoms of withdrawal and detachment from loved ones, depression, insomnia, and anger. Clinical PTSD symptoms also include flashbacks, an inability to concentrate, and self-destructive, self-medicating behavior like drug or alcohol addiction. Self-loathing and rage are constant companions.

The medical definition originally referred to people who personally experienced life-threatening stresses, primarily men returning from battle. And indeed, the US Department of Veterans Affairs has estimated that between 11 and 20 percent of returning soldiers experience PTSD. But in the decades since the condition was first identified, the definition has been expanded to include victims of violence, illness, and natural disasters, as well as those who are rocked by shocks like the death of a loved one and even those who have witnessed others experiencing traumatic events.

By that measure, 90 percent of us will experience trauma in our lifetime—perhaps more since the onset of the pandemic. By some accounts, more than one-third of frontline medical workers have developed PTSD, plus more than one-third of people who survived severe Covid-19. Health-care workers with the condition are more than five times as likely as their peers to consider suicide. Millions more have been traumatized by the deaths of family members and friends, the pandemic shutdown, the economic devastation, and all the resulting uncertainty. The pandemic set off a mass mental health crisis: rates of depression and anxiety have soared, while burnout has skyrocketed to unprecedented levels.

PTSD symptoms don't necessarily go away on their own. In recent decades, neuroscientists have relied on imaging techniques, like functional magnetic resonance imaging, to peer into our skulls and determine which parts of the brain are activated by memories and emotions. And they've found that PTSD isn't simply a psychological condition: extreme trauma can rewire our brains.

For PTSD sufferers, any reminder of the trauma—even something as mild as a sound or a smell—sends their brain and body back into high alert, as if the dreaded event were happening again *right this minute*. Their body pumps out adrenaline, their heart rate and blood pressure skyrocket, and the primitive portion of the brain called the amygdala sets off the fight-or-flight instinct, just as it did during the original awful event. It's as if their high alert system is stuck, like a car alarm that won't turn off. Sufferers can't just will their internal alert system to power down on its own. That leads to a persistently elevated stress level, which in turn manifests in all sorts of symptoms, from insomnia to problems with memory and focus.

Kay Wilson presents an almost textbook case of PTSD: the insomnia, the rage, the intrusive thoughts, the acute sensitivity to noise, and the body on high alert. After the attack, she couldn't hold a conversation without losing the thread. She had trouble remembering the names of her oldest friends; when she looked at them she would see instead the face of the murdered Kristine. She felt numb to the world, yet paralyzed with self-hatred. Not long after she was released from the hospital, she dreamed that the attack itself was all a dream. When she woke up to the reality, she was so traumatized that she willed herself not to sleep again—and for the next decade her body would wake up before she could even begin to dream.

And yet, when I met Kay, I couldn't shake the feeling that there was something more to her case, something that PTSD couldn't explain. Yes, the disorder describes the problems she has struggled with in the years since the attack. But it doesn't account for the other fundamental and very real ways in which Kay has been transformed. It doesn't explain why she is working to help Palestinian children and befriending traditional enemies. What about her pastime of painting brightly colored pictures, her delight in bird watching, and her new appreciation for the beauty beneath the messiness of life? How to explain all that?

Thousands of miles away, psychologists are delving into the answer.

IN THE EARLY 1980s, Richard Tedeschi, a psychologist at the University of North Carolina at Charlotte, began thinking about wisdom. Specifically, he wondered what it is exactly that makes people wise. Lots of people are book-smart, but he wanted to investigate how the brain accumulates and processes wisdom—that is, "knowledge that is gained by having many experiences in life," or "the natural ability to understand things that most other people can't understand," per *Merriam-Webster*. Psychologists have investigated almost every aspect of how we think. Neuroscientists have used multimillion-dollar imaging machines to probe the crevices of our brains. Yet the genesis of wisdom—how we acquire it, where it comes from—has remained a mystery, as enigmatic as understanding the essence of the human soul.

Tedeschi and his colleague Lawrence Calhoun designed a study to try to find the answer. Their first task was to find people who *had* wisdom. Perhaps, they thought, elderly people had some special lock on how to become wise, especially those who had lived through life's most difficult moments, like losing loved ones. That idea got them thinking: maybe not just elderly people, but others who had suffered, might be able to shed light on what makes you wise. And so they went in search of people who had experienced hardship. They spent hours studying the elderly and interviewing people who had severe disabilities or were victims of devastating accidents. What, they wanted to know, had those difficulties taught them?

To their disappointment, they learned pretty much nothing about the origins of wisdom. But they were stunned to discover something else entirely, something they weren't looking for: many of the participants reported positive changes in their lives. They felt stronger than before. They talked about being more open to new experiences and gaining the ability to develop new skills. Some had reinvented their lives entirely. These people didn't simply "bounce back" to their pre-trauma lives. Instead, they had actually bounced *forward*, in many cases moving on to completely new and more fulfilling pursuits.

Tedeschi was particularly struck by one of the participants, a rock musician named Jerry, who had been paralyzed in a car wreck. "This was the one thing that happened in my life that I needed to have happen; it was probably the best thing that ever happened to me," the thirty-four-year-old paraplegic told them, eight years after his accident. "On the outside looking in that's pretty hard to swallow, I'm sure, but hey, that's the way I view it. If I hadn't experienced this and lived through it, I likely wouldn't be here today because of my lifestyle previously—I was on a real self-destructive path."

It didn't seem to make sense. These people had experienced the worst that life could throw at someone. The elderly participants had watched children and spouses die of illness or even suicide. The accident victims, like Jerry, had been cut down in the prime of life. "I was shocked" at Jerry's response, Tedeschi told me. Even more surprising was that "we found he wasn't the only one who said that." When he and Calhoun interviewed other accident victims and disabled subjects, they were awed, he said, by the comments they heard, among them:

- I established a new path for my life.
- I am able to do better things with my life.
- New opportunities are available that wouldn't have been otherwise.
- I changed my priorities about what is important in life.

Before Jerry's accident, he said, he had been a partier and drug abuser. Afterward, with his rock career over, he went back to school. Ultimately, he earned a graduate degree and went to work at a nonprofit that helps rehabilitate homes for disabled people.

He had managed to take the worst that life threw at him and turn it into something positive.

TEDESCHI AND CALHOUN were well versed in the science of PTSD. Yet it was becoming clear to them that the tunnel-vision focus on PTSD's debilitating symptoms was too limited. It obscured other impacts of trauma. It didn't account for what the researchers were seeing as they widened the aperture on survivors. In their studies, many people who experienced PTSD were also experiencing growth—often at the same time.

They needed to understand what was going on. So they sought out others who had survived traumas. Over the next few years, in a series of studies, they and others interviewed those who had endured hurricanes, war, domestic violence, the death of loved ones. These survivors were traumatized, for sure. Many suffered from PTSD. Yet, in each study, a significant number of them also felt renewed. They changed their priorities. They had a sense of new possibilities in life. They had become open to following new paths.

In 1995, the two researchers coined a phrase for the phenomenon: post-traumatic *growth*. They created a checklist of twenty-one ways in which the original group of disabled men and women told them their lives improved after tragedies. The list, taken directly from the mouths of the survivors, included "I developed new interests" and "I discovered that I'm stronger than I thought I was." Together, the items on the checklist encompassed growth in five domains: appreciation for life; relationships with others; spiritual changes; personal strength; and, notably, "new possibilities in life." In a study of 373 people conducted by Marie J. C. Forgeard of the University of Pennsylvania, the majority of respondents also reported increased creativity after trauma.

Since then, the burgeoning field has expanded to encompass

the study of trauma victims of every stripe. Survivors of a New Zealand earthquake, state terrorism in Chile, and train bombings in Madrid have reported positive personal changes. Hundreds of studies have found a similar trajectory in groups as diverse as victims of childhood sexual abuse, sexual assault and domestic violence survivors, military combat veterans, bone marrow transplant patients, and cardiac and heart attack survivors. A 2019 meta-analysis of twenty-six studies concluded that almost half of all trauma survivors ultimately experience post-traumatic growth. It can affect societies as a whole after a communal trauma like wartime or, more to the point, a pandemic.

One of the earliest documented cases of post-traumatic growth came in the aftermath of a horrific European 1987 ferry accident, when the *Herald of Free Enterprise* suddenly capsized on its way from Belgium to England after the bow door was left open. The ferry sank in seconds, throwing men, women, and small children into the freezing waters in pitch blackness, killing 193 of them. In the immediate aftermath, psychologist Stephen Joseph was able to interview survivors, who, not surprisingly, reported suffering nightmares and anxiety. Yet when Joseph interviewed them again three years later, 43 percent reported that their lives and attitudes had changed for the better.

What's more, post-traumatic growth may actually increase over time, a meta-analysis of breast cancer research suggests. In one study of 653 breast cancer patients, women were asked on four separate occasions to rate how strongly they felt about the twenty-one statements used to measure post-traumatic growth, including "I developed new interests," "I have changed my priorities," and "I established a new path for my life." The first time they answered the questions was shortly after they were diagnosed. The questionnaire was repeated six, twelve, and eighteen months afterward. Intriguingly, the researchers found that the women's reports of positive feelings grew each time: the longer they had had to adjust to their new reality, the more strongly they felt that despite facing a potentially fatal illness, their lives had actually improved in some ways.

Some of the most notable high achievers trace their success back directly to traumatic experiences. Sumner Redstone, the billionaire entrepreneur whose media empire included CBS and Viacom, was a relatively obscure lawyer and movie theater owner before almost dying in a horrific hotel fire at age fifty-five. Engulfed in flames that seared half his body with third-degree burns, he climbed out an upper-floor window and hung on by the tips of his fingers to a ledge in order to survive. Only after he recovered did he supercharge his ambitions and embark on his manic empire-building spree. "I think I was driven before, but out of that fire came most of the exciting things I have ever done," he once said.

Tedeschi and Calhoun were the first to put a name to post-traumatic growth, but the syndrome is familiar in literature, history, and religion. In Christianity, Jesus transforms his followers through his suffering; in the New Testament (John 16:20–21), Jesus says, "Truly, truly, I say to you, you will weep and lament . . . you will be sorrowful but your sorrow will turn to joy." Buddhism teaches adherents to embrace suffering. In the Islamic faith, the prophet Muhammad is tested by tribulations including the deaths of his wife and uncle. Literature is filled with tales of heroes and heroines who surmount great odds and come out not just renewed but transformed, from Homer's *Odyssey* to J. R. R. Tolkien's *The Lord of the Rings*, from Toni Morrison's *Beloved* and Margaret Atwood's *The Handmaid's Tale* to Stan Lee's *Spider-Man*.

The concept of growth after struggle was perhaps most famously crystallized by Viktor Frankl, the Holocaust survivor whose seminal book, *Man's Search for Meaning*, posits that people can thrive by finding the meaning even in the most unspeakable circumstances. In recounting his horrific experience in a Nazi concentration camp, Frankl comes to the conclusion that "everywhere man is confronted with fate, with the chance of achieving something through his own suffering." He calls this "tragic optimism," which he defines as "the human capacity to creatively turn life's negative aspects into something positive or constructive."

ASTONISHINGLY, RESEARCH TO date suggests that trauma survivors may experience more growth than clinical PTSD. Yet not everyone gets there. While some people transform their lives, others remain mired in stress and misery. What sets the thrivers apart? Have they discovered strategies that others can follow?

It turns out that there are ways to facilitate and encourage post-traumatic growth. As we've seen, reinventions often follow the cadence of *search*, *struggle*, *stop*, and *solution*. For those who experience trauma, there's a twist on that progression: trauma typically inverts the order, with the catalyst being the trauma—the struggle. That in turn prompts the search—the attempt to make sense of what happened.

Trauma shakes up our core belief systems, our understanding of the world. Suddenly everything we took for granted about the future and about fairness and controllability has been shattered. For survivors, navigating this stage requires understanding that they aren't alone and they aren't crazy, that they are experiencing a normal response to an abnormal situation. In this stage (the search), survivors begin to reconfigure their beliefs about life and the future. The process is somewhat akin to the search for future "possible selves."

That phase is followed by another "period of struggle," as Tedeschi calls it. This is the confusing, often miserable, slog that is common to other types of transformations. It's that unavoidable in-between period of limbo, when survivors have left their old identity and worldview behind but haven't yet figured out what comes next. They can't "bounce back" to where they were—the standard definition of resilience or recovery. That would be impossible. Instead, they are trying to navigate forward, toward something new. "It takes time," Tedeschi told me. "It takes a while to right yourself and figure out which direction you're going to go."

To get through the struggle phase, psychologists have found, survivors need to figure out how to regulate their emotions—through exercise, meditation, or whatever else works for them. They need to open up to others and develop a new narrative around their experience—an account that links the past with the present with where they are going in the future. In other words, those who experience growth learn to tell a cohesive "story" about themselves. A new narrative shows them a path forward, allowing them to go beyond simply trying to reclaim the life that has now been shattered.

Intriguingly, survivors who get through to the other side often cite the same essential ingredient—what Tedeschi calls an "expert companion." The companion could be a professional, like a therapist, but more often than not that person is a friend, a family member, or even an acquaintance who helps them make sense of the world as it is now. With the benefit of an outsider's perspective, the expert companion may see strengths that the survivor is unaware of, or pathways never before imagined. The companion may open the survivor's mind to new ways of thinking and help them illuminate a path forward. Only then is their growth—or even transformation—unleashed.

That was the case for Michael Murphy. In 2007, he was a junior at Virginia's Randolph-Macon College, a history major, and an athlete who played baseball and football. But his world collapsed in an instant when, at a drunken house party, he and a friend decided to climb to the roof to get a view of campus. He slipped, fell twenty-five feet to the ground, landed on his back—and severed his spine.

For three years, he struggled to come to terms with his new life. Yet today, more than a decade later, he said, "It was a weird twist of fate that turned out to be one of the best things to ever happen to me. It opened up a lot of opportunities for me." He began to redefine himself and work toward new goals: finishing a "Tough Mudder" obstacle course (he's now done two), racing in a marathon (a dozen and counting), and learning to mono-ski. He mused in a blog post about how the transformation happened, about what was the turning point. The key, he realized, was to embrace "vulnerability" and refuse to fall into a "'go-it-alone' mentality." His athletic pursuits were supported by a team of friends, and even strangers, who helped him persevere when the odds against him seemed insurmountable. His physical therapy led him to meet his wife. "I've had help, I've asked for help, I've embraced help," he wrote.

That was the case for Kay Wilson too. "I'm blessed to have amazing friends," she told me. "It seems like every personality filled a different need." Her friend Hannah immediately took charge of her care after the attack. Her tour bus driver, a burly Arab Israeli named Khalil, "would waddle into the room, bring some food I'd never eat, and sit there, drinking scotch. He'd say, 'I'll sit with you, and teach you some Arab curses.'" A rotating cast of other friends took turns driving her to appointments, translating for her family back in England, hosting her, and as she recovered, acting as a sounding board as she slowly began processing what had happened to her. These were the people to whom she could tell her story and with whom she could begin to craft a new one. "Every person had a different gift," she said.

THE PERIOD OF struggle can last for years, yet ultimately survivors of even the most horrific tragedies can make it to the other side. In 1993, researchers sat down with ninety-four people who had experienced one of the single most stressful events in life: a child or a spouse had died suddenly in a car accident. Remarkably, when they were interviewed four to seven years afterward, the majority reported at least one positive change, including higher self-confidence and focus on enjoying the present. Almost one-quarter of them said they had a greater appreciation for life. Surprisingly, the number of positive changes they had experienced "significantly" outnumbered the negative changes, the researchers found.

Nobody would suggest that the death of a child or some other monstrous tragedy is a positive. It isn't the awful event itself that leads to growth, Tedeschi stresses. Instead, it's the survivor's response that makes the difference, as they reevaluate their life, their goals and priorities, and search for a new way of framing the trauma.

Often, survivors discover that part of the solution is to help others. Researchers have found that altruism can facilitate and increase post-traumatic growth. You often hear of bereaved parents setting up nonprofit foundations to honor the memory of their children, like Sandy Hook Promise, established to prevent gun violence after the horrific 2012 school shooting that killed twenty-six people in a Connecticut elementary school, most of them first-graders. One study of Scottish cancer survivors found that half became involved with a charity—more than the number of those who rewarded themselves with a dream vacation.

That finding was borne out in interviews I conducted with survivors like Kay Wilson, who founded the after-school program for Palestinian kids after almost being murdered by Palestinian attackers. She hopes to "dispel hatred, whether toward Arabs or Jews," she says. Her charitable work "helps me make meaning out of something so senseless." As we talked further, she paused, then returned to that phrase: it's about *making* meaning, she stressed, not *finding* meaning. That may seem a minor point, but for trauma survivors like Kay it is an essential one: there is no way to find meaning in a random murder, only a way to *make* something more positive in the aftermath.

IN THE WAKE of the Covid-19 pandemic, will we see post-traumatic growth on a large scale? Research on previous mass events—in particular, recent studies focused on the terror attacks of September 11, 2001—suggests that societies as a whole can experience post-traumatic growth. The assault by Al Qaeda, the deadliest terrorist attack in American history, killed almost three thousand people and left the entire country in shock and disbelief. Even though most Americans didn't experience the attacks firsthand, the trauma was felt by almost everyone. Millions watched on television as planes crashed into the World Trade Center towers and witnessed, in real time, the collapse of the towers. They saw the smoldering remains of two other planes, one that crashed into the Pentagon and the other in a Pennsylvania field. More than two decades later, the wounds, both psychic and physical, are still healing. More than two thousand people have died from diseases attributed to inhaling the toxic cloud of dust and smoke.

My colleague Joe and I were among those in the World Trade Center when the first plane hit. When we made our way outside moments later, the sight greeting us was incomprehensible. Above us, smoke billowed out of a massive, ugly gash in the upper floors of the tower. In front of us, cars were pulled up at crazy angles on the sidewalk, abandoned. One was crushed by a giant chunk of concrete. Pulverized plaster drifted down from the brilliant blue sky, almost like snow, the flakes pinging metallically as they hit the sunglasses perched on top of my head. Blank financial forms wafted from the sky. After a few stunned moments of watching, necks craned upward, we hurriedly set off for our *Wall Street Journal* office across the street, assuming this was a horrific plane accident that would be a major news story—only to have our way blocked, first by rows of burning airplane seats and debris on one street and then, when we detoured to the parallel street, far worse. Human carnage, raw and red, was splattered thickly across the pavement and sidewalk.

We picked our way through this hellscape, stepping gingerly, swerving to avoid a headless corpse that someone had inadequately covered with a restaurant napkin. That's when the second plane flew in, just above our heads, crashing with a boom, deep and deafening. Everyone on the street scattered, not even looking up, fueled by a primitive instinct that led each of us to flatten ourselves against the walls of the nearest buildings. Only then did we realize this was no accident; we were under attack.

Like hundreds of others, we ultimately made our way on foot uptown. Another colleague of ours, who had the presence of mind to grab a camera, took photos on that trek. What's astonishing to see now is that, in a photo of the first tower minutes before it collapsed, those heading uptown to flee from the attack don't even turn around. They don't run. Instead, they continue trudging slowly forward, faces blank. Aside from their business suits, they look like hollow-eyed refugees heading toward the border in a war-torn country. The experience was simply too overwhelming to process. Elsewhere in the photo, the people coming from uptown, who hadn't been there, watch wide-eyed in horror.

Not surprisingly, both Joe and I experienced classic posttraumatic stress symptoms afterward—nightmares, flashbacks, jumpiness. Even now, more than two decades later, I avoid watching the televised memorial services and voluminous written remembrances each year, as do many of the people I know who were there. It's one of the classic PTSD symptoms: avoidance. For me and many others I knew at the time, the world cleaved in two, into the "before" and the "after."

Yet in the years that followed, many of us ended up reimagining our lives in fresh new ways. Both Joe and I would leave the paper to try our hand at new pursuits. A few years later, after also surviving a bout with breast cancer, I took a career leap I never would have imagined before: I gave up my secure job to start a new magazine, a risky proposition in the best of times, but too exciting an opportunity to pass up. Unwittingly we were embracing the tenets of post-traumatic growth, including "I have developed new interests" and "I established a new path for my life."

We weren't outliers. The 9/11 terror attacks provided psychologists and neuroscientists with an unprecedented opportunity to follow the trajectory of trauma survivors in real time. One study conducted in the immediate aftermath and then again six months after the attacks had a sample of 1,505 people, including 11 percent who were either there or were close to someone who was injured or killed. It found a correlation between post-traumatic stress symptoms and people who experienced growth afterward. Another study that followed 1,382 adults over three years following the attacks, starting in November 2001, found that more than half (58 percent) reported some kind of positive change afterward.

Shortly before the attacks, psychologists Christopher Peterson and Martin E. P. Seligman had surveyed more than four thousand people for a research project intended to assess character strengths like kindness, leadership, and gratitude. They weren't looking at post-traumatic growth, and they obviously had no idea of the events about to unfold. But when they surveyed their subjects again two months after the attacks, and then again ten months later, the group scored higher each time on qualities such as gratitude, hope, leadership, teamwork, and kindness.

Whether the Covid-19 pandemic encourages similar positive growth is an open question. We are in a different world today than we were in 2001. Back then, the terrorist threat united much of the country; today the pandemic has further divided it. Still, there's at least a faint hope that we will have post-traumatic growth if we can educate ourselves and eventually emerge from this period of struggle to tell a new story about ourselves.

CERTAIN TYPES OF people, like optimists, extroverts, and those receptive to new experiences, seem more likely to be open to post-traumatic growth. But Tedeschi and his colleagues hope to teach trauma survivors of every stripe how to take those positive steps. They want to reframe the conversation around trauma to include concepts like hope and growth, to banish the assumption that PTSD will dominate the life of sufferers, that they will simply have to learn to live with the symptoms. "My least favorite word is 'coping.' It feels like you're asking people to accept a diminished existence," says Josh Goldberg, who cofounded the Boulder Crest Foundation, a nonprofit dedicated to post-traumatic growth. "We owe people better than that."

Boulder Crest, of which Tedeschi is chair, offers free sessions to combat veterans and first responders who are trying to overcome trauma (its unofficial motto: "Struggle is a terrible thing to waste"). Military participants spend a week at its Bluemont, Virginia, campus, followed by eighteen months of check-ins. The program begins by educating them—helping them understand that reactions like anger and numbness are "a normal reaction to an abnormal situation"—and then coaches them on how to regulate emotions, including techniques like meditation, breathing, and immersion in nature. That's followed by disclosure—talking about the impact of the event—and then by sharing their story and finding in it the seeds of growth. The final step is a focus on service—on giving back to others.

The Boulder Crest Foundation has more recently expanded to offer training sessions to first responders, including police officers, health-care workers, and firefighters. The training makes sense for a wider audience as well, Goldberg says. "When we struggle, we think, 'Something is wrong with me. I may never be right again, and nobody else feels the way I do,'" he says. "The irony is, every single person in the world is going to go through the same struggle. . . . There's a universal nature to what we teach. It doesn't matter if you're a first responder or not."

DESPITE ALL THE evidence to the contrary, the medical community still focuses overwhelmingly on the negatives of trauma—the "disorder and brokenness," as Tedeschi says—rather than the potential positives. That negative focus leads to therapies that aim simply to reduce the painful symptoms, which "allows people to live as diminished versions of themselves." He contends that this approach leaves people with "not very satisfying lives." What's more, therapies that focus on the negative often call for revisiting and talking about the trauma, with the idea that repeated exposure will ultimately numb the pain, yet "a lot of people avoid these treatments because they aren't particularly pleasant."

Tedeschi hopes to turn that approach on its head—to focus attention on the potential positive results rather than doubling down on the negatives. "We are trying to change the perspective on what trauma does to people. We feel the mental health system has missed the boat on that."

That view is gaining acceptance. Sally Maitlis, professor of organizational behavior and leadership at University of Oxford's Saïd Business School, has focused her sights on professional dancers and musicians whose careers are cut short by injury. For this group, losing a career is an incomprehensible blow; their occupation is core to their very belief in who they are. "What is my identity if I'm not a performer? Who am I?" as an injured dancer asked her. Yet after spending more than a decade researching this group, Maitlis found that most "manage to create meaningful futures and even feel more fulfilled" than before: "Often, they discover parts of themselves they barely knew existed. And with these discoveries come new ways of understanding who they might become and the work they might do."

The process can't be rushed, she told me. But the way she describes it is quite similar to Boulder Crest's work with veterans. The artists first must grapple with the emotional fallout, often with the help of an expert companion. "People became tearful in the interviews as they shared their distress. . . . A number of them had felt suicidal—that they could not carry on," she says. "Part of the healing process involves regulating those emotions and having someone to talk about it with. When you get to a point where you can tolerate talking about what happened—it wasn't weeks or months, people often spent years trying to get back to their career—there's that piece of even just acknowledging it. You come out of denial. You say, 'This is really true. Now what am I going to do about it?'"

After that, the process unfolds very much in the way that career change unfolds under less traumatic circumstances. It starts with the *search* for information: "Not just thinking, or 'what shall I do?' But a really active process: What have I lost? What is something that I thought about but never tried?" The search is followed by a period of experimentation—that liminal time when you've left your old identity behind but haven't yet fully embraced a new one. "Do something small" to start out with, Maitlis counsels. If you love cooking, don't buy a restaurant; instead, work with someone in the field, or volunteer to shadow a professional.

By following these steps, the artists Maitlis followed have ended up in a variety of different fields, from the dancer who became the director of a health spa chain to the bassoonist who got a doctorate in cognitive science and now specializes in the neuroscience of performance. "You realize parts of yourself you didn't realize you had," as Maitlis puts it. "You are going to show yourself, a lot of the time, that you can not only overcome but go beyond."

Let's be clear: post-traumatic growth doesn't make the grief, sadness, and anxiety disappear. Far from it: post-traumatic growth can coexist with these trauma responses and often does. When researchers followed 103 former Israeli prisoners of war over thirty years, they found that, while the soldiers showed remarkable post-traumatic growth, that didn't diminish their struggles with PTSD. Both had roots in the loss of control they felt in captivity. The two syndromes "overlap, rather than being opposites," the researchers concluded.

In the end, though, learning to contain PTSD while encouraging growth can lead to transformation. That has certainly been the case for Kay Wilson. Some days she feels fine, but on other days a momentary sight or smell will throw her right back into a panic. Her journey hasn't proceeded along one straight line. "I've never been able to do linear. It's more complex than that . . . the whole PTSD thing is one step forward and two steps back." The trauma lives on.

Kay will never be a tour guide again, she still can't sleep, and she still has physical pain. Yet these lingering PTSD symptoms haven't stopped her from becoming a birdwatching guide, a painter, a pianist, and someone who has realized she enjoys giving back to others. She says that focusing her rage narrowly on her attackers has allowed her to open her heart in other ways; it "freed me up not to generically rubber-stamp" all Palestinians as evil. Helping Palestinian kids "gave me meaning to a degree. Terrorism is so meaningless. People who don't even know the name of the person they're murdering. But you have to find some kind of equilibrium, where you can raise your head above the mire."

She rejects the notion of victimhood. "This helplessness has helped me to reinvent. I don't want to be helpless again, ever. I don't want to beg for my life. I want that self-respect and independence," she told me. "A key to the growth was realizing my suffering isn't necessarily worse than somebody else's. It's different. We have terror attacks here, and people are dying of coronavirus. I never say, 'Why them?' So where's the *chutzpah* or hubris to say, 'Why me?'"

She pauses to light a cigarette at her cheery kitchen table. "I have horrible days, but I don't think it nullifies the growth," she says. "I reinvented myself."

5

The "Necessity Entrepreneur"

The Challenges—and Hidden Strengths—of Outliers

Necessity is the mother of taking chances.
—MARK TWAIN

Jane Veron never wanted to leave the workforce. A Harvard MBA who had worked at Bain Consulting and American Express, she loved her career. But she also dreamed of having a family. Like a lot of women, she felt the powerful pull of both—and the frustration of not being able to fully devote herself to either. And so, after she had the second of her three daughters, she reluctantly quit.

For the next dozen years, Jane stayed home in Scarsdale, New York, to raise her kids. She felt fortunate and grateful to be able to afford it. But she was also bereft at the loss of her hard-earned professional identity. "It was twelve years of feeling invisible," she recalls. "I felt this precipitous decline. Your entire identity is wrapped up in work." When she attended events with her husband, she would stumble when asked the inevitable "what do you do?" question. A blank, disinterested look was usually the response she got. "I was passed over, virtually instantly. They looked over my head and moved on to the next person." Encounters like these were especially frustrating because Jane had always imagined combining family and career. "I have so much drive and determination. If the workforce had allowed me to work in a way that *worked*, I would have been valuable. I would have stayed," she says. "But it was untenable."

She poured her excess energy and considerable business skills into neighborhood projects. She lobbied to get a playground built. She revitalized the neighborhood association and then was drafted by others to run it. She worked with local government, the public works department, the schools, and the police to secure a four-way stop sign near the high school. When she went to her business school reunion, her classmates boasted about being named managing directors at investment banks or partners in consulting firms. "I was so proud, I went back to my business school reunion and said, 'I got a four-way stop sign by the high school. It's no easy task.' I felt it gave me purpose."

Still, Jane dreamed of joining the workforce again. She even tried when she was pregnant with her third daughter, looking into a consulting job, but the travel demands weren't realistic for the life she had built. And so, as the kids got older, she doubled down on her community involvement: she chaired the planning board, was president of the League of Women Voters, and became a village trustee.

Finally, after her oldest daughter left for college, she realized, "I need another chapter." By this point, she had been out of the paid workforce for more than a decade and still had two children at home. So rather than trying to pick up where she left off, she pivoted. She pulled together her strands of knowledge about her community and her fellow moms and rolled that into a nonprofit she cofounded called the Acceleration Project, which supports local business owners, especially women and people of color. To advise the owners, she assembled a team of volunteers like herself—women with backgrounds in business and finance who had left the paid workforce to raise kids—to mentor them about balance sheets, marketing, and operations.

The nonprofit aimed to help not just the business owners but the mom volunteers, some of whom were hoping to go back to careers themselves. "I wanted to be able to provide an opportunity for women to use their skills," Jane says, "and prove they weren't just obsolete and had nothing to contribute."

PEOPLE WHO MAKE major pivots in life often do so to chase a particular dream, as Jim Patterson did when he worked on novels from his ad agency desk. But for some, reinvention isn't a choice; it's a necessity. People like Jane who don't fit into the conventional workforce may not be born entrepreneurs. But that may be the only way forward when the world doesn't present them with other options.

Millions are women like Jane who also stepped back from their careers when their kids were young. Children grow up fast, though; in what seems like the blink of an eye, many of these women are revved up and ready to re-engage, fueled by boundless energy and ambition and wisdom. Yet they are shut out of their old industries and ignored by potential employers. These "invisible women" are among the world's great untapped resources. Their old careers are no longer an option, and the gaps on their résumés make it impossible to find work elsewhere. Sometimes automated résumé-screening software trashes their job applications before a human ever sees it. These women often have to claw their way back, sometimes by training for a new industry and sometimes by founding their own business.

Women, along with underrepresented groups like people of color, the disabled, and older workers, face a host of workplace challenges. They often don't have the same access to mentoring and opportunities, they're usually paid less, and they're promoted at lower rates. For example, Black employees comprise 12 percent of entry-level salaried workers (versus 14 percent of the general population), but by the time they reach the senior vice president level that percentage falls to just 4 percent, a McKinsey analysis found. And while Hispanics comprise 19 percent of the population, they make up just 11 percent of entry-level employees and a paltry 6 percent of senior vice presidents and executives.

When executives in these groups do manage to rise to the top, they often get the job only when a company is in dire straits. In a study of female executives, Michelle Ryan and Alex Haslam of the University of Exeter found that female leaders often get a top post only because it's an impossible position, almost certainly doomed to fail, and men don't want it. Then, when the woman can't fix the problem, she gets the blame and is fired—marched right off the dreaded "glass cliff," as the professors dubbed it.

While the glass cliff generally refers to women, it also hobbles marginalized male leaders. In a study of NCAA Division I basketball coaches, researchers at Utah State University found that coaches of color are more likely to be hired when a team has a losing record. These coaches are given less time to turn things around—their job tenure averages almost a year less than that of white coaches—and when they fail, they are almost always replaced by white coaches.

Across industries, meanwhile, Black leaders are penalized more harshly than their white peers for mistakes, and Black women are penalized more than both Black men and white men and women. Reinvention for them often isn't a choice but a necessity.

AS THEY REACH retirement age and beyond, Baby Boomers, too, are finding that the workplace doesn't always have room for them. A recent survey of fifty-seven- to seventy-five-year-olds found that

79 percent of them don't want to retire, either because they can't afford to or because they simply don't want to. In another survey, about the same percentage, 78 percent, said that they had experienced or witnessed age discrimination at work. Ageism is one of the last "isms" that inexplicably seems to be both accepted and considered inevitable. Meanwhile, multiple studies have shown that teams with older workers are *more* productive and innovative and have higher levels of satisfaction.

Perhaps it's no surprise that many seniors are also turning to entrepreneurship to reinvent themselves and their careers rather than try to fit in where they aren't wanted. They're people like Paul Tasner, a San Francisco consumer products executive who was sixty-four years old when, on a Friday night the week before Christmas, his new boss called him into the office and summarily fired him. Paul was in shock. He had never lost a job before. With a background in engineering and a PhD in mathematics, he was an expert on supply chains and manufacturing. He had been working steadily for his entire adult life. The firing was so beyond the realm of his experience that when he joined his wife and friends at a prescheduled dinner that night and announced he had been fired, "they all laughed." They thought it was a joke.

Suddenly out of work, Paul cast about for ways to make use of his skills. "We have a culture that thinks if you reach a certain age, you will be golfing or playing with grandchildren all the time," he says. "I adore my grandchildren, but also want meaningful work." He found some consulting projects here and there, helping companies with supply chain issues, but he felt underutilized. He had the energy and skills and professional contacts to do so much more. "I had over forty years of experience!" he says. "I didn't want to fade away as a consultant." With few if any options in the conventional workforce, he began to look "for something I can do entrepreneurially that speaks to my experience."

Ultimately, at sixty-six, Paul cofounded his own company,

PulpWorks, which converts waste products into biodegradable packaging to replace toxic plastics. "It beats any job I've had, and I've had good jobs too," he told me nine years later, still CEO at age seventy-five. He doesn't earn as much as he once did, but "my kids admire what I'm doing, and my grandkids love what I'm doing. That alone just makes you feel fantastic. . . . For me it's changed the definition of success. I don't think of it in economic terms anymore. You have to pay the mortgage, but I feel incredibly successful. Why shouldn't I? I'm doing good work. I am doing my little part for preventing plastic pollution."

His accomplishments led to a TED talk, which he used to highlight how many others there are like him, with many more to follow. He noted that, by 2050, there will be 84 million seniors in the country, according to census figures. "Can you imagine how many first-time entrepreneurs there will be among 84 million people?" As he told the audience, "Aren't the accomplishments of a seventy-year-old entrepreneur every bit as meaningful, every bit as newsworthy, as the accomplishments of a thirty-year-old entrepreneur? Of course they are. That's why I'd like to make the phrase '70 over 70' just as commonplace as the phrase '30 under 30.'"

WHILE ALL MARGINALIZED groups face barriers, women are especially likely to reinvent their careers—and women of color are even more likely to do so. In part that's because the workplace has been alarmingly slow to acknowledge the needs of working moms. Multiple studies have found that working mothers are considered less competent and less committed to their jobs. An analysis of labor data shows that women as a whole are more likely to be laid off than men; working mothers are the most likely to get the shaft, while men who are dads are the least likely. What's more, while ageism is an equal opportunity offender, it starts earlier for women (at age forty, versus forty-five for men) and hits harder, as evidenced by unemployment rates.

Women overall make up almost half the workforce, and for decades they have received the vast majority of college degrees, yet women are less likely to be promoted than men at every level of an organization. The problem starts early: for every one hundred men promoted to the first rung of management, only eighty-five women join them, McKinsey and the Lean In organization found. Those numbers are substantially lower for women of color—just fifty-eight for Black women. That imbalance grows exponentially at every rung up the ladder, with the vast majority of women boxed out of top jobs because they didn't get the same opportunities and mentoring on the way up. Just 8.8 percent of Fortune 500 CEOs are women—and that's a record high.

Complicating matters, men are more likely to raise their hands for leadership jobs and talk up their qualifications. Women often wait until someone else recognizes their abilities. Lauren Hobart, the CEO of Dick's Sporting Goods, recalled that, while the company's board had identified her years before she got the job, "it isn't something that I ever was gunning for. I was a chief marketing officer, I was getting growth opportunities, I was starting to run e-commerce. I've heard that women often don't see themselves as a CEO, for whatever reason."

Since becoming CEO in 2021, Hobart said, "I've spoken to several other women CEOs. Almost all of them have the same story I have, which is someone else saw it in them before they saw it in themselves." The phenomenon is so common among women that it even has a name: the "tiara syndrome." Coined by Carol Frohlinger and Deborah Kolb, it refers to women's tendency to wait for their achievements to be recognized by others.

When women do lead, their results often top those of their male peers. Financial results rise, debt levels fall, risks are reduced.

Companies with more women in leadership see increased profit-ability and improved stock price performance, studies show. Those firms are also more socially responsible and provide better customer experiences. Yet female leaders are judged far more harshly. A Rockefeller Foundation study found that when a company is in crisis, if the CEO is female, 80 percent of press reports will blame her personally, yet only a minority of such articles blame male bosses. Women's mistakes are remembered longer than those of men, and women face harsher penalties for being wrong.

In a revealing exercise, researchers asked two hundred adults to rate a police chief after reading news stories about a protest rally that spiraled out of control. The only difference was that in some articles, the chief was identified as male, while in others she was depicted as female. When the male chief ended up with twenty-five injured civilians on his hands, participants figured his effectiveness declined 10 percent. But when the chief was female, her effectiveness plunged by 30 percent—and participants demanded that she be demoted, to boot. Victoria Brescoll and her colleagues found a similar reaction, with the woman judged far more harshly than the man, when they gave participants fictional accounts of an error by the chief justice of a state supreme court and by the CEO of an engineering firm.

We've seen the same outcome in real life, not just in academic studies. Female surgeons who lose a patient see 54 percent fewer referrals afterward, according to an analysis of government data, while in the same situation male surgeons experience almost no decline at all. What's worse, when one female surgeon loses a patient, others are also penalized with fewer referrals: *all* women pay the price for one woman's error.

IT ISN'T JUST men who are harder on women. Women can be even harder on themselves. From an early age, young girls are groomed to undervalue themselves compared with boys. Female entrepreneurs routinely pay themselves less than do their male counterparts, and self-employed women take home almost one-third less income than their equivalent male peers. In part that's because female entrepreneurs receive only a tiny percentage of the financial backing that men receive. But it's more than that: research suggests women have grown up internalizing that they are worth less.

One of the most eye-popping studies along these lines involves kids and Hershey's Kisses. First-graders were asked to perform a simple task, and then to set their own pay in chocolate. At six years old, the boys paid themselves more Hershey's Kisses than the girls did! When the experiment was repeated in middle school and high school, this time with cash, the boys paid themselves more every time. Indeed, the pay gap widened the older they got; one set of tenth-grade boys paid themselves *five times* as much as the girls paid themselves.

Perhaps, then, we shouldn't be surprised that at the height of the Covid-19 pandemic female CEOs of start-ups took a 30 percent pay cut—while male CEOs gave themselves a *raise*.

The harsher penalties paid by women makes it both harder for them to make a comeback after a career misstep and more essential to do so, since no one else is likely to step in to bail them out. Female leaders are a whopping 45 percent more likely to be fired than their male counterparts. Yet when *Fortune* magazine surveyed women who lost or left their jobs and fell off of its "Most Powerful Women" list (made up mostly of CEOs), it found that just 13 percent of them were able to find comparable employment elsewhere.

Paradoxically, those barriers have forced women to become champions of reinvention. Despite the odds—or more likely *because* of them—women have become experts at reimagining their careers, and a remarkable entrepreneurial streak among women, and especially among women of color, has only grown in recent years. An American Express report found that the number of businesses helmed by female entrepreneurs soared by more than 20 percent between 2014 and 2019—and at double that rate, or more, for Black, Latina, and Pacific Islander women. Women of color represent 39 percent of the total female population, but a remarkable 89 percent of net new female business owners, the study found.

Many of these women, the study noted, didn't have a choice. They were "necessity entrepreneurs" who "cannot find employment or are unemployed." Others were "flexibility entrepreneurs," boxed out by "workforce policies [that] do not accommodate their caregiving responsibilities." Women started their own companies because they couldn't find suitable work elsewhere. They also were remarkably scrappy—they had to be to survive. Women's businesses are egregiously underfunded. Globally, one-third of all businesses are owned by women, yet in aggregate they face a financing gap of *$1.5 trillion.*

These entrepreneurs give new meaning to the old adage "necessity is the mother of invention." Note that nobody says the *father* of invention. I think there's a reason for that.

MEN'S CAREERS GENERALLY progress in a fairly predictable growth pattern. They follow a straight line that goes up, ultimately plateaus, then ends with retirement. Not so for women. In a study of professional women, organizational psychologist Deborah O'Neil found that women's careers progress through three identifiable stages that mirror the same pattern that we've seen with other types of pivots: the *start→struggle→stop→solution* paradigm. In her taxonomy, the last phase, the solution, is called "reinvention." Almost inevitably, she found, women will need to pivot in their careers and reimagine their trajectory altogether.

In the first stage—what we might consider the search—O'Neil found that women are idealistic about their careers; they proactively pursue opportunities, imagine an unlimited future, and focus on achievement and success. In the second stage, in mid-career, reality strikes hard and a full-on struggle ensues. This is when women's careers often stall: they've been in the workforce for a decade or more and perhaps made it to middle management, but the path forward is now blocked. In O'Neil's study, almost all women in this stage reported experiencing harassment, discrimination, or other toxic interactions. Women she studied were looking for fulfilment but finding a void, she says. They were thinking, "I wanted my career to be an extension of my life, and what brings meaning to me. And I'm just not seeing it."

Conventional wisdom chalks up this frustrating stage to the collision of work and family responsibilities. But we now know that the conventional wisdom is wrong: the career stall is common to women regardless of whether they are married or have children. A Catalyst survey that followed ambitious business school graduates across three continents, for example, found that women who didn't take career breaks still didn't receive the same opportunities as their male counterparts. And a global study of millennial women found that, contrary to popular perception, women in their thirties who quit aren't doing so to start families. The number-one reason they leave is to go elsewhere for better pay, and the second-most common reason is to pursue more attractive professional opportunities. Caring for kids came in a distant fifth place. Yet the damaging myth that women are dialing back their ambition and dropping out to raise kids stubbornly endures—and undergirds decades of unequal pay and promotions.

O'Neil, a professor at Bowling Green State University, refers in her academic papers to this middle period of struggle as the "pragmatic endurance" phase, as women deal with frustrations both at work and at home. When we spoke, though, she offered a more colloquial, and perhaps more accurate, description: "It's just a shit show for these women."

This difficult stage typically leads, O'Neil found—and as we have seen in other transitions—to a stop. Perhaps the woman is laid off, or forced out of her job, or is simply fed up and ready to quit. There might be a trigger like a divorce, the death of a spouse, or kids going off to college. Whatever the impetus, women at this point have hit a wall. They're at an impasse. It's a wake-up call, jolting them out of their complacency and shaking up the status quo.

But there's an upside to this shock to the system. When women are forced to reassess and re-set expectations, that can lead them to reinvent themselves in unexpected and more fulfilling ways. Whatever threw them off track "was devastating in the moment, but it turns into a real opportunity," O'Neil says. In her research, she found that these are the moments that "kicked these women into saying, 'Hmm, okay, it's time to reinvent myself.'" They've entered the solution stage and are prepared to reimagine their futures entirely. "Part of what we found is women's confidence and self-efficacy was beaten down in the second phase" of struggle, O'Neil explains. Refashioning their careers and futures on their own terms is a way to "reclaim" themselves, "to go back out there."

As we've seen with other types of pivots, the stages that O'Neil describes aren't static. The process is cyclical; women may reach one stage, then return to an earlier one. They don't necessarily go through the steps in the same order, although many do follow the general progression from decade to decade as they age. For women in middle age or beyond, the "reinvention" phase is typically thrust upon them whether they want it or not. They are often pushed out of the way—kicked off the career ladder that their male colleagues are still climbing.

Yet when these women do reimagine their careers, they frequently tap into fertile, untapped territories. Many switch to more meaningful and fulfilling work, often in a completely different field, O'Neil found. With surprising frequency, their new careers are geared specifically toward helping others, especially other women. It's "coming to a place of acceptance," where they can say, "'This is who I am and I want to contribute.'"

Wall Street veteran Sallie Krawcheck calls this "the third act" of women's careers. Like O'Neil, she found that the third act is often grounded in "a real sense of mission." Young working moms are told over and over again that "the early years of parenting are going to be tough. Sleep deprivation while trying to establish your career . . . while working to get your kids off to a good start in life . . . is no piece of cake." But after the kids head off for college, "here's what no one else tells you: This time can be a career renaissance for women."

AS INEQUITABLE AS the work world can be for women, it has also toughened them up. It's a stretch to call this a silver lining, but the fact is that when women do lose their jobs, they're more resilient than men. Whether fired, laid off, pushed out, or simply ignored, they're stronger. These ladies have got grit. When they're knocked down, they get right back up and keep going.

That's in part because women have a sort of built-in emotional cushion. Researchers have found that women generally are less likely than men to tie their self-esteem solely to their job. For all of the additional hurdles that women face, that is some recompense. Women tend to have a firm sense of identity beyond the office. That's why, when the job disappears, they don't wallow in self-loathing quite as much as men do.

When psychologists surveyed two hundred unemployed

people, they found that the men had suffered the loss of status far more acutely. "I feel like a loser," one thirty-seven-year-old man reported. "I feel like all the women at the supermarket look at me and know I am unemployed. It's shameful for a man to be without work," said another, a thirty-six-year-old. Women, on the other hand, spoke more about their roles outside of work, whether as amateur athletes, students, parents, daughters, or friends. They also were boosted by the social support they received—more so than the men were. "I have found that my girlfriends and family have been really helpful to me . . . everyone has been so positive that I haven't let things get to me," said a twenty-nine-year-old woman.

I was struck viscerally by this dichotomy on the day in 2009 when *Portfolio* magazine, the business publication I founded, closed, a casualty of the 2008 financial crisis. As our shell-shocked staff cleaned out their desks, I set up a bar with various bottles of pillaged liquor on a communal table. In between packing our boxes, we commiserated over plastic cups of lukewarm wine and scotch. I was immediately struck by the stark difference in the conversations among the men and the women. The men were bereft over the sudden loss of identity, and panicked about the need to get another job right away. This wasn't just about the need for a paycheck. Many of the women were also the primary breadwinners at home. But the women began immediately tapping into alternative identities. They spoke about the opportunity to spend time with their kids or parents or to take some much-needed time for themselves.

That strong self-identity helps put work in its proper perspective, whether in good times or bad. In fact, it's a career "superpower," CNBC correspondent Julia Boorstin says. In her book *When Women Lead*, she describes her worries about going back to work after maternity leave. When she returned, though, she found that she felt even better equipped, more energized, and more creative than before. It was comforting "to know that whatever small indignities befell the workplace 'Julia Boorstin,' there was another identity I could retreat to back at home. My growing family was now the most important thing in my life, so I wasn't as intimidated by my bosses or my interview subjects. Those stakes felt smaller in comparison," she wrote. "Instead of feeling like my womanhood was something that I needed to overcome, it became a kind of superpower that gave me perspective and bolstered me in the most challenging situations."

THIS KIND OF grit is especially necessary for those who belong to more than one marginalized group. I was reminded of that when I caught up with the woman once known as the Budget Fashionista. A decade or so ago, she was a television staple, a funny, personable young blogger and *Today Show* regular with a larger-than-life personality who would prowl the aisles at Marshalls and Target, picking out fabulous finds. I always got a kick out of watching her because she made me feel great about being cheap. She would tell viewers, "I want to save you from committing any fashion violations. I don't want the fashion police coming to your house!" Watching her was almost as much fun as finding last season's Prada sheath dress on the clearance rack.

I hadn't seen her on TV in a while, so I was surprised when I tracked her down recently. It turns out that the Budget Fashionista, whose real name is Kathryn Finney, is now one of the most influential Black technology investors and entrepreneurs in the country. Her most recent business, the Genius Guild, is a hybrid venture fund and tech incubator backed by a $20 million war chest, with a mission to support and invest in companies created by Black founders. In the overwhelmingly white, male technology world, she is literally trying to change the complexion of the industry.

It seemed like an extraordinary pivot for the friendly, frothy budget shopper. Yet when I asked Finney how she had managed to reinvent herself, she seemed perplexed. "I wouldn't call it a pivot. I would call it a continuum. It's who I always was," she said. A surprising number of others I spoke with felt the same way about themselves. Intriguingly, the people who to all outside appearances have made the most radical transformations are the most likely not to see it that way themselves.

The difference in Kathryn Finney's case is that, while she never doubted who she was, almost everybody else did. There were the venture capitalists who spurned her. The tech leaders who ignored her. The potential investor who said he "doesn't do Black women." Even positive news articles praising her success often struck a patronizing tone, like the *Essence* piece that called her "the fairy godmother of tech start-ups."

Black women like Finney face a double bias, discounted for both their race and gender. Adding to that challenge, she found herself at the intersection of two industries, tech and finance, that have been notoriously slow to correct racial and gender inequities. Female founders as a whole are largely shut out by venture capitalists who provide funding to entrepreneurs, receiving just 2 percent of the billions raised in 2021—and Black female founders fare far worse, receiving just 0.27 percent of the total. Venture capital firms are dismissive even before female founders open their mouths: VCs spend 18 percent more time studying male founders' pitch decks than they do reviewing the pitches of all-female teams. Across the board, female entrepreneurs receive smaller loans than men for equivalent businesses, and small-business owners of color are more likely than their white counterparts to be denied credit altogether.

In Finney's case, she had to push through barriers on multiple fronts. She had started her career not in fashion, but as an epidemiologist specializing in global health, working in Ghana. But when her beloved father was diagnosed with colon cancer, she rushed back to his bedside in Minneapolis, abandoning her international ambitions. She was thrown suddenly into that uncomfortable struggle phase. "It was difficult. I had a plan, as most of us do, about what our lives were going to be." Now she had to figure out a new path.

After three months, her father sent her packing, telling her, "Your life isn't here." Kathryn landed in Philadelphia, where in short order she met and married her husband, became CEO of a nonprofit focused on Black women's health—and was devastated when her father succumbed to his illness. She had slammed right into a full stop. It was a low moment. "I was really stressed. My father had passed away and I was a newlywed. My friends were in New York and my family was in Minnesota. In hindsight, I was probably a little depressed, and I was shopping a lot."

That was when her husband—"my expert companion"— suggested that perhaps she could write about her clotheshorse hobby. So she started blogging, writing about budget finds like the shoes she got at the Nordstrom's Rack outlet store. "It was 2002. There was no money to be made on the internet," she says. "It was after the [Internet] bust. . . . I didn't do it for money. I did it because I was bored." But when the Associated Press ran a piece quoting her several months later, the site got so much traffic that it crashed. More press followed, then a book deal and, ultimately, television appearances. The blog grew so popular that Finney was able to quit her day job. The epidemiologist had morphed into the Budget Fashionista.

Yet she was soon right back in *search* mode. As fashion start-ups like Rent the Runway started gaining steam, Finney began thinking about how she could pivot her blog into an online business. She came up with what she thought was a can't-miss idea: a Black female beauty service that would send a box of specialty hair products each month to customers, who often couldn't find the products they needed in local stores. Excited about her plan, she enrolled in a so-called accelerator program, joining a group of about forty-five would-be start-up founders who would receive training, mentoring, and the opportunity to test their ideas in front of an audience. That's when her ambition collided with reality. All but four of the accelerator participants were men. She was the only Black woman. For the first time, "people had no expectations of me. Not low expectations, just no. *We just know you can't do that.*"

She still recalls presenting her idea to the group. She was on her game that day. "I had just done a segment on the *Today Show*, and I'm from Minnesota, so I know how to talk," she recalls. "It was amazing. . . . You could hear a pin drop." She finished with a flourish, elated. She was sure she had nailed it. Then she waited for feedback.

What she got wasn't what she expected. "I don't think you can relate to other Black women," a male colleague opined. His implication was that she was too successful to be accessible to "real" Black women. She was stunned, and infuriated. "As a Black woman, I was in this place of, do I tell him off? If I tell him off, I'm 'the angry Black woman.' It was embarrassing, it was belittling. In hindsight, it was a way to diminish me. It was really difficult."

Finney had slammed right into another *stop* moment. "There was a point at which I was like, 'I'm not going to do it. It's too hard,'" she recalls thinking. Ironically, though, the rejection helped reset her course for the future. In 2012, she sold the Budget Fashionista website and began working with a blogging lifestyle company. She became a frequent speaker at tech conferences, where she was often the only woman of color. She found herself thinking, "I can't be the only Black woman who created something in the tech space."

That realization prompted her to pivot again: she launched a nonprofit, Digital Undivided, to foster growth for start-ups led by women of color. Since nobody had bothered to track how many such founders there were in the first place, she also founded Project Diane, a database of minority female founders named for the civil rights activist Diane Nash. "It was because we needed data to justify our existence," she explains. "I was told over and over again it was too niche for people to care about Black women. . . . It's easy to ignore things if you don't quantify them."

Digital Undivided led in turn to founding the Genius Guild, which goes a step further by investing in Black-owned start-ups and working with the founders to scale their business. Its investments range from a health-care site for women of color to a social media application for "Black nerd" anime fans.

On first glance, Finney's role today seems worlds away from the cheerful blogger gushing about discount shoes. But to her, it makes perfect sense. At every point, "It wasn't a pivot, it was more a logical next step," she told me. "I'm genetically inclined to pivot."

AS FRUSTRATING AS the landscape has been for women and others in marginalized groups, there are signs that the terrain, little by little, may be shifting. Remember Jane Veron, the Scarsdale mom? Her nonprofit and community experience raised her profile to such an extent that in 2021 she was elected the mayor of Scarsdale. She's also still CEO of the Acceleration Project, which has since expanded nationwide. Every element of her journey—taking time off, getting involved in the community, starting the nonprofit—made an essential contribution to her current role.

When she speaks to audiences about her journey from PTA

mom to mayor and nonprofit CEO, it sounds "as if I had planned every step along the way and I can tie it up with a bow," Veron says. "But what I try to share is that when you're in the midst of it, you don't know how it's going to come out. . . . I will assure you that I felt like I was torn in pieces." She hopes she can turn her experience into a way to help others. Among other initiatives at her nonprofit, Veron is attempting to create a flexible workplace where caregivers don't have to make the same difficult choices she did between family and career.

"Barriers existed for both underresourced communities, as well as for those [professional women] who took time off to raise kids," she says. "I felt driven to direct my energy toward addressing social problems. . . . I knew I wanted to use my talents and skills for good."

Morning Joe cohost Mika Brzezinski, who created the Know Your Value campaign to support women's careers, is optimistic that female leaders like Jane, along with new workplace policies—in particular remote work and flexible scheduling—will be game changers. She was especially encouraged when the competition for the *Forbes* "50 over 50" list of high-achieving women, with which she partners, brought in an avalanche of ten thousand nominations, almost all highlighting women who have pivoted throughout their careers. Some didn't even start their trajectory until they were well into middle age or beyond.

"There were so many incredible women over fifty, over sixty, over seventy, over eighty—over eighty and f—ing killing it!" Brzezinski told me. Many are bosses themselves, and have created workplaces that are more welcoming to other women. "I don't look to men for this change," she says. "I'm looking at these powerful women who are staying in the game or reinventing themselves."

These older women are also modeling a new kind of career path, she notes, one that extends over decades, may include multiple pivots, and builds in time to spend on the rest of life, like having a family. "We are discovering a much longer runway than we ever could have imagined," she says. "There's so much more time, so much more opportunity not just to live out their dreams but to live out multiple dreams."

On the other end of the age spectrum, there's some indication that younger generations may face fewer obstacles. Millennials and Gen Zers are more racially and ethnically diverse and notably more tolerant than previous generations, according to Pew Research. Almost half of Gen Zers, those born between 1997 and 2012, are nonwhite, suggesting change is inevitable whether their elders are ready for it or not. Young women are fearlessly reinventing themselves, pivoting or creating from scratch new roles and identities that allow them greater agency over their own lives. They are setting a new standard for their younger siblings.

Among them is tech entrepreneur Ruzwana Bashir. The daughter of illiterate Pakistani immigrants, she grew up in a conservative Pakistani enclave in northern England, where her father was a fruit and vegetable peddler while her mother, who didn't speak English, cared for the family. In their tight-knit community, the men worked as taxi drivers or in factories and the women stayed home. Ruzwana spoke only Urdu until she went to school, and the expectation for her future, she says, was an arranged marriage. Abuse of women and girls was endemic in her community, but not spoken of, for fear of disgracing the family. Ruzwana herself was sexually abused by a neighbor beginning at age ten; "paralyzed by shame," she said nothing about it for years. It was only as an adult that she spoke out and testified against her abuser, risking ostracism from her community; he was sentenced to prison.

For Ruzwana, school became an escape. "It sparked joy in me," she says. She excelled in academics and tested into a school for gifted girls, where her long *shalwar kameez* and traditional

Muslim head scarf marked her as an outsider, the only Pakistani among six hundred students. Still, her outstanding grades won her a scholarship to Oxford. Arriving on campus was a revelation. "Having come from humble beginnings, all of a sudden the world opened up," she told me.

At Oxford, Ruzwana traded in her traditional clothing for jeans and threw herself into campus life and academics. As an outsider, "I was trying to prove I was just as capable as everyone else." She continued in her overachieving ways, ultimately becoming president of the Oxford Union, only the second Muslim to do so (Benazir Bhutto was the first); other predecessors in the post include four British prime ministers. She reveled in learning about different cultures as well. With fellow students, she journeyed to Tanzania to help build a school. She climbed Mount Kilimanjaro. ("I was ill prepared for it, but I made it!") Emerging from her cloistered childhood, she embraced a love of travel and new experiences, traveling to Peru, Bolivia, the United Arab Emirates, Brazil, and Iran.

Like many of her fellow Oxford students, Ruzwana found herself drawn into a career in finance. She snared prestigious positions at Goldman Sachs and at Blackstone. "I followed the path . . . it seemed that's where everyone else was going," she says. But while she was intrigued by some of the work, including Blackstone's massive investment in hotels, she ultimately found it unsatisfying. "I realized you could be successful, but it's not necessarily what ignites my passion."

Yet, as with so many others who ultimately reinvent their careers and lives, it turns out that Ruzwana had been moving toward a new future all along, *searching* for what came next without even realizing where she was heading. Elements of her life that had seemed incidental and peripheral were suddenly coming to the forefront, swimming together to take shape as something new.

There was her youth growing up straddling different cultures. There was her thirst for learning and understanding how others lived. There was her insight into the hotel industry through her work. And capping it all was her insatiable appetite, ignited during college, for travel and experiences.

These separate strands coalesced one frustrating day when she tried to plan a birthday trip to Istanbul with friends. She found herself spending a maddening twenty hours, mostly on the phone, simply trying to arrange tours and sightseeing expeditions. *There must be an easier way*, she thought. That's when inspiration struck. What if she could plan the entire experience, whether a museum tour or a hot-air balloon flight or a kayak rental, with just one click? "It felt like there was an opportunity to build a one-stop shop, and I couldn't find anything that was great that was out there."

Fueled by her new idea, Ruzwana pivoted. She quit Blackstone and headed to Harvard Business School on a Fulbright scholarship. After graduation, she packed her bags and set off for Silicon Valley, hoping to make her dream a reality. She found a like-minded partner in Oskar Bruening, an MIT-trained engineer, and in 2012 they launched Peek, an online marketplace where consumers can book travel experiences like horseback riding or wine tours.

The *struggle*, to be sure, wasn't over. Some of Ruzwana's male peers were making the rounds among venture capitalists and coming back with major investments. But those same investors didn't take her seriously, nor did her female classmates get the kind of respect given unhesitatingly to male founders. One of the VCs asked Ruzwana no questions about herself or her background, then passed on the investment because, he told her dismissively, "We weren't sure you had the grit to build a business like this."

She didn't have *grit*? Ruzwana had already overcome steeper odds than most of us will ever encounter in a lifetime. And she wasn't tough enough? "There's a lot to do still," she says diplomatically.

Despite the VC's boneheaded pronouncement, Ruzwana ultimately did get funding, though less than a male competitor who promptly burned through his much larger investment and failed, she says. She has since navigated other challenges as well. When the pandemic hit, she had to lay off a third of Peek's almost two hundred employees. The company quickly pivoted from travel experiences to homegrown ones—"daycations" like kayaking in Chicago or ziplining in the Ozarks. The local events proved popular, and when restrictions eased, growth resumed and Peek was able to raise additional capital.

By the time I met Ruzwana, at an event for young female founders on International Women's Day at one of Manhattan's more exclusive social clubs, she cut an outgoing, fashionable figure even in that illustrious crowd. While those around her clinked champagne glasses, she sipped on a glass of tea and engaged in animated conversation about fundraising strategies. You wouldn't have suspected what she had to go through to get to that room. But she had turned her struggles into a strength. "I got used to being an outsider," she says. "I was used to having to travel my own path."

Like Ruzwana, other young female founders are increasingly finding success by starting second or even third careers while still in their twenties or early thirties. In the process, they are discovering a remarkably lucrative territory for new businesses that men are often blind to. In 2021, eighty-three female-founded start-ups became "unicorns," so-called because they were valued at $1 billion or more. Recent start-ups geared to women include companies focused on women's health, cosmetics, and connecting neighbors to one another.

These young women are clearing a path that may make it

easier for others to follow. They offer a glimpse of a future that is more hopeful not just for women but for others in marginalized groups. Perhaps someday the challenges of being an "only" will be less of an obstacle and could even spark opportunity. These trail-blazers provide inspiration for others whose paths may currently be blocked.

As O'Neil found in her research on women's career paths, Ruzwana finds more meaning in her second act. In her first pro-fessional incarnation, "I loved the business world, but I realized I wasn't interested in financial engineering." With Peek, "whether renting a boat or taking a class . . . it's an experience that is very joyful. That means a lot to me."

And there's something else too. The company gets thousands of job applications—and a striking number of those applying look a lot like Ruzwana. They're immigrants or first-generation, or women from different kinds of communities. "Having a diverse founder contributes to that," Ruzwana says. "I want to be in a role where you can have a positive impact."

PART II

STRATEGIES FOR SUCCESS

6

Move before You Move (Surprise! You're Already Preparing for Your Next Act)

True life is lived when tiny changes occur.

—LEO TOLSTOY

Will Brown's sprawling grass-fed beef farm in Warwick, New York, is just fifty miles northwest of Manhattan, but a galaxy away from the city. Home is a restored Depression-era farmhouse, surrounded by meadows where sheep and cattle graze. The gentle slopes of the surrounding mountains rise up in the distance.

On a spring day, wearing a torn polo shirt and sturdy jeans, the seventy-one-year-old farmer offers me a tour. He points to where the property line ends, beyond where my eyes can see, at Pochuck Creek—"out of the way place" in the indigenous Lenape Indian language—that ultimately feeds into the Wallkill River. Unhooking a metal cattle fence, he leads the way along a muddy trail through a cow pasture, the air still, the only sounds the chirping of birds and the long grass rustling in the wind.

I stop to admire a flock of sheep in a distant pasture. Suddenly, I jump—a giant, terrifyingly fat black snake is slithering underfoot.

"Snake!" I scream.

Will, a few steps ahead of me, looks laconically over his shoulder without stopping. "What color?"

"Black! A huge black snake! What is it?" I'm shrieking now.

"Black snake." He's a man of few words. "That's what it's called." I scramble through the muck after him, trying to keep up.

We reach his battered Suzuki, and he takes the wheel to show me the rest of his Lowland Farm, which stretches out over a thousand acres and straddles the New Jersey border. We traverse country roads that offer up a curious mix of farmland owned by him and his neighbors—most of them old Warwick farming families who have tended this land for generations—dotted occasionally with massive new suburban luxury homes built on former farmland. He slows as we pass one pasture where his "finishers" are grazing—cows that will be slaughtered in a few weeks' time, bound for farm-to-table restaurants and the local farm store he owns nearby.

"Isn't it hard to slaughter those cows? Don't you get attached to them?" I ask, surveying the herd of majestic bovines in a picture-perfect pastoral scene. He shakes his head. These are young ones, raised for beef, he explains. There's a new crop each year. Every spring the two- and three-year-olds are turned into choice cuts of brisket and prime rib.

Will pauses. Well, he does get attached to the mother cows, he admits. Those he tends to as long as they keep birthing calves, maybe a dozen years or more. The mothers, unlike the calves, have names.

"Do you have a favorite?" I ask.

Oh yes, he nods. "Her name is Bergdorf."

As in Bergdorf Goodman, the upscale Manhattan department store.

And that is the only clue that farmer Will Brown is also a

Harvard-trained economist who spent the first thirty years of his career at J.P. Morgan in London and New York City.

WHEN I FIRST heard about Will Brown, I imagined he was one of those people who quit the corporate world with dreams of moving to the country or running an inn. I envisioned a modern-day *Green Acres*, with that singsong "Goodbye, city life!" But as I got to know him, it became clear that his reinvention was nothing of the sort. It wasn't even planned.

"We never would have decided, 'Let's get a farm,' which is not a very sensible thing to do," he told me. When Will and his wife Barbara bought the farmhouse in the mid-1980s, they were simply looking for an inexpensive weekend place to escape from New York City with their young family. They had no intention of actually operating anything. It wouldn't have made sense in any case; he worked sixty-hour weeks and traveled frequently. Barbara, who had been a research psychologist at New York University, agreed to buy the place on one condition: she "made me promise we'd never have animals."

It took decades, and an endless progression of incremental steps, for that weekend getaway to transform into a full-time profession. It was such a gradual process that Will barely realized it was happening. "The transition happened a piece at a time," he says. "I spent twenty years learning how to do it."

In the popular imagination, transformations are instant, and require no prior preparation. The frog turns into the prince. The poor stepsister sweeping the hearth transforms into Cinderella. Will Brown trades in his business suits for overalls. They all live happily ever after. In real life, of course, imagining some kind of magical makeover is a recipe for disaster. It's much less like a fairy tale and much more akin to Franz Kafka's *Metamorphosis*:

nobody explains to the poor schmuck traveling salesman Gregor Samsa how he's supposed to adjust when he suddenly wakes up one morning as a giant bug. What are the rules? How do you turn over when you're stuck on your back?

Far from being instant, almost all major transformations are gradual, even ones that may look otherwise to the casual observer. I call it the "move before you move." Most people begin edging toward a major transformation, often unknowingly, before they embrace it wholeheartedly. They are in that first stage of transformation, the *search*, without quite realizing it. Throughout my research for this book, this was a constant feature in almost every type of successful reinvention—and an essential one. Giant leaps made without preparation are rare and likely to fail. Instead, those who are successful at making big changes take early steps during the search phase, often before they are aware of what they're doing.

Sometimes those unintentional early moves seem aimless, as if you're spinning your wheels, yet later they turn out to be revelatory. Steve Jobs, as a college dropout, sat in on a calligraphy class for fun—and it later inspired him to introduce multiple computer fonts. Google cofounder Larry Page, who was a serious saxophone player in high school, has said that music is the reason why he prioritized the search engine's high-speed results: "In music you're very cognizant of time. Time is like the primary thing."

If you are contemplating a major transition, you can take some comfort in understanding how this progression plays out. "Moving before you move" means you are doing your homework, even if subconsciously. It suggests, reassuringly, that you're laying the groundwork and are perhaps more prepared than you realize for whatever comes next.

THE BEAUTY OF moving before you move is that, even if you feel a bit lost in the wilderness right now, you're almost certainly moving forward. You'll likely find that nothing you are doing is wasted; you'll call on it later. In the familiar paradigm of *search→struggle→stop→solution*, you may be searching without realizing what you are searching *for*. You don't necessarily know where you will end up, and very often you don't even have a plan. You may well go through a dark period of struggle without seeing where that path is leading. But as uncomfortable as it may be, the key is to lean into the struggle and embrace the mess. It may not make any sense now, when you're still in the middle of it. Sometimes the path isn't clear until you look backward, even if it's obscured by darkness when you look ahead.

What's more, while you may "move before you move" for decades, as Will Brown did, the process doesn't have to take that long. It can unfold quickly, in a matter of a few years, or even months. And it's common to all kinds of pivots, as well as to people at every age. Moving before you move applies just as much to twentysomethings rethinking their identities as it does to "third act" career changers like Will.

Whitney Wolfe Herd, for example, had to reinvent her career from scratch by the time she hit twenty-five. She had cofounded Tinder, the dating app, when she was just twenty-three, and sailed through the search phase. She successfully experimented with new ways to attract young people to dating apps—for example, by traveling around to university campuses and promoting Tinder at fraternities and sororities with flyers, pizza parties, and thongs.

But before she knew it, she was enmeshed in the *struggle*. In a lawsuit, Wolfe Herd claimed that she was sexually harassed at work, alleging, among other things, that a cofounder she had dated sent her abusive text messages and called her a "whore" at a business meeting. (The suit would ultimately be settled.) Two years after cofounding the massively successful site, she was unemployed. Worse, press coverage about her lawsuit had fired up an army of digital trolls, who barraged her with brutally vicious online abuse.

Wolfe Herd had run smack into the *stop*. "I sank into a deep depression," she said. She couldn't sleep and couldn't focus, and she started drinking too much. "At my lowest point, I wanted to die. I was only twenty-four, and already I felt like I was finished. That's the poisonous power of online harassment and abuse—especially when it lands on your phone every morning and follows you everywhere you go."

Yet out of the depths of that struggle came a new idea, an "epiphany," as she called it. She synthesized disparate past experiences, not only what had happened at Tinder but also seemingly random detours, like a high school boyfriend who she said inflicted "severe emotional abuse" (he denied it). "It showed me a very dark side of relationships, and it helped inform my understanding of what was wrong with gender dynamics," she said.

Those pieces coalesced, in the depths of her despair, into an "aha" moment: she would create a digital platform where women could leave compliments for one another. It would be a way to fight the abuse she had experienced in life, reclaim her dignity and self-respect, and in the process help boost other women's self-esteem too. The compliments concept eventually morphed into Bumble, the popular dating platform where women are the ones to make the first move, like a modern-day Sadie Hawkins dance.

She had found her *solution*—and then some. In 2019, Bumble's holding company tapped her to be CEO overseeing both Bumble and Badoo, the world's largest dating site. In 2021, at thirty-one years old, she became the youngest female chief executive to take a company public in the United States. Holding her one-year-old son perched on her hip, she rang the bell on the first day of trading at the NASDAQ exchange. The stock price shot up immediately, and by the end of the day Wolfe Herd also became the world's youngest female self-made billionaire.

Wolfe Herd's outsize success is rare, but in her age group, the speed of her career makeover is not. Younger workers are far more likely than their elders to rethink jobs, career paths, and identities, to reinvent themselves as they go. They intuitively understand the move-before-you-move cadence. They reimagine with abandon. For them, the *search→struggle→stop→solution* paradigm is more of a continuously repeating cycle than a single bridge from one place to another.

Millennials spend an average of just two years and nine months at a job, according to research by CareerBuilder. Gen Zers—those born between 1997 and 2012—spend six months less than that and are now the most job-hopping generation ever tracked. One study found that the average Gen Zer will hold *ten* jobs between the ages of eighteen and thirty-four. What's more, while financial security is a paramount concern, 84 percent of this young generation is also seeking meaning from work. They would even take a pay cut—as much as 21 percent, according to one survey—to find a company that aligns with their values.

On the career front, 62 percent of Gen Zers say they either have started or plan to start a company, making them the most entrepreneurial generation in history. Some 80 percent of the youngest of them, those still in grade school and high school, want to be their own boss. Even among those who don't found their own businesses, their job hopping is an indication that they are searching more actively than their elders for their ultimate career paths and personal identities and are more eager to pivot.

That's a far cry from previous generations. I set off on my path while I was in middle school and stuck to it. When I was in sixth grade, back when I was still pretty sure I would be Mata Hari when I grew up, I joined the fledgling school newspaper. The first article I wrote, about new equipment for the playground, was quoted in the local weekly newspaper. It was the most exciting thing that had ever happened to me. That did it: I had discovered my future. From then on, I knew what I wanted to do and who I wanted to be. I devoured biographies of crusading female journalists like Nellie Bly. I was on a mission.

By high school, I was an editor on the school paper and the literary magazine and spent so much time at the nearby Rutgers University radio station that they forgot I wasn't a student and named me news director. In college, all of my summer jobs were geared to an eventual career in the media. One summer I was the "copy girl" at our suburban New Jersey local daily, charged with sprinting to the printing press as soon as I heard it rumbling to life and grabbing the first four copies off the conveyor belt to hand to the "masthead editors"—the newsroom leaders whose offices surrounded the open floor of the newsroom.

Another summer I was an unpaid intern at a dying magazine, which had the benefit of being in New York City. On those long commuter bus rides, out of sheer boredom, I first picked up my dad's copy of the *Wall Street Journal,* and fell in love. It was the best newspaper writing I had ever read: the front page filled with stories that brought business to life—the struggles, the egos, the boardroom dramas—was as engaging as any bodice-ripping novel or TV show. My singular goal became to get the *Wall Street Journal* internship after junior year, and I threw myself into writing for the college paper. I got the internship, and after graduation, the paper hired me to my dream job, as a cub reporter.

I stayed there for twenty-two years.

THAT WAS THE kind of solid career path that twenty-eight-year-old Lauren Strayhorn imagined for herself too. Her goal was to get a nice, secure corporate marketing job. Her father had worked for one company, General Motors, for almost forty years. That was her intention too—to join one company, stay there for her entire career, and then retire. "Entrepreneurship never came to mind."

Lauren figured that a graduate marketing degree would help set her up for a coveted corporate career. So she enrolled in grad school at Georgetown, while continuing to work full-time in a public relations job. She was a news junkie, but her days were crammed so full that she had no time for TV. To catch up she began consuming email newsletters, a popular way to scour the headlines in short, digestible form.

The problem was that none of the newsletters "looked like me or sounded like me," a young Black professional woman. Soon she was subscribing to twenty newsletters—some mainstream, some geared to millennials, some for multicultural audiences—and spending hours a day weaving together bits and pieces, "having to play Tetris to see what was happening with the news" in a way that was relevant to her.

Lauren wondered if others were similarly frustrated. Putting her graduate marketing classes to use, she interviewed one hundred young Black women. Sure enough, they too said that they couldn't find news targeted to them. Turning her research into a school project, Lauren created a newsletter called "Notedd," which curated a mix of news, culture, and entertainment, aimed squarely at her own demographic. It was a "passion project," she says, one that she enjoyed doing on the side. But it was fun, so she continued working on it sporadically, even after she graduated in May 2019 and took a new full-time job.

When the pandemic hit just a few months later, Lauren, like millions of others, began working remotely. Without a commute or other distractions, she discovered an unexpected silver lining to that uncertain time: "I was now rolling over and working from my bed, and I could put more time and energy into Notedd," Lauren says. She began putting out the newsletter on a regular schedule and ramping up its social media presence. She expanded its offerings, hosting a virtual fitness event and creating a Covid-19 thread for readers to share their concerns and experiences with vaccines: "How does this affect my health, the Black community, Black women?"

She soon realized that her fun side project was a lot more fulfilling than her day job, the one that paid the bills. She began rushing through her "real" work every day so she could spend time with her hobby. "That was my breaking point." Lauren was edging toward a different future without yet realizing it. By experimenting with her newsletter as a school project, then iterating it, she was fully immersed in the search phase. "It was an evolution," she says. But it was evolution over months, not decades. Soon Lauren was wondering if her "side gig" could be something more. She began working with a coach to help her come up with a business plan.

In 2021, with the help of the coach, she quit her job to focus on Notedd. The accidental entrepreneur now spends her days growing her business by working on a subscription model and events. She still takes on freelance work to pay the bills, but her eye is fixed on a future down the line when Notedd becomes self-sustaining and profitable. Lauren is now in that middle phase, the struggle: she hasn't yet fully moved on from her old life working for others, nor has she moved fully into the future, but she feels certain it will be worth the trouble when she does.

"The struggle is real," she says. "But as a Black woman founder . . . I'm trying to set an example that you can pivot, and maybe do another avenue of work like freelance, and still put your time and energy and effort into the passion project." Lauren has discovered an added benefit as well: "For me it was, 'I want to do things I am passionate about. And truly give me joy.'"

Lauren's journey—inching gradually toward a new venture while sticking with the security of a more routine job—is a familiar one for some of the most successful innovators and entrepreneurs. In his book *Originals: How Non-Conformists Move the World*, Wharton psychologist Adam Grant notes that director Ava DuVernay made her first three films while working as a film publicist; *Dilbert* creator Scott Adams didn't quit his job at Pacific Bell for seven years after his comic strip launched; and Nike cofounder Phil Knight sold running shoes out of the trunk of his car for five years before quitting his accounting job to devote himself full-time to his sports apparel company. All of them moved cautiously toward a new identity while remaining firmly ensconced in their old identity—and in a paying job.

"Having a sense of security in one realm gives us the freedom to be original in another," Grant wrote.

AVA DUVERNAY KNEW she wanted to be a filmmaker, Phil Knight knew he wanted to sell athletic gear, and both were taking the necessary steps to get there. Traditional management theory holds that this is exactly the right road map to pursue. We are told that we need to set a goal for ourselves and then carefully plan every step along the way to reach the promised land. In the 1937 self-actualization bible *Think and Grow Rich*—still one of the best-selling books of all time—management guru Oliver Napoleon Hill lays out six steps for success, the fourth of which is: "Create a definite plan for carrying out your desire, and begin at once . . . to put this plan into action." As he wrote, "intelligent planning is essential for success in any undertaking."

And to be sure, if you want to be a surgeon, it makes sense to figure out well in advance what college courses you should take, when and how to apply to med school, what residencies and fellowships to pursue. If you plan to work on Wall Street, you can create a road map that takes you from college major to summer internships to graduate school admissions. When I was a young reporter, one of my twenty-two-year-old colleagues announced that his goal was to someday be the CEO of a media company, and he was planning every step of his career to get him there. (And by the way—he did!)

But as I reported this book I realized how many people don't fall into that neat category. They start down one path, but then life leads them in another. They don't intend to pivot, but their actions propel them in a completely unexpected direction. Often they don't even realize where they are going until they arrive. They are the living embodiment of Steve Jobs's famous observation in a Stanford University commencement address, "You can't connect the dots looking forward, you can only connect them looking backwards."

That was the case for a forty-three-year-old Chicago trial lawyer named Joanne Lee Molinaro, who, without planning to, morphed into perhaps the unlikeliest TikTok star.

The daughter of Korean immigrants, Joanne had established a successful legal career, making partner at a big firm. She was proud of her heritage, and she especially enjoyed the Korean dishes of her childhood. So she was annoyed when, in early 2016, her boyfriend (now-husband) switched to a vegan diet. She at first resisted joining him. "I wasn't on board for a lot of different reasons," she says. "I thought, as a Korean person, I couldn't be vegan. I thought it was really insensitive of this white guy to try to make me vegan."

But she gamely decided to give his plant-based diet a try and set to work "veganizing" his favorite recipes (Italian) and her own (Korean). She substituted marinated mushrooms for beef and tofu for chicken, and she came up with recipes like vegan kimchi fried rice, kkanpoong tofu, and vegan ramen noodles, in addition to the vegan risotto her husband loved. He was so taken with her cooking that he encouraged her to start a YouTube channel, saying, "You're the Korean vegan!"

The nickname stuck. For fun, she set up an Instagram account as well as a YouTube account and began posting her dishes as "the Korean Vegan." It was an amusing distraction, something to take her mind off her work during her limited free time. But between her clever nickname, eye-catching photos, and popular recipes, her posts caught on. Within four years Joanne had amassed seventy thousand Instagram followers and landed a cookbook deal. Yet posting about her vegan cooking was still strictly a sideline. "That's all it was, a hobby," she says. "I didn't even think at that time the notion of making a career out of this existed." Her real job was time-consuming enough, plus she ran marathons and wrote legal commentary on the side, including coauthoring two *Atlantic* pieces taking apart former president Trump's legal challenges to the 2020 election.

After Covid-19 hit, she began for the first time making TikTok videos, "mostly as a coping mechanism for the isolation caused by the global pandemic." She was hardly in TikTok's demographic sweet spot. The biggest TikTok stars are teens like Charli D'Amelio, or young twentysomethings like Addison Rae, who dance and lip-synch to pop songs. Joanne instead offered sixty-second clips of her cooking a dish while telling a contemplative anecdote about her life and loves, often backed by a classical piano soundtrack performed by her concert-pianist husband. In one video, as she assembles a vegan egg and tofu katsu sandwich, she reminisces about her failed first marriage to her college sweetheart. "It was this internal fear of being a failure," she muses softly. "If I could go back in time and give myself some advice, it would be this: think more about what brings you joy and less about what soothes your fear."

Unexpectedly, the TikTok videos exploded. She began attracting millions of fans, many of them less than half her age. "I think just because it was totally different," she says. "And on TikTok, they are craving safety. They crave empowerment. They crave mother energy."

The attention Joanne got in return was equally intoxicating. "When you get feedback in the form of hearts and likes and comments, it's insanely motivating. You want to do more," she says. By the fall of 2021, her Korean Vegan persona was so time-consuming that there was no room left for lawyering. So she quit the firm, though she remains "of counsel" for projects. Today the Korean Vegan has 3 million TikTok followers, large followings on other social networks, a subscription meal-planning app, and a podcast. Joanne's cookbook became a best-seller and she has contracted for two more. The middle-aged lawyer has become a bona fide TikTok star.

"I never in my wildest imagination ever thought that this would be my life," Joanne says. The transition wasn't planned, and it didn't happen overnight; all told, it took about five years. She had edged toward her new identity incrementally, moving before she moved. Her journey wasn't preordained, nor did she have some end goal in mind along the way. People may look at her as an overnight TikTok success, she says, but the truth is that it was the result of years of taking small steps. That's "important to understand," she told me. Otherwise, "it's anxiety inducing" and creates a false expectation that, "if I don't make it overnight, I'll never make it."

Transformations like Joanne Lee Molinaro's are "counterintuitive," Wharton's Grant says. "We've all been told, whether by *The Secret* or *Think and Grow Rich*, or pick your favorite guru, that if you want something, you have to go and make your intentions clear and work toward it." Instead, "here you have people who are sometimes better off almost accidentally stumbling into this opportunity." He says that "one of the reasons it works is because the pressure is off. When it's a hobby, a side hustle, you can play with it. It unlocks creativity. It allows you to be less linear. You get more free associations, you don't have to rush ahead or execute on the first idea you get, and all that tinkering usually leads to something new."

To be sure, while you're in the midst of that nonlinear thinking and tinkering, the payoff isn't necessarily clear. Sometimes it seems like you're just goofing off. You're procrastinating instead of doing something productive. The side hustle may appear to be leading you exactly nowhere.

That's how I felt about my son's obsession with sports when he was younger. He didn't just play sports—he watched sports, talked about sports, and read about sports, especially baseball. He memorized the annual baseball almanacs and could tell you who won the third game of the 1926 World Series (it was the Cardinals over the Yankees—I just asked him) or how many complete games pitcher Jack Chesbro threw in 1904 for the New York Highlanders (forty-eight, ditto). He could quote baseball historian Bill James verbatim. He had a copy of Lou Gehrig's "Luckiest Man" speech tacked on his bedroom wall.

I wished he would be half as invested in his schoolwork. I nagged him every night about getting to his homework. I got frustrated when we sat down to dinner and he insisted that we needed the TV on to watch what he assured me was "the most important game of the year!" (Apparently, they all were.) When would he stop wasting time?

Truly, the joke was on me. His knowledge of sports, all of it accumulated for fun in his spare time, landed him a job after college as a junior producer at ESPN. He has since won two Sports Emmy Awards, while still in his twenties.

Grant might have predicted as much. In one recent research paper studying procrastination, he found that far from wasting time, procrastinators are subconsciously gathering string for breakthrough ideas while they dawdle. He and Jihae Shin tested that theory by asking study participants to write a business proposal. At the same time, they tempted the participants to procrastinate by providing easy access to video clips of Jimmy Kimmel's popular "Mean Tweets" segment, where celebrities do dramatic readings of nasty posts by strangers. The researchers found that those who procrastinated moderately came up with more creative proposals than those who either didn't procrastinate or who put off the task until the last possible second. They concluded that "putting work off can sometimes pay off. Good ideas may come to those who procrastinate."

LIKE THE KOREAN Vegan, many of the people I encountered while researching this book transitioned to a new life along a meandering path, not knowing exactly where their journey was leading. But a subset of them had to figure out how to reinvent the second part of their lives while still in the midst of the first. They had no choice but to be attuned to future pivots because they had chosen a career with a limited life span.

Athletes, dancers, and those in physically demanding roles, like firefighters and soldiers, typically retire early. At a certain point, either their bodies just won't cooperate anymore or they're considered too "old" for a job dominated by fresh faces. These are people who *must* be intentional about reinventing themselves. As a matter of course, they must consciously spend part of their first career contemplating what their second or third one will be. They understand better than anyone the necessity of starting to move before you move. We have a lot to learn from them.

The average NBA player's career, for example, lasts just four and a half years. Basketball great Len Elmore's lasted a decade, including stints with the Indiana Pacers and New York Knicks. Even so, throughout his playing years he kept an eye on life beyond the court. He knew he'd need to earn a living; when he was active in the 1970s and 1980s, NBA players were well compensated, but they didn't bring in the kind of lifetime-of-leisure riches common today. Even the top salaries of his day "would be party money," he says, pocket change for today's highest-paid players. Some of his fellow players ended up bankrupt, drug addicted, or homeless. A 2009 *Sports Illustrated* article reported that within five years of retirement, 60 percent of NBA players went broke. Many had no other skills to fall back on. Elmore wanted to make sure he wasn't one of them.

For him, the key was to hold on to his earliest childhood dreams, from before he had any inkling he would grow into a giant in life and on the court. When he was growing up in the projects of East New York, Brooklyn, his parents had stressed education. His mother, the daughter of sharecroppers, had had to forgo a scholarship to college because the family couldn't afford to send her. His father, a city sanitation worker, had dropped out of school in tenth grade. "I blew my opportunity, but you're not going to," his dad told Len, the oldest of their four children. When his parents scraped up enough money to buy a small house in Queens, they set up a "library" in the basement: a shelf with Bible stories and a set of encyclopedias that they went into debt to buy.

It was the 1960s, a tumultuous decade that witnessed the civil rights movement, the Vietnam War, and antiwar protests. Young Len spent hours in front of the TV, taking it all in. He was mesmerized by Martin Luther King Jr. and Malcolm X; his role model was Paul Robeson, the football champion turned lawyer, singer, actor, and civil rights activist. "I thought I could be a part of change. My philosophy was, 'I want to be in the parade, I don't want to be an onlooker,'" he recalls. "I wanted to be Perry Mason, to give a voice to the voiceless."

But as Len grew—and grew, and grew, ultimately reaching six-foot-nine—athletics took over his life. He had always been a strong athlete, playing baseball and football. Still, it wasn't until high school that a gym teacher, after watching him goof around with friends on a court, encouraged him to join the basketball team. "But I didn't know the rules. My PE teacher saw me running around like Chief from *Cuckoo's Nest*." Len picked up the game quickly, and within a year he was accepted to Power Memorial Academy, a Catholic school renowned for its basketball prowess, where the legendary Kareem Abdul-Jabbar had played just a few years earlier.

Basketball was Len's ticket to college. After he led his high school team to the national championship, schools tried to recruit him, offering money and jobs and dispatching powerful alumni to chat him up. It was a confusing time and, for his parents especially, uncomfortable. "We were bought and sold once. It's not going to happen again," his mother said. Ultimately Len chose the University of Maryland, where by his senior year he was named an All-American and where he still holds the record, five decades later, as the school's leading rebounder.

Although he was a diligent student, Len ended up leaving school with a semester to go and signing with the Pacers. That kicked off a career that would take him to the Kansas City Kings, Milwaukee Bucks, and New Jersey (now Brooklyn) Nets before signing with the Knicks in the summer of 1983. By that point, he was thirty-one years old, and realized that "the end of the basketball road was coming, with knee injuries and getting older and the longevity wasn't as great. I anticipated I wasn't going to play much longer."

Yet throughout his career, those Perry Mason dreams had stayed with him, as had his parents' emphasis on education, reinforced by his college girlfriend Gail (now his wife of thirty-five years). Even as he played pro ball, Len had returned to Maryland for summer school every year until he finished his degree. At work, he had positioned himself as "the locker room lawyer," talking with fellow players and sports reporters about collective bargaining issues. And so, after signing his two-year Knicks contract, he signed on for something completely different: a Stanley Kaplan prep course for the LSAT, the law school entrance exam. "That's the year, you talk about reinvention!" he says. With a year to go on his contract, he left pro basketball for good, trading in luxury hotels and adoring fans for the relatively spartan life of a Harvard Law School student.

I first met Len and Gail not long after that, as neighbors who became close friends, with two terrific sons who have grown up with my own kids. Along the way, I've been continually impressed by Len's ability to pivot in his career. After spending a few years as an assistant DA in Brooklyn, he shifted back into the sports world, first as a television college basketball commentator for CBS and then as a sports agent, then back to television again with ESPN and CBS. In between, he did stints as a corporate lawyer and running an educational tech company.

Then, in 2017, he was slammed by the dreaded *stop*, this one a triple threat: a deadly staph infection that almost required a foot amputation, a heart attack, and, in the ultimate indignity, being laid off from his job as an ESPN commentator. At the age of sixty-five, he realized he had to reinvent himself all over again.

It was a brutal time—"the single most difficult transition," he says. He was thrown back into the *struggle*, that period of leaving one thing behind when you aren't sure of where you are going next. He wasn't even sure he *had* a future. "Did I worry that

I'm not capable and question my abilities? Yes," he says. "But I didn't know anything other than going for it. I had to make a choice: Can I get back into physical condition where I could stay in the workplace and still compete? . . . It requires positive thinking."

To help get himself through that dark period, Len wrote out a list of his experiences and skills, including speaking, sports industry expertise, and legal issues. He kept an open mind about potential ways to reshape those skills into something new, as he had done before. That's when a job listing at Columbia University, to teach sports management, caught his eye. Though he didn't have the academic credentials, his real-life experience—all of it, from his childhood admiration for Malcolm X and Paul Robeson to his basketball career to his law and business endeavors—came together. It was as if all of those pieces of his professional identity were part of a *search* that led almost inevitably to the *solution* for this next phase of his life.

Today Len teaches Columbia courses in athlete activism and social justice as well as in sports leadership. He's combined his early social justice yearnings with his basketball career, media expertise, and athlete activism. Having first chosen a career with an expiration date and then pivoting throughout his professional life, he has become an expert at reinvention. He had the self-awareness he needed to synthesize his past experiences in order to reimagine a different kind of future.

"You have to make a search and line the opportunities up with the expertise you bring, and see if there's a fit. It's like two pieces of a puzzle," he told me. "People who get stuck with one lens don't have the ability to recognize that you can transform" by assembling disparate skills in a new way. "That was the lens through which I was going to look at opportunity."

Grant puts it like this: "You're collecting all these ingredients for a dish that you don't have a recipe for yet"—but that will combine in some deliciously unpredictable way in the future.

LEN'S OBSERVATION ABOUT the importance of rolling up your past experiences when remodeling the future is the key for people who successfully transition to new lives or careers. It takes the right mindset and an openness to fresh challenges. And like Len, whose career took him from the basketball court to the DA's office to the broadcast booth to the college lectern, keeping an open mind and paying attention to the twists and turns in life, even those that seem aimless at the time, can lead you down a completely different and delightfully unexpected path.

Will Brown, for example, certainly never set out to be a famer. The son of a Swarthmore economics professor, he had attended private schools before heading to Harvard and then joining J.P. Morgan after graduation. He and his wife were searching for an affordable weekend house when, at the end of a long day, the realtor convinced them to take a look at an old, failing dairy farm. They made their way over narrow, serpentine back roads, then turned down a bumpy dirt path that had been a road many decades earlier, before finally coming upon a farmhouse and outbuildings nestled amid two hundred acres of farmland. A foot of snow carpeted the ground. It was like entering a time capsule.

"Warwick was left behind. It was backward. Development hadn't hit it because there weren't good roads," Brown recalled. "So you go down this half-mile dirt driveway, and it's an old farmhouse. In there was the wife—the heat didn't work, so they had a kerosene heater. And the minister from the Presbyterian church was there, in his black frock. I thought, *We've gone an hour out of Manhattan and gone back a century*."

He was immediately charmed. Besides, "it was cheaper than

any house in Connecticut." They bought the place, renovated it, and retreated there on weekends for a relaxing escape from their hectic lives in the city. They were content to be observers of farm life. Barbara would take the kids to watch a neighboring farmer milk his dairy cows. Another neighbor hayed the property.

In time, a local man leased their pasture for his elderly mother's beef cows. When the cows escaped their pasture, Will would help shoo them back in. He was there when the female cows gave birth, and he even learned how to castrate the male ones. Slowly, he was absorbing more knowledge of farm work. Within a few years, he began purchasing more of the surrounding farmland, first to get access to the main road, then to help preserve farmland from development. A turning point came around 2003, when the elderly cow owner died and her son decided to sell her herd. "We said, 'We've been taking care of them anyway.' So we decided to buy his sixteen cows," Will recalled. He figured it wouldn't take much effort. "These were beef cows, they're grazing. They don't need a great deal of attention."

Barbara's recollection is slightly different. She was busy with a demanding leadership job at a housing nonprofit in New York City. "Do whatever you want," she remembers telling her husband, "but don't be under the impression that I'm going to call in sick and come up here because a cow is running down the road."

By this time farm life was coaxing Will in further. He left the bank and set up a consulting business, which allowed him to spend more time on the farm. A neighbor would come by in the afternoons to hunt on the property and help care for the herd. He convinced Will to buy his own tractor. "So gradually, we started doing more. And of course the cows have calves, and you start getting more of them." When Barbara left her job in 2008, she too began spending more time on the farm, overseeing the website, marketing, and record-keeping for the growing herd.

It wasn't long before the couple realized that the cattle operation had grown too big and time-consuming to be just a side hustle. Either they had to get out of the farm altogether or they had to figure out how to make it a viable business. There was no middle ground.

City life or farm life? That was the tug-of-war.

"I was the more reluctant one," Barbara admits. Still, farm living was beginning to grow on her. Even as we spoke, she urged me, "Come back in the spring when the calves are born. It is a wonderful, wonderful time. The mother starts licking off the calf the second it appears, and it immediately lifts its head." She sighed. "There are rewards. I'm telling you in a backward way how I got captivated by farming, despite everything."

The farm won.

A FEW WEEKS after we first toured the property, I join Will on his daily rounds. It's a steamy summer Sunday morning, when his erstwhile colleagues would be out playing a round of golf or lingering over brunch in the Hamptons. Instead, I'm riding shotgun in Will's mud-caked open-air utility vehicle, rounding up cows and herding them to new pastures. Every day in the warm months he repeats this same maneuver, moving his herds from one field to the next. Each pasture is marked with a thin metal fence—electrified with 8,000 volts coursing through it. I watch as he cuts the power on one piece of fence, shoos the cows out, then reconfigures the enclosure and flips the power back on. Each time he reaches toward that electrified fence, I wince.

"Don't you worry you'll get shocked?" I ask. He shrugs. "Happens all the time." It's part of the routine.

With the cows in one pasture safely moved, I hang on to the roll bar for dear life as we bump and jolt over grassy fields. When we reach another pasture, he jumps out again to remove a section of the terrifying fence. A herd of cows lounges lazily in the shade nearby, their hooves sunk into a pool of mud and cow dung. I step gingerly out of the vehicle; the ooze sucks greedily at my boots, threatening to pull them under. The cows look at me placidly through unblinking eyes. I realize that their faces aren't black, as I had assumed; they are simply covered with thousands of the flies buzzing all around us and landing in a mass on the cows' snouts.

Will doesn't seem to notice. He slaps cows on their flanks, claps his hands, yells "Ho! Ho!" then jumps back in the vehicle to lead the way to an adjoining pasture. Within a few minutes, the herd is following us obediently, like so many 1,400-pound puppy dogs trotting behind us.

It's hard work, and solitary. There's nothing remotely glamorous about it. This is about as far from *Green Acres* and "Goodbye, city life!" as anything I can imagine. There's definitely no Eva Gabor waiting back at the farmhouse for us with cocktails.

When people think about how lovely it would be to give up the bustle of city life for the peaceful, slower life in the country, this is definitely not what they have in mind. Farm life is grueling manual labor. And this is just the start of Will's day. After moving two herds and repairing a broken water hose line, he pulls up to yet another field. Leading me through an ankle-deep cesspool of cow dung ("This is nothing—you should see it after it's rained"), we emerge onto a field where neat rows of mowed long grasses stretch out for acres, as far as the eye can see. This field will be turned into 800-pound bales of hay later in the day. A hulking tractor sits nearby, waiting for Will to get to work.

It's hard to imagine how a Harvard-trained desk-jockey economist could pivot so comfortably into farm life. Yet when I ask Will about it, he too, like others I've interviewed, describes the change as more of a continuum. In his second career he uses all of his previous experiences, he says, even though, to an outsider, they seem completely disconnected.

As an economist, he'd always been interested in processes and in problem solving, whether farm or factory or finance. "Managing a farm fits very well with that," his wife observes. Part of the challenge and the appeal for Will is to apply his economics brain to the notoriously difficult business of farming. Another attraction is that he oversees every element of the farm operation, from birthing cows to selling steaks, whereas in his corporate job he was one cog in a giant organization. "To me, the farming was one aspect of it. The other appeal was running a small business. You have revenue, expenses, payroll taxes. I'd been a corporate guy. You do whatever your specialty is. You only see your piece of business. This had more appeal."

As with others, Will's reinvention was a gradual process. Perhaps the most important reason for his success, and for his comfort level with farming, is that he began moving toward his new life before he consciously realized he was leaving the old one. He scaled back his consulting business while simultaneously increasing his involvement on the farm. He slowly adjusted to the different rhythms of life, rising with the sun—before 5:00 AM in the summertime—without so much as an alarm clock, even though in his J.P. Morgan days he had to force himself out of bed when the alarm rang at 6:00 AM.

To him, full-time farming is just one more stage of life, no different than going from a corporate job at a big bank to a one-person consulting operation, or becoming an empty-nester when the kids left for college. "Then you start doing farming, and that's different again. Each of these steps was a pretty big change," he says. But "it happened in stages. To be able to do a little bit, do it on weekends for a while, to step into it, was a huge advantage."

As I take my leave, eager for a shower and air conditioning,

Will pauses to see me off. His worn T-shirt is stained with sweat, and his shoes are caked with cow dung and mud. There's no trace of the one-time Ivy League economist in suit and tie. The temperature is fast approaching 90 degrees, even though the early morning sun is barely peeking through the trees.

I maneuver my car out onto the dirt road, the AC blessedly on full blast, as Will turns to go back to work. Hours more of back-breaking labor await him.

He looks happy.

7

Stop What You're Doing

You Deserve a Break Today

No great work has ever been produced except after a long interval of still and musing meditations.

—BRITISH ECONOMIST WALTER BAGEHOT, 1860

I once accompanied a hard-charging colleague on a cross-country business trip to visit clients, with stops in major cities along the way. As we landed in Los Angeles late one night, after an exhausting jaunt through a series of midwestern conference rooms, I begged for downtime, saying I couldn't wait to check into the hotel and get some shut-eye.

My colleague snickered. "Sleep is for suckers," he said.

I've heard variations on that sentiment throughout my working life. Another friend, a media executive, when confronted with a tough challenge, "puts on a pot of coffee," as he puts it. What he means is that he and his wife stay up all night, fortified with caffeine, to try to figure out a solution.

Like my friends, most of us double down and just work harder when we're faced with a stubborn problem. Our inclination is to keep working on a challenge, even when we've exhausted ourselves, when we can't figure out the answer. If we're contemplating a major life change, it's even worse, as we endlessly cogitate through sleepless nights. We're like Sisyphus, rolling that rock up a mountain over and over again, even though we know it'll just come crashing down every time. Or like Boxer, the worker horse in George Orwell's *Animal Farm*, repeating, "I will work harder!" until we collapse.

This is exactly the wrong approach.

As we've seen with "aha" moments, sudden smack-the-forehead realizations often follow a period of distraction. The solution appears only after you stop what you're doing to take a shower, or go for a walk, or go to sleep. But taking a breather isn't just conducive to those rare flashes of insight. It's also essential to the other types of pivots we've explored, whether surviving trauma or overcoming failure or rethinking the workplace. It's an essential element of the now-familiar *search→struggle→stop→solution* paradigm. It's the key to reinvention and creative breakthroughs of all sorts. The unconscious does an awful lot of heavy lifting when we aren't paying attention.

Think about the last time you had a really great idea. Where were you? Were you sitting at your desk at the end of a long day? On your feet after an eight-hour shift? In a two-hour meeting? I'm pretty sure nobody ever came up with a genius idea while sitting on a Zoom call. In fact, a study published in *Nature* magazine found that Zoom meetings crush creativity. Working without stop actually makes us less creative and less able to come up with solutions. Taking a breather to turn to some other activity entirely is far more productive.

Research across multiple fields has confirmed that taking a break, whether to sleep for a few hours or to take a sabbatical for many months, may be the most important, yet most underrated, ingredient in coming up with new ideas and directions. The implications of these findings are immense, not just for our personal sanity but for businesses, schools, and governments that desperately need to rethink their structures to become more innovative, more effective—and more humane.

The problem is that modern society isn't built for taking breaks. Most of us have a hard time willing ourselves to relax. We assume that we're supposed to overcome an impasse or solve a tricky problem by sitting and staring at it. It's built into our culture, our schooling, and our upbringing.

The concept of relaxation itself is suspect. Americans leave one-third of their paid vacation days on the table. During the pandemic, remote workers actually put in *more* hours than they had before, and burnout became endemic. "I'm too busy" is by this point a status-symbol cliché. We venerate the executives who boast about how little sleep they get, like Indra Nooyi, who slept four hours a night while running PepsiCo, or fashion designer Tom Ford, who has said he sleeps only three hours a night, or Donald Trump, who says he needs less than four hours a night. That fetishization was captured in an ad campaign from my own alma mater: "People who don't have time make time to read the *Wall Street Journal.*"

Even with all that, there's an entire industry devoted to telling us we aren't doing *enough.* Books instruct us on how to work harder, faster, and better, how to organize for maximum efficiency, how to emulate the work habits of highly successful people. Consultants charge hefty fees to reorganize workflows and organizational charts. Coaches tell bosses how to squeeze more work out of themselves and their subordinates. Self-anointed experts on YouTube and Substack offer "productivity hacks" that promise us the nirvana of a zero inbox. All of this makes us even busier, with less time than ever to rethink our careers or lives, even though researchers have found there to be no correlation between busyness and productivity.

What's more, if you do happen to carve out leisure time, we

think less of you. A North Dakota State professor's analysis of holiday letters found an alarming increase in references to "hectic," "whirlwind," and "crazy busy" schedules over the past few decades. And when researchers asked people to rate the social status of "Jim," who works ten hours a day plus weekends, and of another Jim who works less than seven hours a day, the overworked Jim outranked his more leisurely counterpart by a long shot. Similarly, when shown a photo of "Anne," who is wearing a Bluetooth headset (presumably working), respondents rated her as higher status than an Anne who is using ordinary headphones (as if listening to music). They gave similar ratings to "Matthew" who buys groceries from delivery service Peapod and the presumably less-busy Matthew who buys in person from Trader Joe's. And when 112 respondents were asked to read a letter from "Daniel," who described his life as "crazy busy as usual," and a letter from Daniel, whose life was "relaxed as usual," the busy Daniel was deemed to be wealthier, to have a better-paying job, and to be in higher demand than the chill version of himself.

The same researchers also analyzed Twitter "humblebrags"—posts that they define as "the act of showing off about something through an ostensibly self-deprecating statement." When they coded 1,100 such tweets, they found that fully 12 percent complained about being just too darn busy. Among them:

Tlaloc Rivas, stage director: "Opened a show last Friday. Begin rehearsals for another next Tuesday. In-between that, meetings in DC. I HAVE NO LIFE!"
Austin Pettis, American football receiver: "Had a lot going on these past few weeks and even more these next two . . . this is wayyyy to much to handle!"
Arthur Kade, actor and model: "I need 2 write a blog with an update on everything!! I have been so ridic busy w meetings and calls that I have neglected my fans."

Josh Sigurdson, journalist and songwriter: "Hi, I'm 16 and I'm publishing 3 books and an album this year. Do you have any advice on how to handle it best?"

Yet staying busy without taking a break is perhaps the least useful way to come up with original ideas. Some of the most storied innovators attribute their success to *not* working. Microsoft cofounder Paul Allen once told me that playing rock music on his guitar at night allowed him to be a better programmer during the day. Even in the early days of the company, when he worked punishing hours, Allen would pull out his guitar to relax in the evenings. He had studied violin as a young child, switched to guitar when he was fifteen, and was a rock 'n' roller for the rest of his life. He saw a connection between the intensity of coding and the relaxation of his music: playing "reinforces your confidence in the ability to create," he said. For him, he explained, playing guitar opened up new avenues in his brain, which in turn helped him reinvent personal computing. In both music and programming, "something is pushing you to look beyond what currently exists and express yourself in a new way."

You don't have to teach yourself guitar or listen to Jimi Hendrix—Paul Allen's inspiration—to get that benefit. Simply daydreaming, allowing your mind to wander, can do the trick. Even in the best of times, we spend 25 to 50 percent of our time daydreaming, a figure that mental health experts believe increased during the Covid-19 pandemic. Most of us consider daydreaming a problem, even a character flaw. The conventional wisdom holds that when we're daydreaming, we're wasting our time. We try to snap ourselves out of it. We yell at our kids and spouses when they stare off into space instead of paying attention to us. We're embarrassed when we're caught spacing out during a meeting. Teachers discipline students for their wandering minds and note as much on report cards.

Yet research suggests that we're actually at our most creative when we're daydreaming. A few years ago, Jonathan Schooler, the UC–Santa Barbara psychologist who studies mind wandering, and a group of colleagues asked almost two hundred writers and physicists to keep a diary of their most creative thoughts each day. He wanted to know not just where and when they had their most original thoughts, but also whether there was a difference between how these two very different types of professionals—the "creative" writers versus the "analytical" physicists—came up with ideas.

Astonishingly, 20 percent of the best ideas of those in *both* groups came while they were doing anything but work. Great brainstorms came to them when they were daydreaming, when they were paying bills—anytime except when they were focused on the problem itself. They were also more likely to solve particularly vexing challenges or impasses during those nonwork times. Not all of their creative ideas qualified as eureka revelations. But those who did experience "aha" moments were far more likely to have them when they *weren't* at work rather than when they were sitting at their desks.

Other research has shown similar benefits from walking, spending time in nature, exercising, sleeping and napping, meditating, and showering. Pretty much any kind of break will do. In a 2015 Australian study, 1,114 people ranging in age from eighteen to eighty-five reported that they solved challenges while cleaning house, exercising, riding on a bus or train, and taking a shower, among other activities. Solutions "often come to me when I stop actively thinking about the problem," as one participant put it. Added another, "Occasionally a solution to a problem will come into my mind when I am say, playing golf." A third said, "The solution comes usually at night either when I'm asleep (It comes in my dream), or I wake up with the solution."

Simply taking a walk seems to have an outsize impact. In one study, creativity soared by as much as 60 percent among participants who were walking versus sitting or being pushed in a wheelchair. Any kind of walking, even on a treadmill staring at a blank wall, seemed to do the trick. When four dozen students were asked to come up with alternative uses for everyday objects, like a button, those who were sitting came up with mundane and conventional ideas, while those who were walking were far more likely to come up with out-of-the-box concepts, like "a doorknob for a dollhouse" or a "tiny strainer."

The creative benefits of walking helps explain why Steve Jobs famously took frequent walks and held meetings on foot, as does Netflix cofounder Reed Hastings. Composers Beethoven, Mahler, Tchaikovsky, and Britten also took daily walks to inspire their work. So did writers from Henry David Thoreau to Haruki Murakami, William James, and Joyce Carol Oates. "All truly great thoughts are conceived by walking," Nietzsche wrote in 1889.

Taking a break in nature has a similar effect. A 2012 study found that after people spent four to six days hiking in the wilds of Alaska, Colorado, or Washington, their scores on a creative problem-solving test soared by 50 percent. If you don't have four days to play with, a Scottish study found that just twenty-five minutes of walking in a park offered some of the same benefits, including reduced frustration and relaxed thinking of the sort that allows fresh ideas to collide and coalesce. Canada even instituted a program in 2022 allowing doctors to prescribe national park passes to patients, citing research that spending time in nature can lower stress hormones and even reduce anxiety about climate change. "There's almost no medical condition that nature doesn't make better," said physician Melissa Lem, director of the PaRx initiative, which helped distribute the passes.

When I worked at Gannett, the publisher of *USA Today*, I tried to take daily walks around the tranquil pond at our suburban Virginia headquarters. Some of my colleagues did the same, and a number of us even began taking meetings while walking the pond. We didn't know why it worked, but somehow it did: we came up with any number of article ideas and storytelling innovations on those little strolls. I noticed the same phenomenon in a very different setting—as a fellow at the Institute for Advanced Study in Princeton, once the academic home of Albert Einstein. The campus encompasses almost 600 acres of woods, with miles of trails, through which some of the great scientists would stroll while contemplating new theories and discoveries. The woods were preserved specifically as "a tranquil environment for scholars engaged in theoretical research and intellectual inquiry."

Taking a break to meditate has similar benefits, researchers have found. Meditation is most familiar these days from apps, like Headspace and Calm, that promote stress relief and improved sleep. But a British study found that those who meditated were also able to learn more quickly, providing empirical evidence in support of the mantra of the New Age guru Ram Dass: "The quieter you become the more you can hear."

NOBODY SAYS THIS is easy. The great masters, from Einstein to Beethoven, could control the cadence of their days, but most of us are slaves to our work schedules. For many, it's impossible to disengage from work, not just during the day but through weekends and sleepless nights. The famed Vietnamese Buddhist monk Thich Nhat Hanh spent the better part of his ninety-five years trying to convince people to take a break and meditate. He was not always successful. "Nonthinking is the secret of success," the influential Zen master exhorted a group of Google employees, of all people, at the Googleplex Silicon Valley headquarters. "And that is why the time when we are not working, that time can be very productive, if we know how to focus on the moment."

When you don't give your brain a rest and allow it to get distracted, it doesn't have a chance to make those remote connections that lead to creative breakthroughs. Recent research suggests that social media scrolling among kids, for example, shuts down potentially creative thinking by preventing them from daydreaming and engaging in quiet contemplation. The *Harvard Business Review* similarly reported that spending too much time on Facebook hurts your ability to focus and learn.

That's why sleep is especially important to juice problem solving. As we've seen with Paul McCartney and "Yesterday," people often report having creative breakthroughs when they slumber. Mary Shelley wrote in her diary in 1816 that she literally dreamed up *Frankenstein* one night after an evening of telling ghost stories with her husband, Percy Shelley, and their friend Lord Byron. The writer John Steinbeck described the phenomenon poetically when he said, "A problem difficult at night is resolved in the morning after the committee of sleep has worked on it."

Rock and Roll Hall of Famer Todd Rundgren, known for iconic 1970s hits like "Hello It's Me," told me one of his best-known songs came to him fully formed, lyrics and all, while he was sleeping. At the time, in 1982, he was recording an album in his signature pop style, yet in the middle of one night, he woke up with a totally out-of-character tune in his head. He stumbled out of bed and wrote down the melody and lyrics: *I don't want to work. I want to bang on the drum all day* . . .

"Bang the Drum All Day" went on to become one of his most lucrative hits, a ubiquitous anthem at parties, on drive-time radio, at ballgames and in commercials. "It's a novelty song. I wouldn't have done it consciously. Such a song was not in my conscious mind," he told me. He felt as if it was bestowed upon him: "It was like a gift to me."

But sleep plays a role in all sorts of problem solving, not just such "aha" moments. When you hear "sleep on it," take that advice literally. In one early experiment almost half a century ago, William Dement asked five hundred students to try to solve word problems before bed. About 20 percent of them dreamed of solutions. Two decades later, in 1993, Harvard psychologist Deirdre Barrett asked seventy-six students to think about a specific problem every night before bed for a week. Some of the problems they chose were existential (what field should I pursue?). Others were decidedly practical (how should I arrange the furniture in my new apartment?). Afterward, almost half of the students reported that their dreams addressed the problem—including the student who dreamed of a furniture layout that turned out to be a perfect fit for her new pad.

An entire body of research has since grown up around the benefits of sleep and dreams, including how we actually *learn* while sleeping. In a particularly devious 2004 experiment, researchers at the University of Lübeck in Germany played a trick on some unsuspecting study participants. They taught the group how to generate a string of numbers from another set of numbers, using an especially tedious method. What they didn't tell participants was that there was a shortcut to the solution. When participants returned eight hours later, those who had slept were more than twice as likely as those who stayed awake to have spotted the shortcut. (The study report made no mention of how furious the sleep-deprived participants were.)

I stumbled onto that insight unintentionally. Back in college, I was a nervous test taker, but a confident writer. So I used to look for courses that had final term papers instead of final exams. That way, I hoped, I would have a better shot at a decent grade. Yet the first few times I tried this failsafe plan, it failed. The problem was that I seemed to always find myself pulling all-nighters just before a paper was due. Toward dawn, I would hit a wall and my brain would shut down. Yet I'd stay stubbornly glued to my chair, forcing myself to stay awake and keep plowing ahead. *Bad idea.*

After a few such miserable episodes, I discovered a trick. When I hit the point when my exhausted brain refused to work, I would stick my rough draft in a drawer. Sometimes I put it aside just for a few hours while I catnapped; on the rare occasions when I planned better, I'd ignore it for several days. Then, when I pulled out the draft and reread it, *boom!* It was like magic. All of its flaws were crystal clear. The solutions appeared right in front of my eyes, and fixing the paper was a cinch. It was actually fun, even relaxing.

I thought my writing trick—which I use to this day, though I can no longer handle all-nighters!—was my own little secret, unique to me. But then I read the memoir of a truly gifted wordsmith, comedian John Cleese of Monty Python fame. I felt an odd shiver of recognition as he described his typical creative process:

> If I wrote a sketch by myself in the evening, I'd often get stuck, and would sit there at my little desk, cudgeling my brains. Eventually I'd give up and go to bed.
>
> And in the morning, I'd wake up and make myself a cup of coffee, and then I'd drift over to the desk and sit at it, and, almost immediately, the solution to the problem I'd been wrestling with the previous evening . . . became quite obvious to me! . . . It was like a gift, a reward for all my wrestling with the puzzle.

Cleese, in other words, passed through all of the now-familiar stages—the search for the sketch idea, the struggle when he got stuck and ultimately stopped, followed by the solution, which arrived after he took a break for a good night's sleep.

Cleese recalled one particularly frustrating episode early in his career when he cowrote a parody of a Church of England sermon that he was sure was pure comedy gold—and then lost it. He turned his room upside down searching for it, with no luck. Finally, he sat down and attempted to re-create it from memory. That's when a curious thing happened. After finishing the reconstruction, he stumbled upon the original sketch that he'd lost and compared the two.

"Weirdly, I discovered that the remembered version was actually an improvement. . . . This puzzled the hell out of me," he wrote in 2020. "I began to realise that my unconscious was working on stuff all the time, without my being consciously aware of it."

CLEESE'S INSIGHT, ABOUT the unconscious "working on stuff all the time," even when we aren't paying attention, is exactly right. It's what happens when we snooze. It's a cruel irony considering that the world we live in values sleep so little. How much sleep did you get last night? Were you tired when you woke up? More than a third of Americans get inadequate sleep, which the Centers for Disease Control and Prevention (CDC) defines as less than seven hours a night. Yet researchers have found that getting less than six hours of sleep is "the main risk factor" for burnout. More rest makes us healthier and more productive: when Ernst & Young studied its own employees, it found that for every ten additional hours of vacation an employee took, his or her performance rating improved by 8 percent. An analysis by University of Minnesota psychologist Erik Klinger suggests that when you're thinking about important life goals, like job possibilities, your ability is "highest during relaxed periods, when the brain's default-mode network dominates, or during sleep."

Getting enough sleep is often an elusive goal, of course. But even napping comes with some problem-solving benefits. Harvard Medical School researchers asked ninety-nine students to memorize a complicated 3D maze on a computer screen, then placed the students virtually "inside" the maze and asked them to navigate to another location. Several hours later, when the students returned to try the maze again, students who had spent their breaks napping for ninety minutes far outperformed those who had stayed awake. What's more, the nappers who also dreamed about the maze performed ten times better than those who didn't.

Scientists have long theorized that sleep helps us both consolidate new memories and selectively forget some older ones, to unclog the brain. When you have too much information swimming around in your head, it's hard to separate out the signal from the noise and to come up with clear new ideas. Sleep allows your brain to brush away the unimportant stuff and focus on what counts. What's more, when the prefrontal cortex—the control center of the brain, a kind of inner parent that regulates rational thinking—powers down, it allows free-flowing thoughts to mix and combine in new ways.

There's evidence that our brains are at their most creative, not when we are deeply asleep, but when we first wake up, still drowsy. Thomas Edison was so certain that his best invention ideas percolated in a dreamlike state "at the edges of sleep" that he would sometimes take multiple naps a day, drifting off with steel balls in his hands that would clatter into metal saucers below him and wake him up if he slumbered too deeply. He may have been credited with saying that "genius is 1 percent inspiration and 99 percent perspiration," but his own actions suggest otherwise.

Edison didn't need to know the latest neurologic research to understand why naps worked. He just knew what to do to coax out his most creative ideas. The same goes for other prolific innovators and leaders. Winston Churchill was famous for his midday naps. Nintendo video game designer Shigeru Miyamoto has said that he came up with Donkey Kong while soaking in the bath. Director Ingmar Bergman is said to have knocked off work by 3:30 PM every day—while directing sixty films. Stephen King, who has written almost seventy books and more than two hundred short stories, typically works just four hours a day and naps in the afternoon.

LONG BREAKS CAN be especially useful. If your job offers paid vacation, take it. People who use their vacation days are promoted at almost twice the rate of those who leave days on the table. Leaders who take off even more extended time come back with fresher ideas. Deborah S. Linnell and Tim Wolfred surveyed sixty-one nonprofit executives who had taken sabbaticals of several months each and found that, in addition to relieving stress, the time away allowed them to "spark creativity," develop "out-of-the-box" thinking, and even introduce entirely new visions for their organization.

UC–Santa Barbara's Schooler credits a sabbatical as the catalyst for his pioneering research on mind wandering. For the first few decades of his career, he researched memory, but after a 1998 sabbatical he realized he wanted to pivot in a new direction. He likens the change to "Jack and the Beanstalk": "A couple of ideas stuck out to me, but those 'beans' I ended up planting led me to mind wandering and other major ideas that I've been reaping ever since." His own experience, he says, suggests that the longer duration of a sabbatical is especially conducive to making "a substantial shift in direction," such as pursuing a new career or specialty.

Isaac Newton was one of the great thinkers who also championed taking exceedingly long breaks. "To arrive at the simplest truth, as Newton knew and practiced, requires years of *contempla-*

tion. Not activity. Not reasoning. Not calculating. Not busy behaviour of any kind. Not reading. Not talking. Not making an effort. Not thinking," George Spencer-Brown, the British polymath, wrote memorably in his 1969 *Laws of Form*, which explored the intersection of mathematics and philosophy.

As we've seen, creativity experts call this kind of time-out the "incubation" period, during which you are consciously ignoring a problem and after which your unconscious rewards you with a solution. Scientists theorize that while you are in an "incubation interval" and occupied with unrelated matters, your brain is able to noodle solutions in the background. What's more, as you engage in other activities, you're vacuuming up additional information that gets thrown into the hopper of your subconscious brain, mixing in even more potential thoughts that can coalesce into new ideas. And finally, the time away allows you to see any problem or challenge with fresh eyes when you return.

Typically, your incubation periods are unique to you. You're cooking, or showering, or running in the park—or, as with Schooler and sabbaticals, taking protracted time away from your daily life. But beginning in the early months of the Covid-19 pandemic, a strange, perhaps unprecedented phenomenon took hold. Everyone's lives were disrupted, all at the same time. Even as essential workers and frontline health-care providers were thrown into a dangerous, exhausting frenzy of activity, the rest of the country came to a screeching halt. Schools were closed, and kids were sent home. Office workers were dispatched to their kitchen tables to work remotely. Grandparents couldn't visit with grandkids; friends couldn't meet for coffee or a meal; movie theaters closed, and sports events were canceled. Every familiar element of existence, from schooling to travel to meals, was turned on its head, and many lives remained upended even after the introduction of vaccines and therapies.

In short, the pandemic forced us *all* to take a protracted break from our routines. Unintentionally, it created a worldwide petri-dish experiment, as millions of us experienced an extended time-out from our everyday lives all at once. "You can basically say Covid has provided everybody with an incubation interval," Schooler told me. That incubation period, when millions of us were suddenly yanked away from our daily existence, became a fertile time for rethinking, which is what led so many of us to reprioritize our lives, reevaluate our goals, and end relationships or dive into new ones. Many of us were reimagining a new path forward.

That incubation period also helps explain why so many millions of people quit their jobs, even though almost one-third of them had no new job to go into. Covid-19 created a perfect worldwide laboratory in which to study how every step of the incubation process plays out. "You're getting time away, which allows for lots of unconscious processes to take place," Schooler explains. "You're exposed to different contexts, different information than you would have been, reading things you wouldn't otherwise." And when the pandemic wanes, "time has passed, so when you finally get back to work, you'll see it with fresh eyes."

That was certainly the case for Lucy Chang Evans, of Naperville, Illinois. The initial shutdown prompted her "to take a much deeper look inside . . . I was a lot more introspective." A onetime Secret Service agent, she had dropped out of the workplace altogether when her kids were young. After a divorce, she went back to work as a civil engineer, the career she originally trained for. But after the pandemic hit, Lucy, then forty-eight, quit her job to help her kids with remote learning while pursuing an online MBA. Her life narrowed to the confines of their small house. Yet while her life became smaller, it allowed her dreams to become that much larger. The forced stop of her previous life opened up some unexpected benefits.

"That clean break took away barriers to my way of thinking," she said. Eliminating the daily commute and "the day-to-day routine that kept me on the same path" freed her up to imagine a different future. The stillness allowed other insights to come to the fore. For starters, Lucy realized she was done with toxic workplaces: "I feel like I'm not willing to put up with abusive behavior at work anymore." She decided to pivot into a more meaningful career, perhaps focused on solutions for the troubled child welfare system. "I want to be able to look my children in the eye and tell them I did something that will benefit their future world."

Her experience has echoed among so many others in the wake of the pandemic. When the *New York Times* asked readers about their New Year's resolutions for 2022, with the pandemic entering its third year, one after another talked about the need to just . . . *stop*. "I resolve to do less and enjoy it more," one reader wrote. "I resolve to remember my boundaries. 'No' is a complete sentence," said another. "I am never going back to sending work-related emails after dinner or on weekends," wrote a third. Said another, "I resolve to put work second. My family and I come first from now on." Added another, "I am never going back to being separated from my children for ten to eleven hours a day as they commute and attend school and after-school programs while I work."

In her book *Do Nothing*, Celeste Headlee argues that not only *can* we work those breaks into our daily lives, but we *must*. "Think back to times in your life when you worked a considerable amount of overtime. Do you think you were in the right frame of mind then to think creatively or carefully?" she writes. "When our minds are idle, we allow ourselves to reconnect with our creativity and re-engage with reflective thought—two activities that are essential to progress."

Even miniature breaks throughout your day can make the difference. Some years ago, while working on my first book, I spent a miserable long holiday weekend on my laptop, staring at the cursor blinking on an empty screen. I had a ferocious case of writer's block. Whatever well of creativity I thought I possessed had evaporated. *Poof!* I had nothing. After four days, I hadn't even written a sentence.

Days later, on a transatlantic plane trip to Switzerland for a conference, I found myself sitting next to Tony Schwartz. Tony, a former journalist, is best known now for ghostwriting Donald Trump's book *The Art of the Deal* and then emerging as one of the former president's harshest critics. But he is also the founder of a consulting firm, The Energy Project, that helps companies balance the work-life equation for employees. My nerves were frayed by exhaustion as we chatted, and I was panicking about the looming deadline for my book. I admitted to him my struggle with writing. "Try the ninety-minute rule," Tony said.

The idea, he explained, is simple: you focus completely on your work for ninety minutes. No emails, no checking your phone, no distractions. But at the end of ninety minutes you *must* stop. You must take a break. It's non-negotiable. It doesn't matter what you do on your break—you can exercise, eat, watch TV, do anything at all, as long as you aren't working. Then you return to your desk and repeat the process. But only three times daily, he cautioned; work more than that and you're depleted.

I tried out Tony's advice—and it worked like a charm. As the end of each ninety-minute session neared, knowing I had a hard deadline fast approaching, it was easier and less emotionally fraught to write something, anything. I would promise myself I just needed to get to the end of this sentence, or that paragraph. I would write down whatever was in my head, focused on beating the deadline. The forced break afterward came as a guilt-free whoosh of relief, knowing I had no choice and wasn't just goofing off. I broke through my writer's block and easily finished the manuscript by my deadline.

Tony's ninety-minute rule has roots in neuroscience. Six decades ago, a sleep researcher named Nathaniel Kleitman discovered the "basic rest-activity cycle": during the night, he found, we go from light sleep to deep sleep and then back again, in approximately ninety-minute intervals. As it turns out, that cycle continues during our waking hours too. By focusing intensely, then taking a break, we refresh our brain and allow thoughts to coalesce. We gain a sense of perspective for the next go-round.

Some people have figured out that cycle on their own. Nineteenth-century naturalist Charles Darwin put in three ninety-minute work sessions a day, punctuated by morning and afternoon walks, lunch with his wife, and a late-afternoon nap. While sticking to that schedule, he managed to write nineteen books, including his seminal *On the Origin of Species*. The French mathematician Henri Poincaré, for his part, structured his workday with just *two* intense sessions of two hours each, one in the morning and the other in the afternoon—a total of four hours.

K. Anders Ericsson, the late Florida State University psychologist, confirmed the validity of this approach with his famous study of violin virtuosos. Ericsson is known now for his discovery, amplified by Malcolm Gladwell in *Outliers*, that experts spend ten thousand hours on their craft before mastering it. But there's a lesser-known element to mastery that Ericsson also found: not only do expert musicians know how *long* to practice—they know when to *stop*.

The virtuosos he studied didn't play for endless hours every day. Instead, they put down their instruments after ninety minutes of what he called "deliberate" practice, during which they focused intensely on their work. In any given day, they didn't play for more than three of these sessions, just four and a half hours total. The best students also tended to take naps during the day, slept an hour longer than their less-accomplished counterparts at night, and spent about twenty-five hours a week on leisure activities. They became virtuosos not just because they put in more cumulative hours than their peers, but because they put in the *right* hours. They had the discipline to practice, but also the discipline to take a time-out. That's what gave their brains the ability to synthesize and store what they learned during practice.

The irony is that, in Ericsson's study, the group of lesser violinists who were deemed merely proficient in their craft had started at the same average age (eight) as their gifted peers and spent the same number of years (ten) studying their instrument. The difference wasn't in their backgrounds. It was in how they learned to manage their time—and just as important, their time *off*.

UNLIKE US, OUR ancestors understood the importance of taking a break. What's more, they didn't feel guilty about it. On the contrary, they celebrated downtime. Aristotle was a big booster of breathing room. He believed that quiet, pleasant contemplation was one of the highest virtues, and one necessary for human well-being. Aristocratic ancient Greeks prized free time because it enabled them to devote themselves to *polis*—contemplating their spiritual, moral, and political lives. The Romans actually had contempt for manual labor, a "vulgar" pursuit for which "the very wage they receive is a pledge of slavery," as Cicero declared in 44 BC. Time to think was similarly prized across Asia, India, and Europe among the ruling classes, and of course, it was the genesis of the sabbath day of rest in Judeo-Christian religions.

The fetishization of busyness is a relatively modern invention, and largely an American one. After Captain John Smith founded the colony of Jamestown in 1607, he decreed that any man found guilty of "idleness" would be banished ("He who shall not work, shall not eat"). Founding father Benjamin Franklin pushed the credo further. He was just forty-two when he retired from his printing business and declared his intention to become a "Man of Leisure." Yet he spent the next four decades in a whirl of activity, as statesman, scientist, author, French ambassador, and, apparently, voracious womanizer. It's no coincidence that he coined adages like "Never leave that till tomorrow, which you can do today," and "Early to bed, and early to rise, makes a man healthy, wealthy and wise." In his 1757 book *The Way to Wealth*, he also advised that "sloth makes all things difficult."

Half a century after Franklin's death, the nature of work was transformed when the industrial revolution introduced rigid working hours to the thousands who began toiling in factories or on railroads instead of at home or on a farm. Schoolmarms taught children more than just reading and writing; they also instructed them that "idleness was a disgrace." Farmers and artisans who used to be paid by the task morphed into factory workers paid by how many hours they labored. Time suddenly equaled money. Economists estimate that the average workweek for nineteenth-century factory workers topped sixty hours, sometimes edging close to seventy hours. The "Protestant work ethic," which held that hard work and thrift lead to heavenly rewards, reinforced the drumbeat of all work and no play.

Work became so all-consuming that pioneering psychologist William James took to the podium to rail against it in an 1896 speech, "The Gospel of Relaxation." He bemoaned "those absurd feelings of hurry and having no time . . . that breathlessness and tension, that anxiety of feature," and warned that "these perfectly wanton and unnecessary tricks of inner attitude . . . idealized by many as the admirable way of life, are the last straws that break the American camel's back." He urged his audience that it was time for them to, so to speak, chill out. They must "unclamp" the brain, he told his listeners, "and let it run free."

A century later, scientists would validate his words—the brain does indeed need to "unclamp" to unleash creativity. But at the time, James's speech mostly fell on deaf ears. By the time the Gilded Age of nineteenth- and early-twentieth-century industrialists like Andrew Carnegie, John D. Rockefeller and J. P. Morgan was ushered in, class divisions between workers and the wealthy were widening. Millions were laboring long hours for barely livable wages. Sixty-hour weeks were common, and six-day weeks the norm. The modern weekend hadn't yet been invented. Leisure was the province only of the idle rich, and they weren't using it for Aristotelian contemplation.

Economist Thorstein Veblen skewered the wealthy industrialists who considered labor a "mark of inferiority" in his 1899 social critique *The Theory of the Leisure Class*. For the rich, leisure time was an "economic expression of their superior rank," which they showed off by "conspicuous consumption" of frivolous luxuries along with "conspicuous leisure" made possible by excessive free time. F. Scott Fitzgerald would crystallize that theory into the "careless people" who "smashed up things and creatures and then retreated back into their money or their vast carelessness" in his 1925 novel *The Great Gatsby*. By the time the German director Fritz Lang made his silent-film masterpiece *Metropolis* in 1927, "leisure" had morphed into an easy cultural shorthand for "evil." The film paints a grim portrait of a dystopian future when factory workers toil ceaselessly underground to power a great city, while the "Club of the Sons"—the privileged offspring of the industrialists who rule the city—frolic on the rooftops above. Lang's message wasn't subtle. In the popular consciousness, hardworking people were noble precisely because of their hard work, in stark contrast to the pernicious lazy rich.

Henry Ford famously pared back the workweek on his Model T assembly lines to five days from six, helping usher in the forty-hour workweek that was codified in 1940. With assembly lines and mass production, it seemed that the tide might finally turn toward a more humane work schedule.

Indeed, economist John Maynard Keynes had predicted, back in 1930, that increases in productivity would whittle the workweek down to fifteen hours by 2030. Nikola Tesla a few years later forecast that robots would replace most human labor within a century. "For the first time since his creation man will be faced with his real, his permanent problem—how to use his freedom from pressing economic cares," Keynes wrote, "how to occupy the leisure."

Ha.

Instead, today we remain a nation of unreformed workaholics. The vaunted ethic has become a Frankenstein monster, a contortion of the Puritan ideal of hard work into a fanatical gospel of busyness: "Busy" has become a religion. We believe we're "wasting time" if we stop for a moment to consider whether we are actually happy with the treadmill of our lives and livelihoods. Fully one-quarter of American workers spend more than forty-five hours a week on the job, and 16 percent of us put in more than sixty hours a week, even though productivity declines and health risks mount precipitously at this level of work activity. For those working more than fifty-five hours, heart disease and stroke risk climb dramatically. A global study of workers in 194 countries concluded that in 2016 excessive work hours led to about 745,000 deaths, making overwork "the largest of any occupational risk factor calculated to date."

YET THERE MAY be a hopeful path forward in all of this—one blazed by Lucy Chang Evans and millions of others like her. The Covid-19 pandemic shook many of us to the core and woke us up to the importance and value of taking a breather, of just . . . stopping. It helped us realize that the old way wasn't working and showed us it was time for a do-over.

We are now in the midst of an unprecedented opportunity to reshape the workplace, the culture of work, and our own attitudes. The workweek most of us grew up with—the standard forty-hour, five-day grind—was outdated even before the pandemic. It was standardized after World War II, built on a military model of strict hierarchies, created by men for men, and based on the assumption that there was a wife to handle duties at home. Sure, that model has been tweaked since then, from open office plans to perks like free food. But despite advances in technology and communication, the nature of work remained essentially unchanged for decades—until Covid-19 struck.

The new emerging paradigm includes intentional breaks and flexibility in work hours, both during the day and throughout the workweek and year. Hybrid schedules, with two or three days a week in the office and the rest remote, are becoming standard. More than one hundred companies have gone further, adopting or experimenting with a four-day workweek. Every piece of research to date has shown benefits from shortening the workweek, and few if any downsides. In a trial in Iceland, for example, workers reported decreased stress and burnout, while productivity remained steady or actually *increased*.

Some companies also are continuing pandemic-era practices such as "recharge days," mandatory full weeks off, no-meetings Fridays, and email shutoffs after hours. Even Goldman Sachs began mandating that employees take at least three weeks of vacation a year. Meanwhile, Salesforce and others have adopted a permanent "work from anywhere" policy, while some other firms, including Pinterest, Uber, and Dropbox, have cut back on planned physical office expansions.

Companies continue to struggle with finding the right balance between remote work and the benefits of the on-site collaborations and serendipitous collisions that lead to new ideas. But it's clear that remote work has helped to free up precious time: Americans in 2019 spent almost an hour round-trip on their daily commute, and lost the equivalent of a soul-crushing nineteen workdays a year to sitting in traffic.

Organizations are embracing these strategies to prevent burnout and increase worker retention, which is all well and good. But the approach deepens the divide between knowledge workers and hourly workers as well as others in jobs that are still inflexible. Which raises the question: What if we designed the workplace so that burnout wasn't a natural by-product in the first place? What if work became better integrated with life as a rule rather than as an exception?

Achieving these goals could set off a domino effect in other sectors, giving us all a bit more breathing room. Take education: The school day for most kids starts way too early. If we're changing the workweek, why not adjust school hours too? For that matter, perhaps it's time to reassess the cadence of the entire school calendar. In health care, the move to telehealth during Covid-19 barely scratches the surface of the types of rethinking that could make medical services more accessible, while also creating a more humane work environment for providers.

In part, these types of changes will require all of us to adjust our own attitudes. We've got to figure out how to stop fetishizing busyness. We have to reframe the way we work, the way we live, and even the way we think. Some people are already doing so. For example, Britt Altizer, of Richmond, Virginia, used to put in long hours managing his family's popular dessert restaurant, while his wife Kari sold life insurance. Their lives were frenetic. They juggled the demands of work with caring for a newborn son. They didn't imagine their days could be any other way.

But during the initial pandemic shutdown, Kari, then thirty-one, had to quit her job to care for their son. Meanwhile, Britt, then thirty, was briefly furloughed. With his days suddenly empty, he began spending time outside, tending to the couple's garden. During those hours alone, "I did some soul searching," he says. Being outdoors brought back memories of growing up on a farm and revived his interest in environmental science, which had been his major in college. "During the time I was home, I was gardening and really loving life. I realized working outdoors was something I had to get back to doing."

The unexpected break from the whirlwind of their daily lives was the catalyst for them to quit their jobs and open a landscaping business together. "We realized the things that were important to us were our family, our house, flexibility, our quality of life, and not so much making money," Kari says. It was a difficult transition; she had always envisioned a lifelong career in business and now had to reassess her own plans and self-image. When restrictions eased, she even tried going back to the corporate world and working in the office—but she soon found that the extra money wasn't worth the trade-off of long hours away from her family. "I can't get this way again, sacrificing quality time with my son and being home just in time to put him to bed," she says, "and forgetting everything I learned during the pandemic."

Their new life, Britt says, is "definitely" more rewarding. "And that's what life is about. About what makes you feel complete, and satisfied." Ironically, it was the pandemic that made it possible. "Covid was a cue for me to reassess," he says. Otherwise, "I may have stuck with it [the restaurant business] forever."

It shouldn't take a global pandemic to give us all the space to breathe. Perhaps now we'll finally heed William James's words from more than a century ago: it's time for each of us to "unclamp" our brain and "let it run free."

8

Find Your "Expert Companion"

...And Be One Yourself

*In everyone's life, at some time, our inner fire goes out. It is
then burst into flame by an encounter with another human being. We
should all be thankful for those people who rekindle the inner spirit.*

—ALBERT SCHWEITZER

As any working mom will tell you, something's got to give. For years, as I clumsily attempted to juggle a demanding job while raising two kids, I gave up not one but two "somethings": cooking and sleep. I'm still working on getting back sleep. But during the pandemic, while working remotely at home, I finally learned to cook. That's when I became perhaps the last person in the country to discover Ina Garten, better known as "the Barefoot Contessa."

As apparently everyone else other than me already knew, Garten is a Food Network star. An instantly recognizable icon with her brunette bob-and-bangs and denim shirts, she has amassed an obsessive following. She has written more than a dozen cookbooks that collectively have sold millions of copies. Her skillet-roasted lemon chicken and Beatty's chocolate cake recipes are to die for.

But she almost didn't do any of it.

Back in 1978, she was on the career fast track, with an MBA and a prestigious White House job as a young nuclear budget analyst. But while it was a glamorous gig, in reality she was bored. She had a lot more fun trying out Julia Child cookbook recipes at home and throwing weekly dinner parties for friends. She was in the *search* stage, looking for another path, with no idea what that might be.

"I was sitting in my office one day thinking, I've got to do something else," she recalled. That's when, flipping through the pages of the *New York Times*, she came across a for-sale ad for a little specialty food shop in Westhampton Beach, New York, a town she'd never visited. It was called the Barefoot Contessa, named for an Ava Gardner film she'd never seen. Yet something about it caught Ina's imagination. She was still thinking about it when she chatted with her husband Jeffrey after work.

"I went home that night and I said to Jeffrey, 'You know, I really need to do something else.'"

"Do what you love," he responded. "If you love it, you'll be really good at it."

"And I said, 'You know, funny you should mention it.'"

The couple drove out to visit the shop, a tiny postage stamp of a place. "I saw this 400-square-foot store, and they were baking chocolate chip cookies. And I thought, *This is where I want to be.*" They put in a lowball offer on the place, figuring that would give her time to negotiate while thinking more carefully about whether she actually wanted to take this crazy leap. Instead, the offer was accepted immediately. "Oh shit! Now I have to do it. It wasn't supposed to work that way," she recalled. Still, with her husband's support, Ina took a deep breath and went ahead with it. And so, back in DC, she resigned from her fast-track job to take the helm of a little store in a sleepy off-season town.

It was not an overwhelmingly popular decision.

"A grocery store!" her parents cried in despair. "Why?"

This was a reasonable question. It seemed madness to throw away an MBA and a prestigious post in order to man the counter at a tiny local store. What's more, it promised to be a daunting proposition for someone with absolutely no experience running anything. Ina was in way too deep. Almost right away, panic set in. "This is the stupidest thing I've ever done in my life," she recalled thinking when she first started. "I'd never been in the food business, I didn't know how to do anything." Again, her husband stepped in. "If you could do it in the first week, you'd be bored in the second week," he reassured her.

While her parents "were anything but supportive," her husband was a rock. With his encouragement, she poured herself into her new life. Building the business was brutally difficult. During the summer season, from May to September, she would work fifteen-hour days, six days a week. She catered as many as ten parties a night. But her efforts paid off. As her reputation grew, she expanded the store, then moved it to East Hampton, where it attracted A-list locals like Steven Spielberg. She began garnering national attention, becoming a recognized food icon in her own right. The nuclear budget analyst's reinvention of herself as a food doyenne was complete.

After almost two decades running her popular store, Ina sold it, looking for a new challenge. At first she cast around, feeling lost, trying to figure out what to do with herself. She had once again left her old life and identity behind without quite figuring out the new one. "I forced myself to go to my office every morning but ended up spending more than a few days reading magazines or copying over my address book," she recalled. It "was the most difficult year of my life."

Again it was Jeffrey who came to her aid. He listened patiently and observed, "You love the food business. Just stay in the game." So she decided to try her hand at a cookbook. At the age of fifty-one, she published the first of what turned out to be a dozen-plus best-selling recipe collections. Her television success quickly followed.

"Those early days of cooking for Jeffrey and my many years running a specialty food store were actually just preparation for what I've found to be my true passion—writing cookbooks," she said. Her husband's encouragement to do what she loved was the "best advice."

"It just takes one person who just believes in you," she explained to Katie Couric. "It could be a teacher, it could be a parent, it could be a spouse. And for me that was Jeffrey, and my whole life turned around."

AS WE'VE SEEN, when making a significant change, we tend to start with a search for new information, often without even realizing what we're doing, as Ina Garten did when she was a young MBA, experimenting with Julia Child recipes and throwing dinner parties for her friends. Then comes that uncomfortable struggle stage, which can drag on for months or even years, when we leave behind our old identity but haven't yet figured out the new one. That's where Garten found herself when she bought the tiny specialty food business ("This is the stupidest thing I've ever done!") and again after she sold the store and plunged into "the most difficult year of my life."

Sometimes, though, to get beyond the struggle and power through to the solution, we need help. We can't quite make the leap on our own. Sometimes we're just stuck in our own heads, endlessly thinking and cogitating and daydreaming but unable to figure out if we are making the correct decision. We can get lost in the whirling gears of our thought process.

That's where an expert companion can make the difference.

I'm borrowing the term "expert companion" here from trauma psychologists, who use it to describe the person or people who help a survivor come to grips with their experience and move forward on a path toward growth. Recall that psychologist Richard Tedeschi found that the expert companion is frequently a key to transformation for those who have endured war, illness, violence or other horrific events. It's the person who will listen to your story, help you manage your emotions, and encourage you as you reconsider your beliefs and goals. This companion doesn't necessarily give advice and certainly doesn't give orders. Instead, it's the person who can see you with a clear eye and help you recognize new opportunities.

That definition sounds to me an awful lot like Ina Garten's husband. He helped her see for herself that her passion was worth pursuing, that it was worth taking a risk to follow a new path and set new goals. He believed in her abilities and saw that she could handle this fresh challenge, even when she wasn't sure of it herself. He was the person who, in the midst of her struggle, gave her the confidence to power ahead and pivot in new, untested directions.

In my interviews with people who have experienced every imaginable type of major transformation, almost all mentioned an outside voice, either another person or a group of people, who helped them find their own way to change. As I reported this book, it became increasingly clear that, in this more colloquial sense, we could all use an expert companion. We all need someone who can hear our concerns and help us clarify our goals and decisions. Not only can we all use an expert companion ourselves, but we can strive to be one to others as well.

In that sense, the expert companion can take many forms. It can be a spouse, as was the case for Ina Garten and Chris Donovan, the telephone repairman whose husband encouraged him to pursue his dream of becoming a shoe designer. I relied on my husband as well when I was considering leaving my longtime, secure job at the *Wall Street Journal* for the risky, uncharted territory of founding a new magazine. For months I was on the fence about whether to take the plunge. My husband steadfastly refused to weigh in, saying that it had to be my decision. But he listened to me endlessly debating the pros and cons, and crucially, he observed that when I talked about this mythical magazine, my demeanor changed, that I lit up in a way he hadn't seen in years. It took his help—listening, reflecting back to me, but not telling me what to do—for me to realize I was ready to take a leap.

Jim VandeHei similarly credits his wife for giving him the "swift kick" he needed to cofound *Politico*. In 2006, when he was a reporter at the *Washington Post*, Jim and his colleague John Harris almost gave up on their plan to launch the political news site. The risks were overwhelming: he had two young kids, he had never managed anything "other than the night shift at Little Caesars Pizza" as a teen, and almost everybody thought the new venture would fail. But his wife Autumn "told us to stop being wimps—and to suck it up," he recounted. She "often knows me better than I do." The site has since become a powerhouse, and VandeHei went on to cofound *Axios*, another political site, as CEO. "We all need an Autumn," he said, a person "whom we trust to give us wise—and often tough—advice."

The expert companion doesn't have to be a family member or even a close friend. Anyone who has a sense of perspective that you lack in yourself can fill this role. Expert companions can emerge from the most unexpected places. One of my college classmates, a British studies major named Christopher Handy, spent years working at art galleries and then in banking and insurance. Early on, in his spare time, he took up flying lessons and traveled frequently to London with his wife Amy. Later, after the couple moved from New York City to Portland, Maine, to raise their children, he also dipped a toe back into acting, a hobby of his while we were in school. He dabbled with voice-over work and acted in some summer stock productions. In 2006, he landed the costarring role in a community theater production of A. R. Gurney's *Love Letters*, a two-person play.

It was there that his costar, whose day job was working as a Delta flight attendant, turned to him one day and announced: "You would make a good flight attendant."

To be clear, this thought had never crossed Chris's mind. His costar caught him off guard. He saw himself more narrowly, as a family man who worked at a bank and did some theater on the side. But his costar, observing him on stage and off, assembled the pieces he had never quite knit together himself. He had an interest in aviation and travel. He was outgoing, loved being on-stage, and had a sonorous voice. He knew how to communicate with an audience. He had a magnetic ability to hold people's attention. His costar snapped those jigsaw pieces into place in a new way and saw, with clarity, where his skill set could take him.

"It was a thunderstruck kind of moment," he said later.

Her "apropos of nothing" comment got him thinking, he said, and set him on an entirely new course. He left his job, researched airlines, and ultimately enrolled in a JetBlue training course. Today Chris is a lead flight attendant for the airline. In 2022, he was tapped to become one of the first attendants for JetBlue's new London route, a position that allows him to make use of his considerable British studies expertise. (In our conversation, he glided effortlessly from the nineteenth-century painter Sir Frederic Leighton to the librettos of Gilbert and Sullivan.) Every chapter of his life—his theater training, his fascination with aviation, his love of travel, even his college major—came together in his new career. He had a long search, followed by a struggle to find the right road, but ultimately it all led him to a job he loves.

"As a lead flight attendant, I get to use my theatrical and voice-over talent to make my cabin safety announcements pleasant—and even entertaining! After all, airline customers are a captive audience; why not make it fun for them?" he said. "But even more than that, I have discovered I enjoy lending a hand and making someone else's day just a little more pleasant."

And it all stems from the observation from that most unexpected of expert companions, his Delta flight attendant costar. "She knew me from my stage presence, from how I use my voice to deliver lines, how I am in front of a large number of people, how I can present myself and present information that is useful in a story," he said. "There is no way I would ever have seen it in myself."

CHRIS'S EXPERT COMPANION had deep knowledge of the airline industry, having been a part of it for more than two dozen years. But the expert companion doesn't need to have expertise in a particular profession; their expertise, instead, is in *you*. Garten's husband is a management expert and the emeritus dean of the Yale School of Management. His entire knowledge of cooking amounts to making coffee, she has said. My husband is a lawyer, with no experience as a journalist (though he *does* cook and also makes awesome coffee).

In fact, there can be a benefit from an expert companion who isn't closely tied to your profession. It's easier for them to have a perspective and clarity that you lack yourself, to have enough distance to see something in you that you don't see yourself. Their observations about you can be revelatory. People who switch careers altogether, or who transform their lives in other ways, are especially likely to cite the influence of someone who had nothing to do at all with the new job.

Consider restaurateur Danny Meyer. As a kid growing up in St. Louis, he was obsessed with food. He swapped sandwiches in the elementary school lunchroom so he could taste how other families lived. His Francophile parents introduced him early to French food. He sampled regional cuisines on every family vacation and learned to cook over an open fire at summer camp. By high school, he was inventing his own creations for his buddies (hello, cheese-stuffed knockwurst wrapped in bacon). After he graduated from college, he traveled around the country for his sales job with a security-tag manufacturer, tasting the cuisine at every stop.

But at some point it was time to grow up. And so Meyer decided to go to law school. At dinner in Manhattan with his aunt and uncle ("Elio's on Second Avenue," he recalls with precision decades later), he lamented that he would be taking the LSAT entrance exams the next day. He wasn't particularly excited about going to law school, he told them, but he needed to quit fooling around and become a real adult.

His uncle wasn't having it.

"Since you were a child, all you've ever talked or thought about is food," the uncle told him. "Why don't you just open a restaurant?"

As Meyer recalls, the idea struck him like a lightning bolt, as "both foreign and like an absolute bull's-eye." He realized he'd been on a *search* for this new career his whole life, from the time he was a kid swapping sandwiches. Now he was in the midst of a *struggle* as he tried to imagine his future. His uncle's simple observation suddenly clarified the entire journey. That comment set him on a path to becoming one of the most successful restaurateurs in the world. "From that moment on, I was off to the races." He never did apply to law school.

Today Meyer's Union Square Hospitality Group, of which he is executive chairman, runs more than a dozen restaurants, including Gramercy Tavern; he also founded the fast-casual Shake Shack chain. Until that evening at Elio's, Meyer told me, "I knew I loved restaurants, but it just never occurred to me that that was a viable career choice."

What a lesser world we would live in if not for Meyer's uncle! Sure, we'd have one more lawyer, but we would be missing out on sublime chocolate shakes, thousands of gourmet meals, and countless restaurant wedding proposals that would have to have been made elsewhere.

And what's true for Meyer is true for so many who never would have made the leap into new ventures without prodding from others. We have expert companions to thank for elevating and promoting some of the greatest leaders in history. As Wharton's Adam Grant points out, quite a few legendary leaders championed their causes only reluctantly, after their talents were discovered and encouraged by others.

Steve Wozniak had to be cajoled by Steve Jobs, his friends, even his mom and dad, into leaving his job at Hewlett-Packard to co-found Apple. Michelangelo didn't consider himself a painter—he was known as a sculptor—and spent two years putting off his assignment to paint the Sistine Chapel ceiling until the pope insisted he start. Martin Luther King Jr. was drafted by colleagues to head up the Montgomery Improvement Association, to lead a bus boycott, and to be the closing speaker at the 1963 March on Washington, where he gave his seminal "I Have a Dream" speech.

"We can only imagine how many Wozniaks, Michelangelos, and Kings never pursued, publicized, or promoted their original ideas because they were not dragged or catapulted into the spotlight," Grant writes.

SOMETIMES, AN EXPERT companion is a work mentor. We know how important it is for career advancement to have a mentor—or better yet, a sponsor. Mentors can give advice, but sponsors can do even more, not only counseling you, but advocating for you and helping you get that next promotion. Both roles are important, but they are typically limited to your career. In some cases, though, a mentor or sponsor sees beyond your work identity and recognizes hidden talents that can help you find a fresh path in your life as well as your work.

Media executive Cyndi Stivers, for example, was a young journalist at *Premiere* magazine when her boss, Susan Lyne, asked her to help with business-side operations as well. Cyndi didn't think of herself as a corporate executive. Yes, she was highly organized, with a talent for streamlining processes and a near-photographic memory, but these qualities "were completely innate," she says, so much so that she had no idea they were particularly special or suited to other kinds of work. "I just assumed everybody could do that." Her boss's recognition ended up redirecting the arc of Cyndi's career and life. She has since taken on multifaceted roles at various media companies, from founding editor in chief of *Time Out New York* to senior executive with Martha Stewart's Living Omnimedia company. At her most recent perch at TED Conferences, she helps recruit top TED speakers and founded a residency program for innovators working on new projects.

"I learned a huge lesson, that when you're taking stock of what you ought to be doing with your life, talk to somebody who has watched you in action and ask them what they think your strengths are," Cyndi says. "I had skills that were so second nature to me, I didn't value them or list them."

Boston Consulting Group even recommends that every chief executive officer find what it calls, in consultant-speak, "a trusted dialogue partner" to fill that role. BCG has calculated that the complexity of businesses has increased exponentially over the past fifty years. "Deep thought and reflection are casualties of this high-pressure and high-stakes environment," it found, and that loss hinders the ability to "imagine untapped opportunities." It recommends that CEOs find time in their overscheduled calendars to meet with a trusted partner who can be "frank and open," providing the CEO with the clarity needed to come up with breakthrough ideas.

Indeed, for anyone considering a pivot, a helpful first step is to write down what *other* people tell you are your strengths. Scarsdale mayor Jane Veron, the Harvard MBA who cofounded a nonprofit to help small-business owners, often coaches female professionals and alumni groups. She instructs the women "to write down what do people tell you you're good at, and that very often you automatically dismiss. You don't think it's hard, so you undervalue what you're good at, that comes easy to you." The results, she says, can be revelatory. We often overlook our own strengths, because they don't seem special to us, yet they can shine neon-bright to others.

VERON'S ADVICE HIGHLIGHTS another key point: while an expert companion may be a close friend or colleague, that person doesn't have to be anyone in your inner circle at all. Your expert companion may even be someone you haven't seen in ages. Multiple studies have found the remarkable power of "dormant ties" (people we've fallen out of touch with) and "weak alliances" (people we only know in passing). These may include people we haven't spoken to in a few years, or with whom we're only tangentially connected. Maybe we worked with them at a previous job, or maybe they're a school classmate. Often, these people are more helpful than those in your current circle whom you've probably already mined for wisdom, contacts, and advice. A previously dormant tie could well lead the way to your next adventure.

Fifty years ago, sociologist Mark Granovetter published a

seminal study on "The Strength of Weak Ties." He asked 282 Boston white-collar workers who had recently switched jobs how they had found their new position. Research findings until then would have predicted that they got their new posts thanks to a close friend or colleague, or perhaps a relative. Powerful associations like those, Granovetter wrote, are naturally "more motivated to help with job information." Such a prediction certainly made intuitive sense. If you are looking for another job or another line of work, wouldn't you rely on people you know well? Wouldn't you approach your mentors and colleagues and close friends?

But Granovetter found that wasn't the case. Instead, the vast majority of job switchers, some 84 percent, had landed their new post through someone they knew only casually. They mentioned old college acquaintances and former colleagues. They talked about running into people by chance, or connecting through mutual friends. Perhaps the job was suggested by an acquaintance of a friend, or a classmate's former roommate, or a colleague's brother-in-law. It is those just outside of your inner circle, Granovetter concluded, who are the most important keys to new opportunity. Those within your own close network know what you know, and they have similar worldviews. It takes the outsider—the casual friend, the former coworker—to bring in fresh information.

Granovetter found that the same dynamic helps to supercharge innovation. Close-knit groups are all familiar with their own work; it takes connecting with distantly related groups to come up with truly breakthrough new ideas. "It is remarkable," he noted dryly, "that people receive crucial information from individuals whose very existence they have forgotten."

These dormant ties can be a font of great advice. About a decade ago, researchers asked 224 executives to reach out to someone they used to know well but hadn't connected with in at least three years. The executives were instructed to choose someone who "might provide information, knowledge or advice that would help you" with a work issue, and to speak with them in person or on the telephone, not via email.

The results were resounding: those they reached out to had far more creative and original ideas than the executives' close ties had been able to offer. When the study participants spoke with their once-dormant connections, they also got right to the point, rather than meandering aimlessly, as we often do in social chats; that approach proved extraordinarily efficient for the time-pressed executives. And because of their shared past, they more readily trusted each other. "Before contacting them I thought that they would not have too much to provide . . . but I was proved wrong. I was very surprised by the fresh ideas," one executive reported back. The experience, added another, "has been eye-opening for me. For one, it has shown me how much potential I have in my Rolodex."

As a side benefit, taking advantage of these kinds of "weak tie" relationships, including those random encounters we have in our everyday lives, also leads to greater happiness. Psychologist Gillian Sandstrom asked people to record every interaction they had during the day—with the doorman who said hello, the barista at the coffee shop, the cashier at the grocery store. She found that those participants with the most weak ties like these were the happiest. What's more, those who had the highest number of these interactions during a given day were happier on that day than on others.

Granovetter's pioneering research was completed long before the invention of LinkedIn and Facebook. But in the social media era, weak ties and dormant connections can be even more fruitful. It's a lot easier to connect with an old school friend when you're already following each other's posts. If you want to track down a former boss or professor, they are just a Google search away. So is your ex-boyfriend's old roommate, who perhaps is in a field you would like to pivot to, or who lives in a city where you plan to move.

Indeed, technology has trumped biology and the human brain when it comes to staying in touch with others. Over your lifetime, you are likely to forge thousands of relationships. But humans are built to juggle only a hundred to two hundred of them at any given time. Beyond that limit, some relationships will lie fallow. In years past, the assumption was always that those distant relationships would eventually wither and die. Not anymore.

Social media has been problematic in too many ways to count, from the spread of misinformation to the rise in bullying. But it has undeniably been productive in at least one way: it has allowed us to build connections and to refresh them, from those closest to us to those on the outermost edges, at a moment's notice. It's easier than ever to go back in time to reconnect.

SOMETIMES YOUR EXPERT companion is an obvious choice, as with Ina Garten and her husband. But the selection isn't always so clear. If you're in need of an expert companion yourself, where do you start looking?

You may well have a person—or people—in your life already. Think about a friend, relative, colleague, or even someone you know only tangentially, whose perspective you value. You may not have imagined them in that role before now, but they are ready for it. The expert companion is someone who "is comfortable with you, so you do not need to change," Tedeschi and his coauthor Bret Moore wrote in *The Posttraumatic Growth Workbook*. He or she will try to see things through your eyes but also can "offer a sense of perspective." It's the person who has "faith in your ability to continue on this path to some unknown destination" and "faith in your ability to do well." At the same time, he or she "points things out that you miss, especially about yourself and the progress you are making."

Of course, finding an expert companion and then asking for candid feedback can be uncomfortable. Many of us are reluctant to seek advice. What if we look weak, or incompetent? We may be especially apprehensive if we are trying to make a good impression on the acquaintance or colleague. We're sure that we'll look dumb and the other person will doubt our abilities.

Yet, as it turns out, the opposite is true: when we ask for advice, others regard us as *more* competent.

In a series of studies, Wharton and Harvard researchers asked students to solve brain teasers or challenging math problems with a partner. Some students were told that they would be judged solely on the accuracy of their answers. Others were told that they would be judged according to how good an impression they made on their partner (which in reality was a computer). Before starting, the students were given three options for communicating with their partner: (1) saying, "Hey, can you give me any advice?" (2) saying, "Hey, I hope you did well," or (3) sending no message at all.

Not surprisingly, students rated on their accuracy eagerly asked for advice. By contrast, students rated on how good an impression they made were less than *half* as likely to ask for help. They were afraid they'd look like idiots, even though asking for advice would have helped them solve the problem. Yet when other students were paired with a partner that was either neutral or asking *them* for advice, they had a higher opinion of the advice seeker. They figured that the person who asked their advice must be quite clever—in part because it's flattering to be asked for help. We tend to think, *He was smart to ask for my advice because I am smart.*

Not only does asking for advice make us look smarter, but doing so also makes us more likable. In a separate study, Harvard researchers analyzed people engaged in "get-to-know-you" chats as well as in face-to-face speed dating conversations. In both cases, they found that people felt more warmly toward those who asked a lot of questions. The questioners seemed to be more caring and understanding. In fact, most of us don't ask *enough* questions, the researchers concluded. As they wrote, "It doesn't hurt to ask."

AN EXPERT COMPANION doesn't even have to actually give advice to be effective. Sometimes just being there is enough. Their most important contribution may be to simply listen. When we have a goal in mind but don't articulate it, it's easy to let it slide. But when we share our goal with someone else, we suddenly feel more accountable. We are more likely to go through with pursuing it. Let's say you want to lose ten pounds. If you keep that goal to yourself and nobody is any the wiser, it's pretty easy to cheat on your diet. But if you're sharing your progress with another person every day, you're more likely to stick to it.

In fact, sharing any kind of goal with someone else makes it more likely that you will succeed. A 2015 study of adults between the ages of twenty-three and seventy-two found that more than 70 percent of those who sent weekly updates to a friend completed their goals, twice the percentage of those who didn't share written goals. That was true regardless of the objectives, which included increasing productivity, improving work-life balance, writing a book chapter, and selling a house.

That meshes with the research that London Business School's Herminia Ibarra has conducted on career change. She found that while thinking about a new path is useful, it can be counterproductive if all you do is cogitate. You've got to share those thoughts with someone else, your own expert companion. If you're stuck in your own head, all you're doing is daydreaming, and that won't get you very far. It's important to also take action, including by "trying out new activities, reaching out to new groups, finding new role models, and reworking our story as we tell it to those around us," she wrote in her book *Working Identity: Unconventional Strategies for Reinventing Your Career*. In other words, seeking an expert companion and asking their feedback or telling them your story is a sign of strength, not of weakness.

Taken together, the research all points to the same conclusion: if all you do is *think* about another path, you will find yourself in an endless circular conversation with yourself. You aren't finding new information or gaining new insights. All of the different methods outlined in the research described here—whether sharing your goals in writing, reaching out to new groups, or telling your story to others—have one element in common. They require articulating where you think you want to go to someone else, and then getting feedback on it. They break through the endlessly repeating, pointless loop in your head.

That's exactly what Glen Mazzara's expert companion did for him. Glen was a logistics manager at a New York City hospital, overseeing budgets and construction projects for the hospital. He didn't love the job. But he had married young and was already a dad. He needed a steady paycheck. For sure, this wasn't exactly his dream job. His fantasy was to be a TV screenwriter. Considering he didn't know the first thing about how to go about doing that, his dream didn't seem terribly practical. Most certainly not when there were bills to pay.

It was his wife's "aunt"—a close friend of her family—who helped him see otherwise. She produced documentaries for PBS, so she knew something about television. Hearing about his day job, how he had to keep the plates spinning at the hospital while wrangling various constituencies, she observed, "A lot of what you do is like TV production." Once he shared his goals with her, they became real. Her encouragement was "a turning point," he told me. "She took me seriously."

Her reflection was enough to prompt Glen to start writing in earnest. It took effort; he didn't own a computer, so he would get to the hospital at dawn to steal a few hours of writing time before the workday began. Ultimately, after penning three spec scripts that went nowhere, he was able to snare an agent. Starting as a writer on the 1990s Don Johnson vehicle, *Nash Bridges*, Glen ultimately worked his way up to become an executive producer of *The Shield* and showrunner for *The Walking Dead*, among many other credits.

THERE ARE NO doubt opportunities in your life not just to *have* an expert companion but to *become* one yourself. The key is to be nonjudgmental and patient. Your role is to ask questions and help them see new perspectives, not to dictate what they should be feeling or thinking, or to tell them what to do. The idea is to give them feedback that will help them understand where they're going, how realistic it is, and what they've already accomplished. As Tedeschi and Moore write, "An expert companion offers ideas about what might be happening without acting like a know-it-all."

In Tedeschi and Moore's world of psychology, the expert companion is often a family member or friend, but may also be a therapist who is trained for the role. Similarly, while your expert companion is likely to be someone you already know, there is a parallel in that it may instead be a trained career coach or life coach.

That was the case for Khemaridh Hy. The son of Cambodian immigrants who settled in New York after fleeing their country's civil war, Khe (pronounced "Kay") was a studious, dutiful son. He followed the successful first-generation playbook: he got good

grades, went to Yale, and pursued a career in finance after graduation. His career all went according to plan. By the time he hit thirty-
one, he had been promoted to managing director at BlackRock, the
prestigious investment firm. Yet while he liked his colleagues and
the financial rewards, "something was off," he says. He was toiling
through twelve-hour days and feeling "comfortably numb. You're
not unhappy, but you're definitely not happy. You don't particularly
love the work you do, but you don't hate it."

He couldn't figure out why he wasn't more satisfied. He had
financial security, a great job title, and was rewarded with the en-
vious glances of his peers at cocktail parties. Yet somehow none
of that made a difference. "I had a lot of insecurities that I grew
up with as a result of being shy and nerdy and being outside of
the culture. . . . You think a lot of that goes away with success and
money," he says. "And then you have a taste of it, and you realize
those feelings don't go away."

To ease his boredom, Khe threw himself into side projects. He
blogged anonymously about music, set up networking parties, and
played around with various kinds of productivity software. On a
vacation, he started a newsletter he called "RadReads," sharing life
hacks and links to interesting pieces he was reading elsewhere.
"Those things lit me up. I realized that 5 percent of my activities
were bringing me 99 percent of my happiness," he recalls. "I said,
'Imagine if you could do that all day.'" His feelings were further
"crystallized" after he and his wife had a baby daughter. He'd had
enough. When he had saved enough money to last at least eighteen
months, he quit.

Khe's was hardly a "take this job and shove it" move. Leaving
BlackRock was a fraught decision. He was thirty-five years old, he
had started a family, and he didn't have another job lined up. "My
parents were not okay with this. 'We fled Cambodia, sacrificed
our whole lives, and three years after you get [the promotion], you

quit?' And my wife is, 'What do I tell people you do when I meet new moms?'" It didn't help that almost every day he'd get a text from a friend or former colleague casually asking, "What are you doing these days?" The lack of a professional identity was crippling. "It almost drove me back into the workforce."

That's where his expert companions came in. Khe began working with a life coach, who "gave me a lot of tools to really just navigate the emotions that were coming through." A second coach, a self-described "practical philosopher," helped him explore questions like "Why am I obsessed with work?" The coaches helped him understand the kind of life he *did* want. The family moved to California, where he could indulge in his passion for surfing. He focused on his weekly "RadReads" newsletter and found that his musings on life and recommendations on productivity resonated with other midcareer professionals. His posts ranged from "Why do so many successful people fear being broke?" to "What would you do for a Bezos Bod?" As the newsletter gained traction, it caught the attention of CNN, which in an article dubbed him "the Oprah for Millennials."

Since then, Khe has grown his business, hiring full-time employees and teaching an online productivity course that combines his time management coaching with his philosophizing on life issues. As he describes it: "Come for the productivity, stay for the existential."

With the help of his expert companions, Khe has engineered a career that allows him to fit his work into his life, rather than vice versa. He doesn't schedule meetings before 11:30 AM, so that he can surf in the morning and help get his kids ready for school. He has dinner with his family every night. Though he doesn't earn anything close to the seven figures he made in finance, he says that isn't the point. He currently works about thirty-eight hours a week, with a goal to shave that down to thirty hours. If he wanted to earn more, he would have to work longer hours, he reasons, and "all I would want to do is buy back time, to surf more." Since he already has the time, "I don't need to make more money to buy back more time."

These days Khe has taken on coaching clients himself, becoming a professional expert companion for others. When we spoke, he sported a fashionably scruffy beard and black T-shirt; a surf board was propped up behind him. After he quit his finance job, "it was very scary for four years," he says. "But I'm not scared anymore."

AS FOR INA Garten, after more than fifty years of marriage, her husband Jeffrey is still her expert companion. He drops in occasionally on her most recent cooking show, *Be My Guest with Ina Garten*. Her book *Cooking for Jeffrey* is a virtual paean to her spouse, with affectionate stories about how they met when she was still a high school student and he was a college classmate of her big brother. And of course the book includes his favorite recipes, from Perfect Roast Chicken to Limoncello Ricotta Cheesecake. Jeffrey appears on the cover, smiling next to Ina, a slice of chocolate layer cake in hand.

The cookbook's description of Jeffrey could be the textbook definition of an expert companion. "It was Jeffrey who first encouraged me to turn what I considered more of a hobby or pastime into my career," Ina writes. "His words started me on a journey that has led to a life and happiness beyond any I could have imagined. I already loved to cook for Jeffrey, but he helped me realize I could do more with that interest."

The ultimate companion, he inspired her to find that path on her own, without telling her what to do. "I often say that he was the first feminist I ever knew; he believed that I could do anything I wanted to do," she writes. "He's the reason I love to cook and also the person who continually encourages me to do what I love."

IT IS EXTRAORDINARY how an expert companion, even if it's someone we've lost touch with for a while, can lead us to new horizons. My own experience on this front has been profound. One of the kindest, funniest, and most talented reporters I ever worked with was Jeff Zaslow. We were colleagues at the *Wall Street Journal* for years, before I headed off to start a magazine and he embarked on a second career as a prolific author, including cowriting the autobiographies of both Gabby Giffords and Chesley "Sully" Sullenberger.

We hadn't seen each other in a couple of years when I published a *New York Times* op-ed about the death of my demanding childhood music teacher and the outpouring of tributes from his former students who belatedly appreciated the life lessons he had taught us. In the piece, I described the emotional experience of returning to my teacher's memorial service, toting my long-neglected viola, so that I could participate in an alumni concert in his memory. I thought I was nuts for feeling so strongly about a teacher I had barely seen since high school. Yet when I arrived at the rehearsal, I found three generations of former students—now accountants and lawyers and teachers—who had flown in from every corner of the country with their old instruments in tow, because they felt exactly as I did. Our group of mostly lapsed musicians created a symphony orchestra the size of the New York Philharmonic. It was among the most powerful experiences I've ever had.

When Jeff read that piece, he picked up the phone and called me from Chicago. "You have to write a book about this," he announced, with barely a "hello." I hadn't seen it that way; I had spent my career up to that point as a business writer and editor, not a weaver of sentimental tales. "I don't do that kind of writing," I protested. In fact, I only wrote the piece at the insistence of a good friend—another expert companion!—to whom I'd recounted the experience over dinner.

But Jeff had a clearer view of my skills, my potential, and even my personality than I did. He knew that underneath the no-nonsense editor exterior was someone who weeps at Hallmark commercials and still sobs uncontrollably during reruns of *Beaches*.

"I'm going to call you every day until you realize this is a book!" he said, laughing, but also *really* meaning it. He even sent me samples of book proposals to show me how the process works. Seeing myself through his eyes, understanding how he viewed me, was revelatory. He helped me come to the realization that I actually did want to pivot, to try my hand at narrative, emotionally charged storytelling. Ultimately, his clear-eyed view helped lead to the book *Strings Attached*, which I cowrote with my teacher's daughter, the Chicago Symphony violinist Melanie Kupchynsky, to tell the story of her dad's heartbreaking, inspiring journey from Ukrainian war refugee to pied piper of classical music.

I had the good fortune of getting to know Jeff well when we worked together, and the even better fortune to rekindle our close friendship. He was the ultimate expert companion. Tragically, he died not long after in a car accident, at just fifty-three years old.

We never know what life may bring tomorrow. You might be reluctant to reach out to that person you haven't spoken to in years. You might be shy, or embarrassed. You may fear that they will be offended or annoyed. But give it a try. You almost certainly won't regret it—and it may well prove to be life changing.

9

Lessons from Play-Doh

Bringing Brands Back from the Dead

If I have learned nothing else in my years here,
my biggest lesson is you have to constantly reinvent this company.
That's how you get to be 103 years old.

—GINNI ROMETTY, FORMER CEO OF IBM

If you had lived in the United States a century or so ago, it's likely your walls would have been filthy, courtesy of your home's coal heater, which would have kept you toasty but left behind a nasty residue. To get rid of the stuff, you'd head to your local hardware store and pick up a cleaner formulated especially to scrub off that sticky coating.

Today almost all of those cleaners are gone. Except one: Kutol.

If you're thinking, *I never heard of Kutol*, that's because you know it better by another name. Unlike its competitors, Kutol's owners reimagined their product. They added coloring and a pleasant, vaguely vanilla smell, stripped out the detergent, and then reintroduced it—as a child's toy.

Today Kutol is known as Play-Doh. It has generated billions of dollars in sales and remains one of the best-selling toys on the planet.

Play-Doh's reinvention story is particular to its owners and its time. Yet its spectacular pivot from obsolete cleaner to iconic kids' toy holds lessons for companies of all kinds. Its story provides insights into why some businesses and brands disappear, while others are reimagined in ways that propel them to even greater success. At a time when the average life span of a company is only about ten years, Play-Doh's story offers lessons in how organizations can pivot and appear just as relevant today as they did half a century ago. As a window into the kinds of business environments that encourage innovation, Play-Doh offers other institutions a lens through which to view how they might think about navigating change.

Throughout this book we've met individuals who made remarkable pivots. Some have reinvented their career, like James Patterson. Others have remade their lives after unimaginable trauma, like Kay Wilson. A few have stumbled onto "aha" moments that led to ingenious innovations, like Art Fry with Post-it notes. Many have pioneered the road to reinvention unintentionally, like economist-turned-farmer Will Brown, or out of necessity, like stay-at-home-mom-turned-entrepreneur Jane Veron. We've seen how these individuals navigate a "Reinvention Road Map"—a similar progression of stages they go through when they pivot, whether in life or at work. They *search* for information; they often *struggle* as they leave behind old identities before fully embracing new ones; and they frequently face an impasse that *stops* them in their tracks, before finding the *solution*. We've seen the similarities between those who change careers, who bounce back from trauma, who turn their lives around after a shattering failure.

Their examples provide insights into how individuals navigate a changing world. But what about businesses, where most of us work? They face infinitely more complex challenges. Their leaders need not only to rethink and reinvent products but to adjust to the new and evolving needs of employees and customers. They must be sensitive to changes in both the marketplace and the culture at large.

These kinds of complicated evolutions—or revolutions—are different for every organization. Yet, while there's no exact science, businesses that have pivoted successfully share common themes. Their trajectories often mirror those of individuals. Typically, companies and brands that come back from the brink do so only after leaders have been *searching* for a solution and have had to endure a painful *struggle*, replete with dead ends and frustrating tail-chasing. There may even be an almost extinction-level *stop*. The pivot may take the organization in a wildly different direction. Sometimes it isn't about tweaking an existing product as much as about reimagining an entirely different purpose from what the product was designed for in the first place.

There's an added element as well. Almost always, the answer comes from people who are outside of the established power structure. It's the person or group that has a clearer perspective than those in the inner circle. There's a parallel here with the expert-companion role that, say, Ina Garten's husband played in her transformation into the Barefoot Contessa: he recognized strengths and opportunities that she didn't know she had. Within companies, too, it often takes someone outside the C-suite to convince, shake up, and open the eyes of those in leadership.

Rarely do you hear of a CEO, no matter how visionary, having the brilliant brainstorm that turns around a company. Apple's Steve Jobs didn't dream up the iPhone himself. It was a pet project of engineers and designers working deep within the company. In fact, not only did Jobs have no inkling of what they were working on, but when he did learn about it, he at first argued against it. He thought a "smart" phone would be a gimmick, and that the product wouldn't appeal to anybody but "pocket protector" geeks.

His employees were the ones who convinced him to make the bet on the phone, which he then wholeheartedly championed, transforming an entire industry.

Like the iPhone, a great reinvention idea might originate with rank-and-file employees in the trenches, or even with outsiders, like customers or vendors. They can reimagine a product with a freedom not available to the managers who focus on today's sales and tomorrow's quarterly profits. They aren't bound by tradition or "that's the way we've always done it" thinking. Another crucial element is that they succeed only when leaders like Jobs have the confidence to hear them out and embrace their fresh ideas—or have the good sense to step aside and get out of the way.

There's a reason why Post-it notes originated in the bowels of 3M, with Art Fry working on his own time, rather than as a top-down corporate initiative. Recall that 3M allowed its employees to work on their own passion projects 15 percent of their time. Fry took on the challenge of reinventing an otherwise useless adhesive on his own. When he needed support from other departments—whose bosses had no intention of lending their employees out to him—those colleagues used *their* 15 percent time to work with him. It was the renegade nature of this project, executed without the official sanction of the company, that enabled them to transform a failed adhesive into one of the most successful products in 3M's history. Other companies have adopted similar programs, like Google's 20 percent side project time, which jump-started the creation of Gmail and Google News.

Major product categories owe their very existence to outsiders who saw what insiders missed. One of the unlikeliest grew out of the newfangled bandages that Kimberly-Clark manufactured for wounded soldiers during World War I. Its great innovation was to make the dressings from wood pulp, which was both more absorbent and cheaper than cotton. After the war ended, military demand dried up. But something odd was going on. Nurses had begun hoarding the stuff, not for their patients but for themselves. They had figured out that the bandages had an awesome off-label use: for their monthly periods.

Up until then, women for centuries had dealt with their menstrual cycles by using rags (thus the awful idiom "she's on the rag") or homemade pads. But nurses had now figured out a better way. They realized, well before the company did, that there was not only another use for the product but also a massive untapped pool of potential customers—almost half of the adult population. Kimberly-Clark ultimately introduced Kotex (named for the pads' "cotton-like texture") menstrual pads in October 1919. The global feminine hygiene category is now valued at $39 billion.

More recently, a sales rep at the chemical giant BASF inadvertently discovered an entirely new category of household cleaners. That was the last thing on his mind when he made a visit to a Japanese construction company. His only goal that day was to extol the virtues of BASF's insulating and soundproofing foam. Unfortunately, he clumsily knocked over a cup of coffee onto a blueprint on the desk. Mortified, he grabbed a chunk of the spongy insulating foam and apologetically began wiping up the spill. The foam did the trick. But it also did something else: it erased the blueprint.

Back at the office, the sales rep shared the story with one of his colleagues, a chemist. Ordinarily, that water-cooler chitchat would have been the end of it. "In the past, this discovery might well have been dismissed within BASF as a mere novelty," a "seemingly irrelevant" data point, INSEAD business school professor Ben Bensaou writes. After all, salespeople and chemists inhabit different worlds, and besides, BASF had a $2-billion-a-year research and development operation.

But by a fortunate twist, the company was in the midst of

breaking down those traditional silos between departments as part of a cascading series of changes intended to supercharge innovation. And so, instead of ignoring the sales rep's discovery, company leaders took note. They brainstormed different ways to think about the insulation. Ultimately, they forged a partnership with Procter & Gamble, which in 2003 repurposed the foam into what became a massive hit: Mr. Clean Magic Eraser. Today the company markets at least half a dozen variations of the Magic Eraser, which has become a familiar household staple (including at my house) for erasing scuff marks and crayon from walls.

Bensaou argues that companies trying to innovate or reinvent themselves today must follow a similar path, by empowering employees at every level to come up with new ideas. Most organizations "fail to recognize *the entire organization*, including all the people who work for it, has a role to play in the innovating engine," he writes. He describes the equivalent of the expert companion—someone who has the perspective and the insights to help reinvent the future: "Once you take *innovating by anyone, anytime, anywhere* as your goal, you can begin turning your organization into a true innovating engine."

That was certainly the case with one of the most remarkable reinventions I've come across. It's the story of how an outright flop turned into one of the most profitable pharmaceuticals of all time.

JOIN ME IN the small town of Sandwich, England. Sandwich is a throwback in time, a quaint medieval outpost hard by the White Cliffs of Dover. If you were to travel here, you might amble through the ancient stone Fisher Gate, dating back to 1384. You might wander through the winding, narrow cobblestone streets in the town center, or climb to the top of the St. Peter's Church tower to take in the view of the surrounding bucolic countryside. Perhaps you'd cap off your visit with a pint at the fifteenth-century George & Dragon pub.

Sandwich is a quiet place, barely more than a village. Its current population tops out at under five thousand people. Over the centuries, it has been best known as the birthplace of . . . well, you know. According to lore, in the eighteenth century John Montagu, the fourth Earl of Sandwich and a gambling addict, became so engrossed at the gaming table that he refused to leave even during mealtimes, instead ordering his valet to bring him salt beef between two slices of bread. Supposedly, others also began ordering "the same as Sandwich!"

It was in this unlikely town, a place that seems to belong to an entirely different century, that the pharmaceutical giant Pfizer set up a laboratory outpost in the 1950s. And it was here in 1986 that scientists came up with a treatment for angina, a condition in which narrowed arteries can't pump enough blood through the heart. They hoped their compound, known as UK-92480, would alleviate the chest pain caused by the condition by selectively blocking an enzyme called PDE5 and allowing blood vessels to expand.

Ian Osterloh, one of the scientists at the lab, vividly remembers hearing about the drug for the first time in the late 1980s. Osterloh, an unassuming Brit whose slight build, thinning hair, and mild demeanor betrayed no hint of the epic role he would someday play in millions of lives, was a bit skeptical. He was just being realistic; pharmaceutical drug development is a painfully slow, often fruitless process, often "a source of frustration and disappointment," as he put it. "I wasn't thinking this is going to change the world, or anything like that," he told me.

Still, the angina drug was promising enough to at least begin testing it. Unfortunately, early studies using healthy volunteers were disappointing. When given the medication three times a day, the volunteers suffered muscle aches, headaches, and indigestion. There was also another, somewhat bizarre, side effect. The male participants "reported increased erections several days after the initial dose," recalls Osterloh. It was an annoying obstacle blocking the path to success for treating a *real* ailment. "None of us at Pfizer thought much of this side effect at the time," he says. The finding was considered so tangential that the lead investigator "only mentioned it reluctantly," at the very end of a meeting to report results: "He was embarrassed about it."

A small trial conducted with angina sufferers was no more auspicious. While the medication was "moderately helpful," it was clear that patients would ultimately experience those same aggravating side effects. The trade-off wasn't worth it.

Under ordinary circumstances, the drug would have been abandoned, another disappointment. "The drug had no future for its original condition, angina," Osterloh told me. "Most people assumed the drug would die." And indeed, interest evaporated. The angina drug was a bust.

That could have been the end of this story. In countless similar cases, in industries around the globe, it is. A potential new product is tested, the results are underwhelming, and the product is abandoned. The company moves on to try something else, searching for more fruitful solutions.

Sometimes, though, within the germ of a failed product is a successful one. Sometimes there's a person or a group of people who look at the misfire through a different lens and see a glimmer of something new, something they didn't set out to look for in the first place. Such was the case with Osterloh and his Sandwich colleagues. They couldn't help but notice the persistent reports of that bizarre side effect, that men were getting erections. Slowly it dawned on them that maybe they were looking at this drug the wrong way. Forget about angina. Could it instead be used as an impotence treatment?

Osterloh and his team were able to shift their focus in this completely new way because they had a freedom most of their colleagues didn't. They were far removed from New York headquarters, separated by 3,500 miles, multiple time zones, and an ocean. Nobody outside of the United Kingdom even knew what they were up to. "In Sandwich, there seemed to be more freedom to do exploration, and not have to have everything micromanaged from the other side," Osterloh told me. Set loose from bureaucratic meddling, the small team of scientists had a perspective unavailable to their bosses. They were able to think creatively and to look at their discovery with fresh eyes.

The *struggle* stage, though, was just beginning. No one knew if there even *was* a market for an impotence drug. None had existed before. At the time impotence was largely considered a psychological condition, not a physical one. The few people from outside their team who heard about it were skeptical. Some thought it was unbecoming for a company of Pfizer's stature to even explore some sort of sex drug. *Eew!* "There were people who thought this isn't a major condition, that we should be doing cancer and heart disease," Osterloh says. "Others thought it was a psychological condition. We'd been teaching that 90 percent of it was psychological, back in the seventies." What's more, "I don't think anybody had any idea how common this was. Some might have thought there was no market for it."

Osterloh and his colleagues, though, were intrigued enough to test the drug as an impotence treatment instead—and had enough autonomy to make that decision on their own. In 1993 they recruited a couple of dozen men in Bristol. After taking the medication, each participant was brought to a private room in the lab, fitted with a device called a RigiScan that measures the girth and hardness of the penis, and then shown erotic films. The results were impressive. "Several of us were very enthusiastic and making the case," Osterloh recalls. Still, resistance was fierce:

one of the top people "on the clinical side in Sandwich was very against it, and he tried to set hurdles that were very high," he says. "I think if it had been just his decision, we wouldn't have been doing the studies."

Despite that internal pushback, Osterloh and the group persevered, recruiting three hundred men from the United Kingdom, Sweden, and France. This time the outcome was too overwhelming to dismiss: 90 percent of the participants responded to the highest dose. In fact, the results were so extraordinary that, in an unheard-of development for a clinical trial, participants began begging for more of the medication. Although they were anonymous—identified only by number—some of them reached out directly to the researchers in Sandwich, outing themselves as they pleaded for additional doses.

"I was like a man who was drowning, and when your drug came along, it was like you threw me a lifeline from the shore," one man wrote to the researchers, imploring them for more. "And now I'm in the water again. You've taken my lifeline away, and I'm going to drown."

Only then did the rest of the company notice—as did the general public, when news stories began emerging about the miracle drug. Crucially, the new direction got buy-in from the company's then-CEO, William Steere Jr., who became a powerful advocate. Clever marketing also played a role. "Impotence is a loaded term, and pejorative," says Janice Lipsky, who ultimately led the medication's marketing team. In early focus groups with male patients, "there was a lot of shame. One man teared up when he was telling us about his experience . . . he felt he couldn't touch or hug his wife because he might get her hopes up."

That insight was behind the team's rebranding of impotence as "erectile dysfunction," a then-obscure technical phrase that had a pleasingly clinical, less emotionally fraught sound to it.

"It was all about destigmatization," Lipsky says. That in turn informed the first television commercial, with former senator Bob Dole, a prostate cancer survivor, talking about the side effect of "erectile dysfunction, ED, often called impotence. You know, it's a little embarrassing to talk about ED, but it's so important to millions of men and their partners that I decided to talk about it publicly." He didn't mention a brand name.

After the Pfizer drug was approved by the Food and Drug Administration in 1998, it went on to become one of the biggest blockbusters in company history. The failed angina medication led the way to creating an entirely new drug category; today the market for erectile dysfunction drugs is estimated at close to $3 billion. Yet if it hadn't been for mild-mannered Osterloh and his small but mighty team of true believers in a far-off medieval village—folks who weren't pulling the corporate strings and who had the creative insight to rethink the drug's purpose—the world might never have been introduced to UK-92480, the little blue pill now known as Viagra.

OSTERLOH AND HIS colleagues benefited from the autonomy that comes from working far removed from headquarters. They were a collaborative group, determined to push through a protracted period of *struggle*, fend off the naysayers, and pivot nimbly. Ultimately they succeeded through below-the-radar, incremental experimentation. From the time Osterloh first learned about the proposed angina drug until the day Viagra itself was introduced, a decade had passed—ten years of trial and error, with many fits and stops along the way.

Yet if the circumstances had been just slightly different—if Osterloh and his colleagues hadn't been so insistent on continuing the trials, if leaders had ordered them to stop when the angina treatment didn't work, if the CEO hadn't become an advocate—Viagra never would have happened.

Which raises the question: How many other undiscovered Viagras are there? How many failed products might have been reinvented in new ways instead of relegated to the dustbin of history? How many failing brands might *still* be revived if only bosses were confident enough to listen to their employees and customers?

Anyone who's been around large corporations is familiar with the stilted top-down attempts at "ideation" and "transformation" that almost always go nowhere. I once got sent on a corporate retreat where we were supposed to choose our "spirit animal." More than once I've sat through painful corporate exercises like pinning colored dots to mission statements tacked to a wall. It's become fashionable in recent years for companies to appoint a "chief transformation officer" to lead the efforts to reinvent the whole company, a typically pointless exercise in box-checking more than in true reinvention. And yet, as often as I've had to participate in tortured corporate "ideation" exercises, I've also seen potentially transformative ideas bubbling up organically from people in the trenches, only to be killed, or simply ignored, by those in power.

Osterloh, too, is well aware of how fortunate he and his team were. At multiple points during the development process, Viagra could have died an untimely death. "For a project to succeed, you have to have the right structure, the right resources, and the right people," he told me. "We were in that sweet spot where this could thrive."

NOT EVERY BUSINESS is able to make that transition. Plenty of them are ill equipped to reinvent their products or themselves. What is it that separates those that succeed from those that fail, those that live from those that die? In other words, how can a company make sure it's a Netflix, not a Blockbuster? The answer depends in part on company leaders' ability to evaluate "expert companion" insights not just about what *to* do, but at least as important, about what *not* to do.

Netflix itself provides an instructive example. It famously started out as a DVD rental-by-mail company before pivoting to digital streaming, and then pivoting again to become an entertainment behemoth, spending billions of dollars a year on content ranging from *The Crown* to *Stranger Things* to *Squid Game*.

The company is famous for its corporate culture manifesto, first outlined by cofounder and CEO Reed Hastings in a 125-page slide deck that was once described as "Silicon Valley's most important document ever." Some of its tenets have been deservedly ridiculed, like its insistence that employees who are doing fine should be fired ("adequate performance gets a generous severance package"), an approach that has prompted comparisons to *The Hunger Games*. And the culture manifesto didn't prevent the company from making significant missteps, like wildly overspending on undistinguished programming. That said, some of its core tenets—valuing candor, asking for feedback—were key to its survival, in particular by incentivizing employees outside of the power structure to innovate. At pivotal moments, Netflix leaders have trusted their own expert companions within the ranks, prompting them to shift or even reverse their own decisions.

In the early 2000s, for example, company leadership was betting on a new way to distribute videos: a "Netflix Box." Customers, who would have their very own box at home, would choose the film they wanted to watch the next day, and then the Netflix Box would download the film overnight. (Downloads were slow in those days!) The company's leaders asked for volunteers to work on the project. Just one raised his hand. "Volunteering to lead a new initiative is a very stupid thing to do at Netflix," according to the volunteer, Robert Kyncl, who had started his career in a talent agency mailroom. "The company's culture prides itself on relentless focus, dispassionately eliminating business initiatives that are not core to the overall strategy. You can work on something for years only to find that project mothballed during a quick meeting."

Kyncl was supposed to focus on the Netflix Box. Instead, the Czech native, who in his teens had been a professional cross-country skier, discovered something else: YouTube videos, then still a new invention. "I saw grainy videos of snowboarding accidents," he recalled, "and people lighting their kitchens on fire, and I saw that those videos were attracting massive viewership numbers." He realized that viewers didn't need the slow, laborious process of downloading high-quality movies on a bulky box at home. They could watch directly from the internet. They could *stream* films. "Witnessing the popularity of YouTube was a revelation," he wrote. "And it caused us to stop our launch and pivot to a service that would allow consumers to stream movies remotely instead of downloading them."

Almost a decade later, when Netflix was perfecting streaming in 2015, a lower-level employee helped spur another about-face. At the time, you could still watch Netflix shows only when your device was connected to the internet. You couldn't download a program onto your computer if, say, you were taking a plane trip or going someplace without internet access. Employees kept bringing up the question of downloading, but top executives would shoot it down. They figured that not enough customers would be interested, and that implementing the function would take precious time and focus away from perfecting streaming.

One Netflix executive, though, wasn't convinced. He enlisted a company researcher named Zach Schendel to look into video downloading in countries where it was available. Zach found that, contrary to expectations, it was wildly popular. An Indian commuter downloaded shows to watch while he was carpooling to work. A German customer downloaded shows in the living room, where the internet connection was strong, and watched while cooking in the kitchen, where the connection was weak. The response was unequivocal. Zach took the findings to his boss, who brought them to his boss, and so on all the way up to Hastings, the CEO. Netflix changed its policy, doing an about-face and embracing downloads.

"Let me be clear, I am nobody in the company. I'm just some researcher," Zach said. "Yet I was able to push back against a strong and publicly stated opinion from the top leadership to rally excitement for this feature. This is what Netflix is all about."

EMPLOYEES INSIDE AN organization often have an edge in spotting new ideas and potential pivots, but senior leadership can sometimes play that role too. That's especially true when leaders are brought in from outside the organization. While they almost certainly face multiple challenges, they also have the benefit of bringing a fresh perspective unburdened by the "we don't do that here" mentality.

One classic example is the legendary auto executive Robert Lutz, known for his flamboyant antics as well as his role in transforming multiple carmakers. As Paul Ingrassia described him in a 2001 *Wall Street Journal* profile, "Mr. Lutz doesn't do anything 'appropriate,' at least not on purpose. He likes fast planes, fast cars and fat cigars. He flies his own fighter jet and helicopter" and views corporate "touchy-feely team-building exercises" with "undisguised disgust." Lutz was notorious for his outsize gestures—like when he introduced the Jeep Grand Cherokee at the 1992 Detroit

Auto Show by driving it up the steps of the convention center and smashing through a window.

When then-sleepy Chrysler brought in Lutz in 1986, the company needed a facelift. It had skimped on new-product development and got little respect from the industry. "Chrysler products were basically nobody's first choice," Lutz told me with characteristic bluntness. "You go to a party and people say, 'Who do you work for?' and you say, 'Chrysler,' and they give you a pitiful glance and pat you on the shoulder."

Backed by a small team of supporters who also came from outside, Lutz decided that "what this company needs is something totally unbelievable, something nobody in the US automobile industry has ever done before," he recalled. "What you need to do when you want to change perception is you have to do something truly awesome." That "something truly awesome" became the Dodge Viper, an insanely showy, completely impractical convertible sports car that had no air conditioning, no power top, no ABS brakes, and "made no apologies," as Lutz said. It was, in the words of one reviewer, "as subtle as a sledgehammer and as civilized as a civil war," making it, naturally, "an old-school gearhead's dream."

There was plenty of internal pushback. Lutz had no research to back up his crazy idea when, inspired by a weekend drive in the country in his Cobra roadster, he announced it one Monday. Corporate finance executives thought the $80 million development budget should be used for more practical purposes, like paying down debt. Marketers worried that the car's $50,000 price tag—more than double the cost of a typical Dodge—would be a nonstarter. Yet Lutz's intuition proved right: when the car was introduced in 1991, it was a sensation. The Viper changed perceptions about the company and led the way for a string of hits, including the PT Cruiser ("with its head-turning, Chicagogangster lines," as Ingrassia described it) and the redesigned Dodge Ram.

Lutz contends that his outsider status was key to the turnaround. He and his team "often described ourselves as a band of misfits, cast off from larger, more serious companies and driven by the underdog's desire to show our worth," he said. They may have been top executives, but they never lost their outlaw perspective, which allowed them to take the company where it might never have otherwise ventured.

Lutz used the same playbook when he jumped to General Motors in 2001—at sixty-nine, an age at which most of his peers had long retired. There, in a signature move, he championed the introduction of the Chevy Volt plug-in hybrid, intended to both change the perception of GM as a technological laggard and steal some of the spotlight from the media darling Toyota Prius. "You do something startling, shocking, unexpected—primarily to change the minds of the media and the public about what the company stands for," he told me. "The Viper and the Chevy Volt were done for identical reasons."

There, too, he faced off against naysayers. "Almost nobody wanted it except for me and a hardy band of co-warriors," he said. When you do something truly outside the box . . . people are hoping it will fail." Those people included some colleagues: "The toughest battle I ever fought was at GM, to get the Volt approved, even though I was the vice chairman." Ultimately, what allowed Lutz's team to innovate was the perseverance of their small group. "We had a hardy band of people who really knew what they were talking about and were able to bat down the resistance."

His experience with his "band of co-warriors" points up another crucial factor in corporate reinvention: small teams are often more innovative than larger ones. When University of Chicago researchers analyzed more than 65 million papers, patents, and software products, they found that smaller teams tend to come up with disruptive breakthroughs, while large teams tend to simply iterate on existing developments. Each type of group has its place, but if you want to invent—or reinvent—something truly novel, you're best off starting with a small band.

Small teams aren't just superior when it comes to cars and pharmaceuticals. The wisdom of starting small was as true for the hardy group of 3M renegades who invented Post-its, as it was for the nurses who figured out Kotex. It was the case with the brave engineers and designers who championed the iPhone. These small teams can essentially play the role of the "expert companion."

That holds true on a more modest scale as well. At both the *Wall Street Journal* and *Condé Nast*, when I was tasked with coming up with new products, my rule of thumb was to start with a team just big enough to share a pizza and a pitcher of beer around a table. When we created "Weekend Journal," a popular section devoted to readers' leisure pursuits, the ideas underpinning it—*Let's use our business expertise to write about wine . . . or buying a used car . . . or vacation travel*—were ones that bubbled up around company cafeteria tables. A few years later, our small team created "Personal Journal"—which translated daily news stories about oil prices and interest rates into what-it-means-for-you consumer articles—during a series of intimate get-togethers in local coffee shops in the wake of 9/11, when our downtown office was uninhabitable. Until researching this book, I had no idea that our highly anecdotal approach has been validated by science.

Another key factor in every one of these cases, from Magic Eraser to the Dodge Viper, is that the ideas coming from outside were ultimately heard by—and embraced by—leadership. Too often, internal agitators are ignored, pushed aside, or marginalized. Bruce D. Fischer and Matthew Rohde of Elmhurst College found as much when they studied a manufacturing company that was trying to encourage innovation in its ranks. The company asked employees to submit ideas and incentivized them to do so by holding a monthly drawing among entrants, with the winner receiving a $50 gift card.

At first, the idea seemed to work; in its initial year, new ideas poured in, almost 180 of them. But over time the number dwindled to barely more than a dozen or two a year. When the researchers asked employees why they weren't coming up with new ideas anymore, the answer was clear: a lack of follow-through from the bosses. Sure, they might get a gift card, but what about their ideas for innovation? Why wasn't the company making use of their suggestions? And why weren't the employees getting any feedback when the ideas were rejected? Employees felt "like management is not listening to them," the researchers found.

The story was the same at a utility company the researchers studied. When they asked accountants, marketing specialists, and engineers about innovation, employees overwhelmingly said they were stifled by "a lack of follow-through" and a lack of feedback. That put a damper on their motivation, even more than other issues like time pressures or the extra workload. "When an idea is not acted upon, it serves to erode employee motivation to innovate," the researchers concluded. To take advantage of that outsider perspective, the wisdom of their corporate "expert companions," the boss needs to listen.

AT COMPANIES LIKE Pfizer and Chrysler, the challenge was to rethink an existing product. But what do you do if the only product you make is obsolete? What if there's no amount of tweaking that will save it?

That was the conundrum facing the makers of Kutol wallpaper cleaner. It had been a big hit when it was first introduced in 1933 by Cincinnati brothers Cleophas and Noah McVicker. At the time, coal was the major fuel used to heat American homes. It was cheap and plentiful, but it was also filthy, depositing a layer of soot over walls and floors. That was especially problematic for wallpaper, which in those pre-vinyl days was literally made of paper and was easily ruined by scrubbing. So housewives used a cleaner known as wallpaper dough—a putty typically made from flour, salt, and detergent—which they would rub along their walls to collect the filth.

Kutol brand wallpaper dough provided a tidy living for the extended McVicker family, a coal-mining clan of Scottish immigrants. Cleo McVicker, a hard-charging, larger-than-life personality, proved to be a charismatic leader. A bit of a daredevil, he was an accomplished athlete who piloted his own plane—and had survived two plane crashes, including one in a New Jersey swamp. He generously handed out jobs to various relatives and hoped that his teenage son Joe would eventually follow him to take over the business.

But it all imploded one rainy November night in 1949, when Cleo piloted his four-passenger plane to Rhode Island, to visit Joe at Brown University. In contrast to his father, Joe was a gentle, contemplative soul who, despite all efforts to toughen him up at a military school when he was younger, was drawn to Eastern religions and spirituality. He had been planning to visit the Abbey of Gethsemani monastery in Kentucky, home to the famed Trappist monk and spiritual leader Thomas Merton. His dad was infuriated. He was heading to Brown to talk some sense into the boy.

And so, as instructed, young Joe waited for his dad outside a Providence hotel. The hours ticked by. Joe waited. And waited. It was dawn when he finally learned that his dad's luck had run out: his plane had crashed in a meadow just outside of town. At forty-six years old, Cleo was dead.

His death was a family tragedy. But it also ignited a business crisis. In an instant, the family's future was wiped out—and Joe's plans along with it. His mom, who inherited the family business, needed help. Her son's spiritual quest would have to be put on hold, perhaps indefinitely. Family called. And so, after graduation, Joe dutifully returned home to Ohio, bringing along his new bride, Harriet, a classmate and concert pianist who shelved her own dreams, giving up a place at the Yale School of Music. Now, in the summer of 1952, she found herself in the midst of a difficult pregnancy with the first of their four children, ensconced as a housewife in Cincinnati instead of as a pianist at a conservatory.

Worse was yet to come. Days after their first child was born, Joe was diagnosed with Hodgkin's lymphoma, a deadly blood cancer for which, at the time, there was no cure or even established treatment. Doctors gave him just months to live. And so the couple deposited their newborn baby girl with his mother and took off to Boston for an experimental therapy using a brutally powerful dose of radiation. Depleted, they then headed to Mexico in hopes of a long-shot cure. It would be a full year later before they returned to Cincinnati, where their toddler daughter Juliet refused to go to Harriet. Juliet didn't recognize her own mother.

Joe had managed to battle back from the disease. But while he was preoccupied with his recovery, the family business had taken a shellacking. In the wake of World War II, coal was quickly giving way to cleaner fuels like electricity, oil, and natural gas. While more than half of all US homes were still heated by coal in 1940, that figure plummeted to just 12 percent by 1960, ultimately dwindling to less than 1 percent in the decades afterward. Walls weren't covered in soot anymore. Fewer housewives were buying Kutol wallpaper cleaner, and some stores stopped carrying it altogether.

With Kutol a declining business, the family company was in crisis. And now it was Joe's problem. The company was hurtling ever more quickly toward disaster. Cash was running out, and it was clear that the end was imminent. The collapse of the company would mean financial ruin not just for the business but for the entire extended family. "Kutol was teetering. They were in a place where, 'we need to make some hard decisions,'" his daughter Juliet told me decades later. Joe McVicker wasn't yet twenty-five years old. But the weight of the world—and the future of his family—lay heavily on his shoulders. Life had never looked so bleak.

That's when Joe's expert companion miraculously appeared, in a most unlikely form: a nursery school teacher who happened to be his sister-in-law.

WHILE JOE STRUGGLED to save his dying wallpaper putty business, his wife confided their troubles to her sister, Kathryn Zufall, a young New Jersey housewife who ran a preschool. Known to all as Kay, she had recently settled in the small town of Dover with her husband Robert, a newly minted urologist who was starting to build his medical practice.

The Zufalls were an exceptionally resourceful pair. Dr. Zufall fixed the plumbing with surgical tape and installed after-market seatbelts in the family car himself. His wife was a force of nature who barreled through any obstacle in her path. "The brassy Mrs. Zufall," as a local publication once described her, wasn't afraid to pick a fight with town officials, and she regularly badgered politicians about her various projects. When she wanted her kids to have music lessons, she brought in an out-of-town teacher and set up a studio for him in a spare room to teach local kids. Then she turned her four daughters into a string quartet, insisting that they practice before and after school every day and fill out a daily practice chart of their hours.

"She was difficult to live with as a mother. She was very critical. She could be supportive but mostly just demanding. Fortunately, the things she demanded were good for you," said her daughter Margaret "Peg" Zufall Roberts, who went on to become a professional violist. "There were times you couldn't stand her. But you almost always lived to regret it, because if you didn't do what she said, you discovered on your own that it was the right idea."

Perhaps not surprisingly, when Kay Zufall needed child care for her growing brood, she fixed the problem herself by starting a nursery school at the Presbyterian church. That's what she was preoccupied with when, as Christmas approached in 1955, she paged through a nursery school magazine in search of craft ideas for her students.

Dr. Zufall—as sharp as ever when I tracked him down decades later at age ninety-six—vividly recalls what happened next. She stopped short as she browsed the pages. She got that look in her eyes that he knew so well. Then she turned to her husband and waved the magazine in front of him. "We could save Joe's business!" she announced. The article that had caught her eye described how wallpaper putty could be used to make little toys, like modeling clay. Kay's immediate instinct: *Couldn't that work for Kutol too?*

She and her husband decided to find out by, as they always did, trying it themselves. Grabbing Kay's rolling pin, they flattened the stuff out on the table in their tiny kitchen. Then, using cookie cutters, they made Christmas ornaments, which they hardened in the oven and hung with string on a two-foot-tall tree. Delighted with the results, they phoned Joe in Cincinnati. "Joe," Kay announced to her brother-in-law, "I've got the solution to your business."

Kay's brain wave came at just the moment when Joe had run out of options. He had furiously been searching for a way out. Mortgage his house? Sell the business? It seemed like he was finished. Now he had a lifeline. After Joe flew out from Cincinnati to get a look at the Christmas ornaments in person ("He was desperate," Dr. Zufall says), he was sold. Not only could he repurpose Kutol wallpaper cleaner as modeling clay for kids, but he could use the same cans, the same extruders, the same factory, and almost the same product. It was genius.

Joe was surrounded by vats and vats of dough all day in his factory. Yet it had never occurred to him that there was any other use for the stuff. He didn't imagine any possibility beyond its proscribed purpose as a cleaner. It took an outsider to make the connection, someone who was free from all preconceived notions about Kutol, to shift the frame and think about the product not as a cleaner but as a toy.

Back in Cincinnati, Joe and his wife, along with a chemist named Tien Liu, set to work. They tweaked the wallpaper recipe to ensure that it was nontoxic so that kids wouldn't be harmed if they ate it. Dr. Liu reduced the salt content and added scents, introducing that now-famous Play-Doh aroma. The McVicker kids—literally an in-house focus group—were called into the kitchen to play with the stuff. They became frequent visitors to the nearby factory as well, sometimes roller-skating along its shiny floors among the vats of dough. "Today, in this digital world, people forget to sit around a table and put one and one together," his daughter Mary Noyes told me. "It's the simple things we need to see. It might be right in front of us." Speaking of her father, she added, "He was really good at that."

Joe and his Uncle Noah even came up with the perfect name. Excited, they called the Zufalls to proudly unveil it. In their New Jersey kitchen, Kay and her husband both got on the line to hear the good news.

"We're going to call it 'Rainbow Crafts Modeling Compound,'" Joe announced.

"Wait a minute, we'll call you back," the couple told him.

Dr. Zufall and his wife looked at one another: "We both said, 'We've got to have a better name than that,'" Dr. Zufall recalls. "We had to have a short, snappy name that sounds like fun." Ultimately, it was Dr. Zufall who hit on one they both liked. "This was my contribution to the whole thing, the name. That was my idea," Dr. Zufall says. "I have done some writing in my day. But the only two words of mine that ever became famous were 'Play-Doh.'"

The creation of Play-Doh required that outsider's ability to reimagine a dying product. But it also demanded buy-in from leadership, and Joe proved an indefatigable cheerleader. He traveled to toy fairs around the country, "almost like a covered wagon with stuff falling out the back," his daughter Juliet recalls. He distributed it to local schools and invited schoolchildren to tour the Play-Doh factory. He even wrote a Play-Doh musical, composing the songs himself. It played to great acclaim at the local community theater ("it was a big hit in our small little town," Juliet told me), though sadly it has been lost to history.

Perhaps his greatest stroke of salesmanship was convincing Bob Keeshan, better known as Captain Kangaroo, to feature Play-Doh on his weekday children's TV show, in return for a cut of sales. Soon, five-year-old Juliet, wearing a party dress and with a ribbon in her hair, was trotted out to play with it on camera.

"Captain Kangaroo set the thing on fire like dry pasture," she says.

JOE'S INVENTIVENESS, AT a time when Kutol's imminent demise was about to take down his family and all his employees, was in some ways counterintuitive. Conventional wisdom holds that creativity gets strangled when we're in such dire financial straits. But paradoxically, extreme deprivation can also be at least as great a catalyst. It's a frequent hallmark of the most creative business transformations.

One case in point is the news industry, where local news has been decimated in recent years as print publications have died and advertising dollars have migrated to digital platforms. More than two thousand local papers have been shuttered just since 2005, and the carnage shows no signs of abating. Yet the local journalists I worked with at Gannett, which owned more than one hundred local and metro newspapers in this resource-starved environment, were remarkably creative. They were a font of fresh ideas for how to reach their audiences. Despite the extra workload they bore in depleted newsrooms, and in the face of steadily declining resources, they came up with a riotous, delightful array of new products, events, and business ideas. Across the news industry, much of the most innovative work on revolutionary business models and new ways to reach audiences is being done right now at the local level, where the financial vise is tightest.

A University of Notre Dame study helps explain why. In case studies of a dozen entrepreneurs and other problem solvers in rural India, the researchers found that those with the fewest resources were especially inventive—because they had no choice. A student came up with an ingenious automatized system to pull in clotheslines during the rainy season. A farmer who couldn't afford basic equipment converted a motorcycle into a multipurpose vehicle that plowed, sowed seeds, weeded, and sprayed. A mushroom grower came up with a motorized composting machine. "People who have money cannot make new things," the grower told the researchers, "because they don't feel the need."

The entrepreneurs referred to their methods in Hindi as *Jugaad*, which translates roughly into "hack." Just as we've seen with those who bounce back successfully from failure, these inventive entrepreneurs succeeded through trial and error, iterating one step at a time. They also were unconcerned with conventional thinking about how things "should" be done. In fact, they were dismissive of what others might think and confident that they knew better. "Today, if you ask anybody, they would say that I can solve any problem," declared Kotari, the farmer.

So it was with Play-Doh. As sales of the modeling compound grew, potential advisers came calling on Joe. Harvard Business School types would give him advice on how to grow his business, "and he said no. And they said, 'You will fail. You will be eaten alive.'" But just like the mushroom grower in India, he ignored them, convinced he knew better. "Follow your instinct. That's all he had," Juliet says. "He did the opposite of what they said. He had no experience. He went with his gut."

His gut proved correct. The company's sales exploded, and in 1965 Joe sold the business to General Mills for $3 million— $26 million in today's dollars. The payday landed him a prime spotlight in a *Time* magazine cover story that year headlined, "Millionaires: How They Do It," alongside future icons like Broadway producer Hal Prince and Gulf & Western chair Charles Bluhdorn. Joe McVicker was just thirty-five years old.

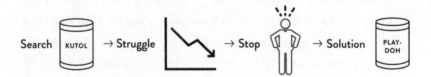

Today Play-Doh is owned by Hasbro, the toy giant. The family is no longer involved, though Play-Doh's legacy runs deep. Play-Doh's riches allowed Joe to return to his original passions— pursuing Eastern religion, meditation, and yoga. Ultimately, he and Harriet divorced, and he spent the remaining decades of his life on his spiritual quest in California, Colorado, and India, where he lived in an ashram before passing away at age sixty-one.

Meanwhile, Kay, who gets accolades in the annals of corporate history, didn't receive a dime for her contributions. Ultimately, the two families fell out over an unrelated feud between the sisters. The Zufalls did just fine, however. After Dr. Zufall retired from his practice, he and his wife set up a clinic for underserved immigrant residents in a church basement; today there are full-fledged Zufall Community Health Centers in multiple New Jersey towns.

In many ways, Play-Doh's metamorphosis provides a playbook for brand reinvention. The company's leaders *searched* for a conventional solution to declining Kutol sales and endured a painful *struggle* that almost ended in a *stop*—near-bankruptcy—before they came up with the *solution*: a reinvention of the product that had nothing to do with its original purpose. Its transformation stands as a testament to the importance of those outside the power structure, whether employees, or customers, or your "expert companion" sister-in-law. And it shows how absolutely essential it is for leadership to recognize a great reinvention idea and then run with it. Joe McVicker may not have come up with the idea of marketing wallpaper putty as modeling clay, but once he recognized it as a viable idea, he devoted himself fully to ensuring that Play-Doh got a successful rollout. Every one of those steps was key to a successful reinvention of the family's company.

The irony is that Joe McVicker could have saved himself a lot of trouble if he'd listened to another outsider in the first place. Long before his sister-in-law Kay came up with the idea of reinventing wallpaper cleaner as a kids' toy, a worker approached Kutol's executives in the office one day. He brought with him a collection of clay figures, which he laid out on a table. "This wallpaper hanger came down and showed us a bunch of little animals he had molded out of our wallpaper cleaner," Joe's brother-in-law and coworker Bill Rhodenbaugh recalled years later. Joe and Bill sent the man with his little clay figures away, not realizing the massive missed opportunity they had just blithely let slip from their grasp.

"We all thought this guy was wonderful, but jeez, the light never went on," Bill marveled later. "Here it was, right in front of us!" But at that moment, they were blind to it. They didn't have the ability to imagine Kutol as anything but a household cleaner.

It makes you wonder how many employees, customers, and sisters-in-law are out there today with transformative ideas of their own. Right now there are almost certainly failing brands and even entire companies that could be revived with a new life and even a wholly different purpose . . . if only the boss will listen.

Epilogue: Next!

A Tool Kit

Wherever you are is the entry point.

—KABIR DAS

Play-Doh's transformation, from soot cleaner to child's toy, was a response to a world that was rapidly changing. It came at a mystifying time when the product and the company's original purpose had become obsolete, a moment in history when it was hard to imagine what could come next. In a very real sense, we are living through a similar period right now. Every few decades, our culture is rocked by seismic changes. The one we're experiencing now, in the wake of a pandemic, political unrest, and economic uncertainty, is especially discomfiting. We're in the midst of historic upheaval. It's no wonder that so many of us have felt unmoored, or confused, or fearful as we try to figure out what comes next.

As change accelerates, though, so does the urgency to understand how to navigate it. That's why it's instructive, and even reassuring, to understand how the people we've met in these pages have done so successfully. Some have figured out new careers, or a new purpose for their lives, while others have bounced back from failure or invented a place for themselves in a world that seemed to be excluding them. They've had grand "aha" moments that led to reinventions from Post-it notes to Viagra. They have managed, when feeling stuck in life or at work, to shake themselves out of complacency or inertia and move forward in breathtakingly imaginative ways.

Those we've chronicled have faced very different kinds of challenges and reacted in very different ways. Yet there are common threads that bind their stories together and lessons they learned that are instructive for the rest of us. In broad strokes, as we've seen, they tend to go through similar stages: *searching* for new information, *struggling* as they try to move from one way of living or working to an unfamiliar new path; perhaps hitting an impasse that *stops* them cold; and ultimately coming up with the *solution*, a way to successfully navigate the transition.

Beyond those stages, they've shared valuable insights. First, even when we feel stuck, or as though we are spinning our wheels, we aren't static. We are moving forward, searching, even if it isn't visible to us at the time. Whether it's lawyer Joanne Lee Molinaro, whose attempts to appease her vegan husband led to her new identity as the "Korean Vegan," or Alan Greenspan, whose early music career ultimately led him to economics, the seeds of where you will go next already exist in what you're doing now. You may not consciously know where your twists and turns are ultimately taking you, like Harland David Sanders, who washed out in multiple jobs, from lawyer to tire salesman, before realizing his potential as Kentucky Fried Chicken's Colonel Sanders. But you may well be on your way already, not recognizing all the hard work you are actually doing now.

Second, we need to learn to lean into the journey of getting from here to there—in other words, to acknowledge the *struggle*. TV executive Marla Ginsburg endured defeat after defeat, losing her livelihood and almost losing her son, yet each element of her journey allowed her to reinvent a more fulfilling life for herself as a clothing designer. Scarsdale mayor Jane Veron endured more than a dozen years of feeling invisible as a stay-at-home mom before turning her skills into becoming a nonprofit CEO and civic leader. Life, as they've proven, isn't a fairy tale; frogs don't suddenly turn into princes. Instead, life is a series of stops and starts and iterative moves that may not be comfortable and that almost certainly won't be easy—but that are necessary.

And finally, those who have made successful pivots have almost all learned to take a breather, to *stop* every once in a while. They ultimately—if sometimes belatedly—realize that taking a break isn't a sign of weakness, but of strength. Keith Reinhard put all his waking brainpower into the McDonald's ad account—yet he invented the Hamburglar in his sleep. The pandemic shutdown gave Kari and Britt Altizer the space to realize they wanted to change careers and reorient their lives around family instead of work. For comedian John Cleese, those breaks that result in fresh insights were "like a gift, a reward."

We need to stop fetishizing busyness and take the time to, as William James once put it, "unclamp" our brains. In truth, that's one concept I'm still working on, with limited success so far. But I'll keep trying, with the help of expert companions like my husband. Which brings up a final key point: it's okay to seek help when you need it—to find your own expert companion, and to be one to others as well.

TO BE SURE, every life and every organization is different. Still, the scores of people I interviewed, along with scientists and researchers across multiple fields, have come up with smart, straightforward strategies to ease transitions. Here are a few action items adopted from their playbooks.

SEARCH

Try on "possible selves." James Patterson thought of himself as a novelist even while working at an advertising agency; telephone repairman Chris Donovan imagined himself as a shoe designer decades before he took steps to become one. Psychologists Hazel Markus and Paula Nurius coined the phrase "possible selves" to describe how we envision our futures: what we want to become, or could become, or even fear becoming. We may imagine our future selves as happier, more confident, thinner—or we may reenvision our lives and careers altogether. Conjuring these "possible selves" can help make them real and lead to meaningful change.

Take small, iterative steps. Contrary to the myths we've grown up with, from Cinderella to Spider-man, there's no such thing as overnight transformation. Almost every transition stems from a series of often small, maybe even unnoticed and unintentional moves in a new direction. Whether it's young Ina Garten inviting her friends to home-cooked dinners long before becoming the Barefoot Contessa, or economist Will Brown spending years gradually learning to mend cattle fences and castrate cows on weekends before becoming a farmer, every successful transition is actually an immeasurable number of often tiny, even imperceptible steps forward.

Listen to your gut. Clea Shearer and Joanna Teplin started their massively successful organizing business, The Home Edit, on pure "gut instinct," they have said. Top executives who have access to mountains of data similarly often ignore it and go with their gut when it comes to spending decisions. It may seem counterintuitive, but sometimes too much information gives us a false sense of security and actually leads us to make objectively wrong decisions. And while gut instinct may *seem* disconcertingly unscientific, it's often actually a reflection of our own expertise and of pattern recognition. Our bodies sense this and begin leading us in the right direction before our brains catch up. As neuroscientist Antonio Damasio has said, "The separation between mind and body" is probably "fictional."

STRUGGLE

Lean into the struggle. The middle step of any transition is both the most difficult and the most overlooked. The stories we tell ourselves about successful transformations tend to minimize this crucial in-between period. But there are no shortcuts. In creativity, this is the "incubation period": you're stumped by a problem, then wake up in the middle of the night suddenly knowing the solution. For career changers, it's the "liminal" period when you've left one identity behind but haven't embraced the new one. For trauma survivors, it's the "period of struggle" that precedes personal growth after enduring tragedy. It's why machete attack survivor Kay Wilson could emerge as a philanthropist, and how scientist Katalin Kariko endured decades of setbacks before her breakthrough that led to the Covid-19 mRNA vaccine.

Create a CV of failure. Everybody flops sometimes. But failure can be more instructive than success. When scientist Melanie Stefan first put together her CV of failure, it helped her realize she had been trying to fit into the wrong mold for her career and led her to pivot in a more fulfilling direction. Northwestern's Dashun Wang found that people who "just miss" a successful outcome early on—like competitive athletes who start out as fourth-place finishers—are more likely to excel later. Laying out your misfires can help you assess whether you should soldier on or give up and redirect your efforts.

Talk to an "expert companion." Trauma experts have found that survivors can achieve post-traumatic growth by talking with a person who knows them well. In a broader sense, all of us could use an expert companion. As a young man, Danny Meyer was considering law school when his uncle told him, "Since you were a child, all you've ever talked or thought about is food. . . . Why don't you just open a restaurant?" That moment set Meyer, founder of Union Square Hospitality Group, on a path to becoming one of the most successful restaurateurs in the world. "I knew I loved restaurants, but it just never occurred to me that that was a viable career choice back then," Meyer told me. Without an outside nudge, "It may have been something I wasn't able to see."

Reach out to your network, especially your "weak ties." If you're looking for a new direction or new opportunities, your best bet may be your dormant ties—people you haven't spoken to in years—or your "weak" ties, people you know only casually. Reams of research, including an analysis of LinkedIn data, have found that when you're job hunting, people in your larger network are far more likely to help surface a job opportunity than those closest to you. What's more, when researchers asked 224 executives to seek work advice from someone they hadn't connected with in at least three years, the executives found that they received more creative ideas and fresh insights from these distant connections than from their close ties.

Take action. Thinking about a new path is useful, but cogitating alone won't get you very far. It's important to act. It's fine to start small. Try taking a course, picking up a hobby, or even talking to others on a different path. "Do something differently that's manageable," said Jocelyn Nicole Johnson, who was a Charlottesville, Virginia, public school art teacher for decades before publishing her lauded first book, *My Monticello*, at age fifty. "But start. . . . You have to start somewhere."

Share your goals. When you share your aspirations with someone else, you're more likely to achieve them. A 2015 study of adults between the ages of twenty-three and seventy-two found that more than 70 percent of those who sent weekly updates to a friend completed their goals, twice the percentage of those who didn't share goals. That was true regardless of the objectives, which included increasing productivity, improving work-life balance, writing a book chapter, and selling a house.

STOP

Take a break. A shower, a run, a nap—or a sabbatical, if possible.
Drexel's John Kounios has found that distracting yourself when you're stuck is often the best way to solve a problem or come up with a new idea. In a 2015 survey of 1,114 people, Linda Ovington and colleagues at Charles Sturt University in Australia, found that 80 percent reported solving challenges while in the shower, exercising, commuting, in nature, or sleeping. Indeed, an entire body of research has grown up around the benefits of sleep, which, scientist theorize, allows tangentially related thoughts to mix and combine in new ways that coalesce into breakthrough ideas. Longer breaks, like sabbaticals, are a luxury—but also can be revelatory. Nonprofit leaders who took advantage of sabbaticals came back with ideas on how to transform their organizations.

Daydream. Even in the best of times, we spend 25 to 50 percent of our time daydreaming, a figure that mental health experts believe increased during the pandemic. The good news is that, in a study of physicists and writers, psychologists at UC–Santa Barbara found that 20 percent of their most original ideas arose while daydreaming. What's more, the ideas they had while daydreaming were more likely to solve "an impasse on a problem and to be experienced as 'aha' moments" than when they were consciously focused on their work.

Try the ninety-minute rule. Psychologist K. Anders Ericsson found that virtuoso violinists tend to focus on deliberate practice during ninety-minute sessions, followed by a break. This pattern works beautifully for other pursuits as well. If you're stuck on a challenge, try focusing completely on your work for ninety minutes. No emails, no checking your phone, no distractions. But at the end of ninety minutes, you *must* stop. It doesn't matter what you do on your break—you can exercise, eat, watch TV, anything at all, as long as you aren't working. Then you return to your desk and repeat the process. Almost inevitably working this way will be more productive than working without a break. I've tried the rule myself while writing this book and can vouch for the fact that it works.

SOLUTION

Remember, nothing is wasted. You may feel like you're spinning your wheels during any transition, but even if you don't realize it, there is a method to your madness. Kathryn Finney tapped into all of her experiences, from her Yale epidemiology studies to her incarnation as the "Budget Fashionista," to become a tech investor in Black-owned businesses. Len Elmore combined his childhood Perry Mason dreams, his interest in civil rights, his pro basketball career, and his unofficial role as locker room lawyer, into his career teaching sports management and advocacy at Columbia University. Almost everyone I interviewed had a similar perspective on past efforts, including their failures.

Be open to the unexpected. Where you go next may not be where you planned. One of the most important insights I learned in my reporting was that people who made the most extraordinary pivots often got there by following meandering and unexpected paths. Khe Hy's goal in life was to become managing director of a prestigious financial firm, yet once he got there he realized that what he actually wanted was meaningful work along with time for family and surfing. Chris Handy, working at a bank, never gave a thought to becoming a flight attendant—until his community theater costar recognized his potential in that profession. When management professor Erik Dane asked people about epiphanies that led them to switch careers, they reported being "open to the possibility of being transformed." Keep your mind, eyes, and heart open and who knows where you might go.

Change is iterative . . . and continuing. Wherever you are now, the journey isn't over. I was especially inspired by those I interviewed who are continuing to reinvent themselves long after retirement age, like Paul Tasner, who's running his start-up at age seventy-five, and Dr. Robert Zufall, who coined the name "Play-Doh" and was still going strong at ninety-six. We could all learn something from chemist Spencer Silver, whose failed adhesive led to the invention of Post-it notes: at age eighty, he reinvented himself as a painter. And I was blown away by his co-inventor Art Fry, who, when I interviewed him several times on the cusp of turning ninety, was still indulging his curiosity. As he confided when we spoke, he was still "working on a couple of inventions." That's a goal we can all aspire to.

WITHOUT A DOUBT, stepping into the unknown can be frightening. But it's also exhilarating. And it's reassuring to know that, as these remarkable people and others have proven, there are concrete strategies that are available to every one of us. There's a Reinvention Road Map to guide us to what's next in how we live, love, and lead.

Harnessing the insights from those we've met in these pages, realizing that the process plays out in its own time and in ways that may initially seem mysterious but that are propelling us forward, is instructive. Meanwhile, new research into the science of change continues to expand our understanding and illuminate what before had been a dark and inscrutable path. This new knowledge of the methods and mysteries behind how we change can help us not only navigate—but even enjoy—the journey.

Acknowledgments

I am forever grateful to the people in these pages—both the individuals who generously shared their stories, and the researchers and experts who helped place those journeys in their proper context. You continue to inspire me every day.

Every writer, once in their life, should be so fortunate as to have an editor like Peter Hubbard at HarperCollins/Mariner Books. His wise guidance and suggestions made this book immeasurably better. I am deeply indebted as well to Molly Gendell, who shepherded the manuscript with good humor, speed, and grace despite the challenges of the pandemic. Huge thanks as well to Elsie Lyons for her terrific cover design, and to Cynthia Buck for her meticulous copyediting. This is my second book with HarperCollins, and I am so grateful for the support of publisher Liate Stehlik, along with Ben Steinberg, Allison Carney, Rachel Berquist, Tavia Kowalchuk, Kendra Newton, and the rest of the team. And what a pleasure to work again with Sharyn Rosenblum!

I will never be able to adequately thank Suzanne Gluck, who is not only an extraordinary agent, but a brilliant reader, tireless advocate, and wonderful friend. Thanks as well to Nina Iandolo for her help, and to the superb team at Harry Walker Agency, especially Don and Ellen Walker, Kimberly Lilienstein, Kara Hoke, and Alexa Sternschein.

Many friends and colleagues helped give birth to this book—brainstorming, giving advice, sharpening its themes, and every once in a while providing a shoulder to cry on. I'm especially grateful to the *WSJ* "brain trust" of brilliant editors and friends: Eileen Daspin, Edward Felsenthal, Alix Freedman, Laura Landro, Eben Shapiro, Amy Stevens, and Hilary Stout. I'm indebted as well to Elyse Klayman, Peggy Kalb, and Nancy Better for their brainstorming prowess, and to Nancy for reading the manuscript and offering razor-sharp comments that gave these pages a welcome polish.

Andrew Heyward not only was an indefatigable partner in crime during the reporting and writing process, but he also introduced me to economist-turned-farmer Will Brown. Thanks as well to Debbie Spero for leading me to Marla Ginsburg; to Elyse Klayman for introducing me to Jane Veron; to Kevin Delaney for sending me to Khe Hy; to Debra Spark, who first found Chris Handy; to podcaster Nancy Meyer for putting me in touch with Art Fry; to Ryan Buxton, who connected me with Lauren Strayhorn; and to Cyndi Stivers who led me to Paul Tasner. My gratitude goes out as well to the many others who helped refine my thinking, among them Bruce Feiler, Adam Grant, John Kounios, Richard Tedeschi, Roger and Ann McNamee, and Ann and Andrew Tisch. Both Gary Rosen at the *Wall Street Journal* and Lucas Wittmann at *TIME* magazine shepherded several of my articles during the reporting process that helped solidify the book's themes. I'm grateful as well to CNBC colleagues who invited me to discuss these issues on air, including Andrew Ross Sorkin, Becky Quick, Joe Kernen, Maxwell Meyers, Mary Duffy, and Dan Colarusso.

Sara Krolewski's fact checking went above and beyond. She didn't just verify facts, spellings, and figures; she dug into histories, lawsuits and patent applications, and made every page better. Thank you, Sara.

Finally, infinite thanks to my family. My kids, Andrew and Rebecca, and awesome son-in-law, Sam, first inspired me to take on this topic. My endlessly patient and loving husband, Tom, is my rock. Reporting and writing this book during the pandemic, with both of us working in close quarters from home, couldn't have been easy for him. But he handled it as always by offering his love, humor, encouragement, and the world's best gin and tonics. I love you forever.

Notes

Introduction: Getting There from Here: The Stages of Reinvention

3   *He was the man behind:* "Burger King—Ultimate Weapon," *AdAge,* January 30, 1983, https://adage.com/videos/burger-king-ultimate-weapon/1238 (accessed May 24, 2022).

4   *I don't recall:* "*Black Market,* by James Patterson," *Kirkus Reviews,* May 15, 1986, https://www.kirkusreviews.com/book-reviews/james-patterson/black-market-2/.

4   *He's written or cowritten:* Laura Miller, "How James Patterson Became the World's Best-Selling Author," *New Yorker,* June 13, 2022, https://www.newyorker.com/magazine/2022/06/20/how-james-patterson-became-the-worlds-best-selling-author; Karen Heller, "James Patterson Mostly Doesn't Write His Books. And His New Readers Mostly Don't Read—Yet," *Washington Post,* June 6, 2016, https://www.washingtonpost.com/lifestyle/style/james-patterson-doesnt-write-his-books-and-his-newest-readers-dont-read/2016/06/06/88e7d3c0-28c2-11e6-ae4a-3cdd5fe74204_story.html.

4–5   *More than 250:* Alexandra Alter, "James Patterson Is Starting Imprint for Children's Books," *New York Times,* May 28, 2015, https://www.nytimes.com/2015/05/29/business/media/james-patterson-best-selling-crime-novelist-is-starting-an-imprint-for-childrens-books.html.

5   *Multiple Patterson books:* Hayley C. Cuccinello and Ariel Shapiro, "World's Highest-Paid Authors 2019: J. K. Rowling Back on Top with $92 Million," *Forbes,* December 20, 2019, https://www.forbes.com/sites/hayleycuccinello/2019/12/20/worlds-highest-paid-authors-2019-rowling-patterson-obama/?sh=6ca6a0ec733a.

5   Vanity Fair *dubbed him:* Todd Purdum, "The Henry Ford of Books," *Vanity Fair,* December 10, 2014, https://www.vanityfair.com/culture/2015/01/james-patterson-best-selling-author.

6 *In a 2020 survey:* "What Do You Want to Be When You Grow Up?," Trade Schools, Colleges and Universities, June 23, 2020, https://www.trade-school s.net/learn/childhood-aspirations.

6 *high school basketball:* "Estimated Probability of Competing in Athletics beyond the High School Interscholastic Level," NCAA Research, September 24, 2013, https://www.wiaawi.org/Portals/0/PDF/Publications/probabilitybeyondhs.pdf.

7 *"We don't let go":* William Bridges, *The Way of Transition: Embracing Life's Most Difficult Moments* (Cambridge, MA: Perseus Book Group/Da Capo Press, 2001), 58.

7 *"Many have been reviewing":* Peggy Noonan, "A Plainer People in a Plainer Time," *Wall Street Journal*, May 22, 2020, https://www.wsj.com/articles/covid-will -make-america-a-plainer-place-11590103104.

7 *Millions quit:* Ben Casselman, "More Quit Jobs than Ever, but Most Turnover Is in Low-Wage Work," *New York Times*, January 4, 2022, https://www.nytimes. com/2022/01/04/business/economy/job-openings-coronavirus.html; "The Big Quit: More than a Third of Professionals Leave Jobs without Another Lined Up, According to Korn Ferry Survey," Korn Ferry, January 20, 2022, https://www .kornferry.com/about-us/press/the-big-quit; S. Mitra Kalita, "The New Rules of Quitting," *Charter*, January 11, 2022, https://time.com/charter/6138353/ne w-rules-of-quitting/.

8 *A 2021 Pew survey:* Kim Parker, Ruth Igielnik, and Rakesh Kochhar, "Unemployed Americans Are Feeling the Emotional Strain of Job Loss; Most Have Considered Changing Occupations," Pew Research Center, February 10, 2021, https://www.pewresearch.org/fact-tank/2021/02/10/unemployed-americans -are-feeling-the-emotional-strain-of-job-loss-most-have-considered-changing -occupations/.

8 *85 percent were looking:* Jane Kellogg Murray and Audrey Eads, "2022 Outlook: Trends and Predictions for Job Seekers," Indeed, February 17, 2022, https:// www.indeed.com/career-advice/finding-a-job/trends-and-predictions.

8 *The average person:* "Number of Jobs, Labor Market Experience, Marital Status, and Health: Results from a National Longitudinal Survey," US Department of Labor, Bureau of Labor Statistics, August 31, 2021, https://www.bls.gov/new s.release/pdf/nlsoy.pdf.

8 *You might be fired:* Mason Walker, "US Newsroom Employment Has Fallen 26% since 2008," Pew Research Center, July 13, 2021, https://www.pewresearch.org /fact-tank/2021/07/13/u-s-newsroom-employment-has-fallen-26-since-2008/; Douglas A. McIntyre, "The Death of Journalism? Here's How Many Newspapers Have Shut Down in the Past 15 Years," *USA Today*, July 24, 2019, https:// www.usatoday.com/story/money/2019/07/24/journalism-jobs-2000-american -newspapers-close-15-years/39797141/; Isabella Simonetti, "Over 360 Newspapers Have Closed since Just before the Start of the Pandemic," *New York Times*, June 29, 2022, https://www.nytimes.com/2022/06/29/business/media/local -newspapers-pandemic.html.

8 *71 percent of millennials:* Brandon Rigoni and Bailey Nelson, "Few Millennials Are Engaged at Work," *Gallup News*, August 30, 2016, https://news.gallup.co m/businessjournal/195209/few-millennials-engaged-work.aspx.

12 *Herminia Ibarra:* Herminia Ibarra, "Reinventing Your Career in the Time of Coronavirus," *Harvard Business Review*, April 27, 2020, https://hbr.org/2020/0 4/reinventing-your-career-in-the-time-of-coronavirus.

12 *"incubation period":* Simone M. Ritter and Ap Dijksterhuis, "Creativity—The Unconscious Foundations of the Incubation Period," *Frontiers in Human Neuroscience* 8, no. 215 (2014), https://www.ncbi.nlm.nih.gov/pmc/articles/PMC 3990058/.

14 *When researchers:* Kaitlin Woolley and Ayelet Fishbach, "Motivating Personal Growth by Seeking Discomfort," *Psychological Science* 33, no. 4 (2022): 510–23, https://journals.sagepub.com/doi/pdf/10.1177/09567976211044685?casa _token=fQczoZjap74AAAAA:jbyWn6pDfPafxSWdkG1vfkE3zhfMNFtq7yTd Ba0zlkReHX0a9QRIdghEtqpmHsnoVoHdO7BDs8ZY.

14 *"When people can positively spin":* Ayelet Fishbach, "Get Comfortable with Feeling Uncomfortable," *Behavioral Scientist*, February 7, 2022, https://behavior alscientist.org/get-comfortable-with-feeling-uncomfortable/?utm_source=convertkit &utm_medium=email&utm_campaign=The+WIFFME+approach+to+getting +what+you+want%20-%207574484.

14 *Shawn Achor:* Shawn Achor, "Positive Intelligence," *Harvard Business Review*, January/February 2012, https://hbr.org/2012/01/positive-intelligence.

14 *In literature:* Joseph Campbell, *The Hero with a Thousand Faces* (Princeton, NJ: Princeton University Press, 1971).

15 *Arnold van Gennep's:* Arnold van Gennep, *The Rites of Passage* [1909] (Chicago: University of Chicago Press, 1960), 21.

15 *Katherine May's:* Katherine May, *Wintering: The Power of Rest and Retreat in Difficult Times* (New York: Riverhead Books, 2020), 10.

15 *In his 2020 book:* Bruce Feiler, *Life Is in the Transitions: Mastering Change at Any Age* (New York: Penguin Press, 2021), 147, 327.

15 *Brené Brown, in* Rising Strong: Brené Brown, *Rising Strong: How the Ability to Reset Transforms the Way We Live, Love, Parent, and Lead* (New York: Random House, 2017), 26–27.

15 *Consider the words:* Eliza Goren, Shefali S. Kulkarni, and Kanyakrit Vongkiatkajorn, "2020 in One Word," *Washington Post*, December 18, 2020, https://www .washingtonpost.com/graphics/2020/lifestyle/2020-in-one-word/.

15 *It's "depleting":* Anne Branigin, "We Asked You for One Word to Describe 2021. Here's What You Said," *The Lily*, December 31, 2021, https://www.thelily.com /we-asked-you-for-one-word-to-describe-2021-heres-what-you-said/.

15 *"It's OK":* Susan Biali Haas, "Covid-19: It's OK to Feel Overwhelmed and Be Unproductive," *Psychology Today*, March 25, 2020.

15 *"You're Not Lazy":* "You're Not Lazy: Why It's Hard to Be Productive Right Now," CNET.

16 *he told me:* Author interview with Chris Donovan, April 20, 2021.

18 *With no prospects:* Author interview with Chris Donovan, January 27, 2022.

19 Boston *magazine:* "Best of Boston, 2020 Best Shoe Designer: Chris Donovan," *Boston,* https://www.bostonmagazine.com/best-of-boston-archive/2020/chris -donovan/ (accessed May 25, 2022).

20 *His literary success:* Jonathan Mahler, "James Patterson Inc.," *New York Times Magazine,* January 20, 2010, https://www.nytimes.com/2010/01/24/magazine /24patterson-t.html.

20 *"pushy and violent":* Author interview with James Patterson, December 22, 2020.

21 *"wanted to be a writer":* Author interview with James Patterson, February 24, 2021.

22 *In 1986:* Hazel Markus and Paula Nurius, "Possible Selves," *American Psychologist* 41, no. 9 (September 1986), https://web.stanford.edu/~hazelm/publications /1986_Markus%20&%20Nurius_PossibleSelves.pdf.

22 *When you imagine:* Geoff Plimmer and Alison Schmidt, "Possible Selves and Career Transition: It's Who You Want to Be, Not What You Want to Do," *New Directions for Adult and Continuing Education,* no. 114 (2007), http://phd .meghan-smith.com/wp-content/uploads/2016/01/2-Possible-selves-and-career -transition.pdf.

23 *"Even in happier":* Ibarra, "Reinventing Your Career in the Time of Coronavirus."

23 *"Try something small":* Isaac Fitzgerald, "It's Never Too Late to Publish a Debut Book and Score a Netflix Deal," *New York Times,* September 28, 2021, https:// www.nytimes.com/2021/09/28/style/jocelyn-nicole-johnson-my-monticello -debut-book.html?tpcc=nlbroadsheet.

24 *"It just cleared":* Author interview with James Patterson, December 22, 2020.

24 *Almost immediately:* James Patterson, Twitter post, December 12, 2018, https:// twitter.com/jp_books/status/1072923677598121984.

24 *She passed away:* Barnegat Bay Island, NJ, Facebook post, December 4, 2018, https://www.facebook.com/BarnegatBayIsland/photos/a.2566521130032378 /2566530823364742.

25 *fifth he had published:* "James Patterson Books in Order," jamespattersonbooklist .com, https://jamespattersonbooklist.com/james-patterson-books-in-order/ (accessed May 25, 2022).

25 *"I knew I wasn't":* Author interview with James Patterson, December 22, 2020.

25 *He befriended:* Author interview with James Patterson, February 24, 2021.

26 *"That's the big":* Author interview with James Patterson, December 22, 2020.

26 *"In theory":* Author interview with James Patterson, February 24, 2021.

27 *"I'm in this traffic":* Author interview with James Patterson, February 24, 2021.

27 *"It was my job":* Author interview with James Patterson, December 22, 2020.

29 *"Good romantic":* Nora Krug, "How Stacey Abrams Turned Heartbreak into a Career Plan—and Romance Novels," *Washington Post,* October 22, 2018, https:// www.washingtonpost.com/entertainment/books/how-stacey-abrams-turned -heartbreak-into-a-side-hustle-as-a-romance-novelist/2018/10/22/1bc44dfc-bb 8a-11e8-bdc0-90f81cc58c5d_story.html.

29   *Figure skating:* Alison Beard, "Life's Work: An Interview with Vera Wang," *Harvard Business Review*, July/August 2019, https://hbr.org/2019/07/lifes-work-an-interview-with-vera-wang.

30   *His career as an author:* Author interview with James Patterson, December 22, 2020.

Chapter 1: Is It Time to Jump?

31   *In some ways:* Alan Greenspan, *The Age of Turbulence: Adventures in a New World* (New York: Penguin, 2008), 21.

32   *Soon he also:* Greenspan, *The Age of Turbulence*, 23.

32   *After he:* Greenspan, *The Age of Turbulence*, 24, 25.

32   *"It was not quite like":* Greenspan, *The Age of Turbulence*, 26.

33   *"The experience of playing":* Greenspan, *The Age of Turbulence*, 27.

33   *"I started looking":* Author interview with Alan Greenspan, September 25, 2013, conducted for Joanne Lipman, "Is Music the Key to Success?," *New York Times*, October 12, 2013, https://www.nytimes.com/2013/10/13/opinion/sunday/is-music-the-key-to-success.html.

33   *"I was apprehensive":* Greenspan, *The Age of Turbulence*, 29.

34   *"People tend to do":* Author interview with Alan Greenspan, September 25, 2013.

34   *"I wasn't confident":* Greenspan, *The Age of Turbulence*, 29.

34   *Self-help guru Tony Robbins:* Mia Doring, "Here's Why Tony Robbins Should Definitely Not Be Your Guru," HeadStuff, September 17, 2018, https://headstuff.org/topical/science/heres-tony-robbins-definitely-not-guru/.

34   *We need "to take on the status quo":* Josh Linkner, *The Road to Reinvention: How to Drive Disruption and Accelerate Transformation* (San Francisco: Jossey-Bass, 2014), 2.

35   *Researchers have found:* Mark Egan, Gregor Matvos, and Amit Seru, "When Harry Fired Sally: The Double Standard in Punishing Misconduct," *Journal of Political Economy* 130, no. 5 (2022): 1184–1248.

35   *The most frequent regret:* Bronnie Ware, *Top Five Regrets of the Dying: A Life Transformed by the Dearly Departing* (Carlsbad, CA: Hay House, 2019), 44.

37   *When John R. Graham:* John R. Graham, Campbell R. Harvey, and Manju Puri, "Capital Allocation and Delegation of Decision-Making Authority within Firms," *Journal of Financial Economics* 115, no. 3 (2015): 449–70.

38   *Graham told me:* Author interview with John Graham, October 30, 2020.

38   *I reached out to:* Author interview with Shabnam Mousavi, October 27, 2020.

39   *The "calculations can provide":* Shabnam Mousavi and Gerd Gigerenzer, "Risk, Uncertainty, and Heuristics," *Journal of Business Research* 67 (2014): 1671–78.

39   *"Gut feel was suppressed":* Author interview with Shabnam Mousavi, October 27, 2020.

39   *"Okay, I'm a thirty-three-year-old":* Clea Shearer and Joanna Teplin, *The Home Edit: A Guide to Organizing and Realizing Your House Goals* (New York: Clarkson Potter, 2019), 13.

40   *"It was obvious":* Shearer and Teplin, *The Home Edit*, 13–14.

40   *"Not the most advisable":* Shearer and Teplin, *The Home Edit*, 14.

40   *They took advantage:* Jessica Dailey, "How The Home Edit's Pro Organizers Built a Lucrative—and Controversial—Empire," *New York Post*, October 1, 2020, https://nypost.com/2020/10/01/how-the-home-edits-professional-organizers-built-a-lucrative-empire/.

41   *"We both have the ability":* Shearer and Teplin, *The Home Edit*, 14.

41   *In a 2002 experiment:* Daniel G. Goldstein and Gerd Gigerenzer, "Models of Ecological Rationality: The Recognition Heuristic," *Psychological Review* 109, no. 1 (2002): 75–90, DOI:10.1037//0033-295X.109.1.75.

42   *In other experiments:* Benjamin Scheibehenne and Arndt Bröder, "Predicting Wimbledon 2005 Tennis Results by Mere Player Name Recognition," *International Journal of Forecasting* 23 (2007): 415–26, http://www.scheibehenne.de/scheibehenne_broeder_2007.pdf; Thorsten Pachur, Peter M. Todd, Gerd Gigerenzer, Lael J. Schooler, and Daniel G. Goldstein, "The Recognition Heuristic: A Review of Theory and Tests," *Frontiers in Psychology*, July 5, 2011, https://www.frontiersin.org/articles/10.3389/fpsyg.2011.00147/full; S. Herzog, "The Boundedly Rational Fluency Heuristic: How Ecologically Valid Is Recognition Speed?," unpublished master's thesis, University of Basel, Switzerland; Ralph Hertwig and Peter M. Todd, "More Is Not Always Better: The Benefits of Cognitive Limits," in *Thinking: Psychological Perspectives on Reasoning, Judgment, and Decision Making*, edited by David Hardman and Laura Macchi (West Sussex, UK: John Wiley & Sons, 2003), 213–31, http://library.mpib-berlin.mpg.de/ft/rh/RH_More_2003.pdf.

42   *Newfoundland students:* Brent Snook and Richard M. Cullen, "Recognizing National Hockey League Greatness with an Ignorance-Based Heuristic," *Canadian Journal of Experimental Psychology* 60, no. 1 (2006): 33–43, https://www.researchgate.net/publication/7163968_Recognizing_National_Hockey_League_greatness_with_an_ignorance-based_heuristic.

42   *And in one unintentionally:* Andreas Ortmann, Gerd Gigerenzer, Bernhard Borges, and Daniel G. Goldstein, "The Recognition Heuristic: A Fast and Frugal Way to Investment Choice?," in *Handbook of Experimental Economics Results*, vol. 1, edited by Charles R. Plott and Vernon L. Smith (Amsterdam: North Holland Publishing, 2008), 993–1003, https://doi.org/10.1016/S1574-0722(07)00107-2.

42   *In one experiment:* Timothy D. Wilson, Douglas J. Lisle, Jonathan Schooler, and Sara Hodges, "Introspecting about Reasons Can Reduce Post-Choice Satisfaction," *Personality and Social Psychology Bulletin* 19, no. 3 (1993): 331–39, https://www.researchgate.net/publication/240281868_Introspecting_about_Reasons_can_Reduce_Post-Choice_Satisfaction.

43   *"changed people's minds":* Timothy D. Wilson and Jonathan Schooler, "Thinking Too Much: Introspection Can Reduce the Quality of Preferences and Decisions," *Journal of Personality and Social Psychology* 60, no. 2 (1991): 181–92.

43   *"deep and abiding emotional":* James C. Cobb, "What We Can Learn from Coca-

Cola's Biggest Blunder," *Time*, July 10, 2015, https://time.com/3950205/new-coke-history-america/.

44 *It has said it collects:* "Amazon.com Buyer Fraud Service Gains Scalability, Cuts Costs in Half Using AWS," AWS, https://aws.amazon.com/solutions/case-studies/AmazonBuyerFraud/ (accessed May 18, 2022).

44 *A BBC reporter:* Leo Kelion, "Why Amazon Knows So Much about You," *BBC News*, https://www.bbc.co.uk/news/extra/CLQYZENMBI/amazon-data (accessed May 18, 2022).

44 *Amazon founder:* Jeff Bezos, "2018 Letter to Shareholders," Amazon, April 11, 2019, https://www.aboutamazon.com/news/company-news/2018-letter-to-shareholders.

44 *"People don't know":* Dave Smith, "What Everyone Gets Wrong about This Famous Steve Jobs Quote, According to Lyft's Design Boss," *Business Insider*, April 19, 2019, https://www.businessinsider.com/steve-jobs-quote-misunderstood-katie-dill-2019-4.

44 *"It isn't the consumer's job":* Peter Noel Murray, "How Steve Jobs Knew What You Wanted," *Psychology Today*, October 13, 2011, https://www.psychologytoday.com/us/blog/inside-the-consumer-mind/201110/how-steve-jobs-knew-what-you-wanted.

44 *"There's always skepticism":* Alison Beard, "Personal Productivity: James Patterson," *Harvard Business Review*, March 2012, https://hbr.org/2012/03/james-patterson.

45 *Yet sure enough:* Xiaohong Wan, Daisuke Takano, Takeshi Asamizuya, Chisato Suzuki, Kenichi Ueno, Kang Cheng, Takeshi Ito, and Keiji Tanaka, "Developing Intuition: Neural Correlates of Cognitive-Skill Learning in Caudate Nucleus," *Journal of Neuroscience* 32, no. 48 (2012): 17492–501, https://www.jneurosci.org/content/32/48/17492.full.

45 developed *intuition:* Christof Koch, "Intuition May Reveal Where Expertise Resides in the Brain," *Scientific American*, May 1, 2015, https://www.scientificamerican.com/article/intuition-may-reveal-where-expertise-resides-in-the-brain/.

46 *When they watched:* Amy McCaig, "In Decision-Making, It Might Be Worth Trusting Your Gut," Rice University, Office of Pubic Affairs, December 14, 2012, http://news2.rice.edu/2012/12/14/in-decision-making-it-might-be-worth-trusting-your-gut/.

46 *But when cognitive psychologist:* Gary Klein, Roberta Calderwood, and Anne Clinton-Cirocco, "Rapid Decision Making on the Fire Ground: The Original Study Plus a Postscript," *Journal of Cognitive Engineering and Decision Making* 4, no. 3 (2010): 186–209.

47 *Neuroscientist Antonio Damasio:* Antonio Damasio, *Descartes' Error: Emotion, Reason, and the Human Brain* (New York: Penguin, 2005), xii–xiii.

47 *As he writes:* Damasio, *Descartes' Error*, 117.

47 *"He was a more effective":* "Learning, Feedback, and Intuition," Judgment and Decision Making, July 16, 2013, https://j-dm.org/archives/744; Robin M. Hogarth, *Educating Intuition* (Chicago: University of Chicago Press, 2001), 85.

48 *It quickly raised:* Benjamin Mullin and Lillian Rizzo, "Quibi Was Supposed to Revolutionize Hollywood. Here's Why It Failed," *Wall Street Journal,* November 2, 2020, https://www.wsj.com/articles/quibi-was-supposed-to-revolutionize -hollywood-heres-why-it-failed-11604343850.

49 *At heart:* James Surowiecki, "Quibi and the Perils of Ignoring the Wisdom of the Crowd," Medium, October 23, 2020, https://marker.medium.com/quibi-and -the-cult-of-the-visionary-entrepreneur-3ca1e694fc9c.

49 *"Instead, they witnessed":* Mullin and Rizzo, "Quibi Was Supposed to Revolutionize Hollywood."

49 *Chris Donovan:* Hailey Bishop, "Chris Donovan's Designs Dominate the Streets Well beyond Boston," Style Boston, https://blog.styleboston.tv/17044/fashion /his-shoes-are-works-of-art/ (accessed May 18, 2022).

49 *Brian May:* David J. Eicher, "Brian May: A Life in Science and Music—the Full Story," *Astronomy,* July 23, 2012, https://astronomy.com/magazine/2012/07 /brian-may---a-life-in-science-and-music---the-full-story; "Discography: Queen," AllMusic, https://www.allmusic.com/artist/queen-mn0000858827/discography (accessed May 18, 2022).

49 *Sociologist Diane Vaughan:* Glenn Collins, "Drifting Apart: A Look at How Relationships End," *New York Times,* December 8, 1986, https://www.nytimes .com/1986/12/08/style/drifting-apart-a-look-at-how-relationships-end.html; Diane Vaughan, *Uncoupling: Turning Points in Intimate Relationships* (New York: Oxford University Press, 1986).

50 *Google's two founders:* Mike Swift, "Google's New CEO Is Smart, Highly Focused and Strong-Willed," *Mercury News,* January 21, 2011, https://www .mercurynews.com/2011/01/21/googles-new-ceo-is-smart-highly-focused-and -strong-willed/; "Larry Page's University of Michigan Commencement Address," YouTube, May 4, 2009, https://www.youtube.com/watch?v=qFb2rvmrahc.

50 *"We almost didn't":* John A. Byrne, "World Changers: 25 Entrepreneurs Who Changed Business as We Knew It," (New York: Portfolio/Penguin 2011).

50 *Perhaps the most audacious:* Andrew Ross Sorkin, "The Dress Code Is Relaxed, but the Courting Is Intense," *New York Times,* November 10, 2006, https://www .nytimes.com/2006/11/10/technology/10deal.html.

51 *Rumor had it:* "Meta Platforms, Inc. (FB)," Yahoo! Finance, https://finance.yahoo .com/quote/FB/.

51 *He stayed on at NYU:* Greenspan, *The Age of Turbulence,* 29.

52 *"The most important economic":* Author interview with Alan Greenspan, September 25, 2013.

Chapter 2: Learning to Love the Struggle

53 *In 2003:* Author interview with Marla Ginsburg, June 28, 2021.

56 *Supreme Court:* Katie Reilly, "'I Wish You Bad Luck.' Read Supreme Court Justice John Roberts' Unconventional Speech to His Son's Graduating Class," *Time,*

July 5, 2017, https://time.com/4845150/chief-justice-john-roberts-commencement-speech-transcript/.

56 *"If you don't fail":* Thorin Klosowski, "What the Best Commencement Speeches Teach Us about Failure," *Time*, April 11, 2017, https://time.com/4845150/chief-justice-john-roberts-commencement-speech-transcript/.

56 *Stories of soaring:* Taylor Locke, "3 Times Mark Cuban Failed before Becoming a Billionaire: 'You Only Gotta Be Right Once,'" CNBC Make It, February 11, 2020, https://www.cnbc.com/2020/02/11/times-mark-cuban-failed-before-becoming-a-billionaire.html.

57 *Even under the best:* Jeffrey Kudisch, "Career Coach: Turned Down for a Job? You Are Now One Rejection Closer to Success," *Washington Post*, March 10, 2017, https://www.washingtonpost.com/news/capital-business/wp/2017/03/10/career-coach-turned-down-for-a-job-you-are-now-one-rejection-closer-to-success/.

57 Atlantic *writer:* Derek Thompson, "Workism Is Making Americans Miserable," *Atlantic*, February 24, 2019, https://www.theatlantic.com/ideas/archive/2019/02/religion-workism-making-americans-miserable/583441/.

57 *Psychologists call this:* Kate Morgan, "Why We Define Ourselves by Our Jobs," BBC, April 13, 2021, https://www.bbc.com/worklife/article/20210409-why-we-define-ourselves-by-our-jobs#:~:text=There%20are%20some%20common%20signs,space%20for%20hobbies%20and%20interests.

58 *"The whole point of intelligence":* Carol S. Dweck, "The Perils and Promises of Praise," ASCD, October 1, 2007, https://www.ascd.org/el/articles/the-perils-and-promises-of-praise.

58 *students in one study:* Xiaodong Lin-Siegler, Janet N. Ahn, Jondou Chen, Fu-Fen Anny Fang, and Myra Luna-Lucero, "Even Einstein Struggled: Effects of Learning about Great Scientists' Struggles on High School Students' Motivation to Learn Science," *Journal of Educational Psychology* 108, no. 3 (2016): 314–28, https://www.apa.org/pubs/journals/releases/edu-edu0000092.pdf.

58 *"Failure is":* Author interview with Xiaodong Lin-Siegler, September 25, 2020.

58 *Dashun Wang:* Author interviews with Dashun Wang, May 18, 2021, and February 8, 2022.

58 *Jamaican sprinter:* Intersecondary School Sports Association, Boys and Girls Athletics Championship, "Complete Results—All Rounds," April 11–15, 2000, http://www.cfpitiming.com/class_1_boys_results.htm (accessed June 8, 2022); OlympicTalk, "Asafa Powell, Former 100m World Record Holder, Does Not Enter Jamaica Olympic Trials," *NBC Sports*, June 24, 2021, https://olympics.nbcsports.com/2021/06/24/asafa-powell-olympics/.

58–59 *In academia:* Yang Wang, Benjamin F. Jones, and Dashun Wang, "Early-Career Setback and Future Career Impact," *Nature Communications* 10, no. 4331 (2019), https://www.nature.com/articles/s41467-019-12189-3.

59 *the Matthew Effect:* David A. Shaywitz, "The Elements of Success," *Wall Street Journal*, November 15, 2008, https://www.wsj.com/articles/SB122671469296530435.

59   *They embodied:* "What Does Not Kill Me Makes Me Stronger: Revision History," Wikipedia, last modified June 8, 2022, https://en.wikipedia.org/w/index.php?title=What_does_not_kill_me_makes_me_stronger&action=history (accessed June 8, 2022).

59   *Their success:* nobelPrize, Instagram post, January 28, 2021, https://www.instagram.com/p/CKliwohAQcS/?utm_source=ig_embed&ig_rid=32725f9a-4310-4885-ab38-4e8cea99df16.

59   *"What these results":* Author interview with Dashun Wang, May 18, 2021.

60   *Those who turn failure:* Dashun Wang and James Evans, "Science Reveals the Tipping Point between Success and Failure," *Fast Company*, January 16, 2020, https://www.fastcompany.com/90451983/science-reveals-the-tipping-point-between-success-and-failure.

60   *"You are learning":* Author interview with Dashun Wang, May 18, 2021.

60   *Eerily, the same:* Yian Yin, Yang Wang, James A. Evans, and Dashun Wang, "Quantifying the Dynamics of Failure across Science, Startups, and Security," *Nature* 575 (2019): 190–94, https://www.nature.com/articles/s41586-019-1725-y.

61   *"forces of invention":* Author interview with Xiaodong Lin-Siegler, September 25, 2020.

61   *We don't often hear details:* "Harry Potter Author: I Considered Suicide," CNN, March 23, 2008, http://edition.cnn.com/2008/SHOWBIZ/03/23/rowling.depressed/index.html.

61   *Before he found fame:* Roger Connors and Tom Smith, *The Wisdom of Oz: Using Personal Accountability to Succeed in Everything You Do* (New York: Penguin, 2016), 115.

61   *Thomas Edison was fired:* Victoria Dawson, "The Epic Failure of Thomas Edison's Talking Doll," *Smithsonian*, June 1, 2015, https://www.smithsonianmag.com/smithsonian-institution/epic-failure-thomas-edisons-talking-doll-180955442/.

62   *As he famously:* Erica R. Hendry, "7 Epic Fails Brought to You by the Genius Mind of Thomas Edison," *Smithsonian*, November 20, 2013, https://www.smithsonianmag.com/innovation/7-epic-fails-brought-to-you-by-the-genius-mind-of-thomas-edison-180947786/.

62   *Basketball great:* "ForbesQuotes: Thoughts on the Business of Life," *Forbes*, https://www.forbes.com/quotes/11194/ (accessed June 8, 2022).

62   *That focus:* Juliet Macur, "Nathan Chen Is Winning by Not Trying So Hard to Win," *New York Times*, February 9, 2022, https://www.nytimes.com/2022/02/09/sports/olympics/nathan-chen-is-winning-by-not-trying-so-hard-to-win.html.

62   *Wang compares:* Author interview with Dashun Wang, February 8, 2022.

63   *Indeed, when 143:* Janet Rae-Dupree, "If You're Open to Growth, You Tend to Grow," *New York Times*, July 6, 2008, https://www.nytimes.com/2008/07/06/business/06unbox.html.

64   *The "fail fast":* Ken Tencer, "'Fail Fast, Fail Often' May Be the Stupidest Business Mantra of All Time," *Globe and Mail*, March 13, 2015, https://www.theglobe

andmail.com/report-on-business/small-business/sb-growth/fail-fast-fail-often
-may-be-the-stupidest-business-mantra-of-all-time/article23407206/.

64 *"We say fail"*: Author interview with Dashun Wang, February 8, 2022.

64 *That was certainly*: Issam Ahmed, "Scientist's mRNA Obsession Once Cost Her
a Job, Now It's Key to Covid-19 Vaccine," *Times of Israel*, December 17, 2020,
https://www.timesofisrael.com/the-hungarian-immigrant-behind-messenger
-rna-key-to-covid-19-vaccines/.

65 *I was up*: Ahmed, "Scientist's mRNA Obsession Once Cost Her a Job."

65 *The experience prompted*: Damian Garde and Jonathan Saltzman, "The Story of
mRNA: How a Once-Dismissed Idea Became a Leading Technology in the Covid Vaccine Race," *STAT News*, November 10, 2020, https://www.statnews.com
/2020/11/10/the-story-of-mrna-how-a-once-dismissed-idea-became-a-leading
-technology-in-the-covid-vaccine-race/.

65 *"the starter pistol"*: Damian Garde and Jonathan Saltzman, "The Story of
mRNA: How a Once-Dismissed Idea Became a Leading Technology in the Covid
Vaccine Race," *STAT News*, November 10, 2020, https://www.statnews.com
/2020/11/10/the-story-of-mrna-how-a-once-dismissed-idea-became-a-leading
-technology-in-the-covid-vaccine-race/.

65 *"I was fortunate enough"*: Author interview with Katalin Kariko, June 8, 2022.

67 *Computational neurobiochemist*: Author interview with Melanie Stefan, September 28, 2020.

68 *"As scientists"*: Melanie Stefan, "A CV of Failures," *Nature* 468 (2010): 467.

68 *"People are just"*: Author interview with Melanie Stefan, September 28, 2020.

70 *"Most of"*: Johannes Haushofer, "CV of Failures," https://haushofer.ne.su.se
/Johannes_Haushofer_CV_of_Failures.pdf (accessed June 10, 2022).

70 *sharing failures*: Alison Wood Brooks, Karen Huang, Nicole Abi-Esber, Ryan W.
Buell, Laura Huang, and Brian Hall, "Mitigating Malicious Envy: Why Successful
Individuals Should Reveal Their Failures," *Journal of Experimental Psychology* 148,
no. 4 (2019): 667–87, https://www.hbs.edu/ris/Publication%20Files/Mitigating
%20Malicious%20Envy_b763904a-ac7a-4981-8e4e-52da0640efa9.pdf.

71 *The idea, he wrote*: Kudisch, "Career Coach: Turned Down for a Job?"

71 *"Usually it's just"*: "I Can See Any Failure as a Chance," The Nobel Prize, August 25,
2022, https://www.nobelprize.org/i-can-see-any-failure-as-a-chance/ (accessed
June 10, 2022).

71 *Upon his return*: Katie Kalvaitis, "Penicillin: An Accidental Discovery Changed
the Course of Medicine," Healio, August 10, 2008, https://www.healio.com
/news/endocrinology/20120325/penicillin-an-accidental-discovery-changed-the
-course-of-medicine.

72 *"One sometimes finds"*: Siang Yong Tan and Yvonne Tatsumura, "Alexander
Fleming (1881–1995): Discoverer of Penicillin," *Singapore Medical Journal* 56,
no. 7 (July 2015): 366–67, https://www.ncbi.nlm.nih.gov/pmc/articles/PMC452
0913/#:~:text=He%20named%20the%20'mould%20juice,was%20exactly
%20what%20I%20did.%E2%80%9D.

72   *One who learned:* Josh Ozersky, "KFC's Colonel Sanders: He Was Real, Not Just an Icon," *Time*, September 15, 2010, http://content.time.com/time/nation/article /0,8599,2019218,00.html.

73   *By the time:* William Whitworth, "Kentucky-Fried," *New Yorker*, February 14, 1970, https://www.newyorker.com/magazine/1970/02/14/kentucky-fried; Colonel Harland Sanders, *The Autobiography of the Original Celebrity Chef* (Louisville, KY: KFC Corporation, 2012), https://www.kfc.ro/documente/Cartea _Colonelului.pdf.

73   *Legend has it:* "The Failures of 5 Famous Entrepreneurs," Smarter Business, https:// smarterbusiness.co.uk/wp-content/uploads/2019/10/The-Failures-of-5-Famous -People.pdf.

73   *He had learned:* Whitworth, "Kentucky-Fried."

74   *"If you let":* Author interview with Marla Ginsburg, January 25, 2022.

74   *Her designs were:* Author interview with Marla Ginsburg, June 28, 2021.

75   *She willed herself:* Author interview with Marla Ginsburg, January 25, 2022.

75   *In a 2016 study:* Bas Verplanken and Deborah Roy, "Empowering Interventions to Promote Sustainable Lifestyles: Testing the Habit Discontinuity Hypothesis in a Field Experiment," *Journal of Environmental Psychology* 45 (2016): 127–34.

76   *As London Business:* Herminia Ibarra, "The 3 Phases of Making a Major Life Change," *Harvard Business Review*, August 6, 2021, https://hbr.org/2021/08/the -3-phases-of-making-a-major-life-change?ab=hero-subleft-2.

76   *"That was a long, lonely":* Author interview with Marla Ginsburg, June 28, 2021.

76   *"I finally got":* Author interview with Marla Ginsburg, January 25, 2022.

77   *Then he handed:* Author interview with Marla Ginsburg, June 28, 2021.

77   *"Help will come":* Author interview with Marla Ginsburg, January 25, 2022.

78   *"I feel like":* Author interview with Marla Ginsburg, June 28, 2021.

78   *"Reinvention makes":* Author interview with Marla Ginsburg, January 25, 2022.

78   *"You have to":* Author interview with Marla Ginsburg, June 28, 2021.

Chapter 3: Eureka!

79   *made up of tiny spheres:* "United States Patent: Acrylate Copolymer Microspheres," Google Patents, https://patents.google.com/patent/US3691140A/en (accessed May 10, 2022).

79   *The spheres "had fabulous":* Author interview with Spencer Silver, March 4, 2021.

80   *"It was my baby":* Author interview with Spencer Silver, March 4, 2021.

80   *for his annoying refusal:* "History Timeline: Post-it Notes," Post-it, https://www .post-it.com/3M/en_US/post-it/contact-us/about-us/ (accessed May 10, 2022).

80   *"Everybody else is singing":* Author interview with Art Fry, March 2, 2021.

81   *The company reportedly:* Nick Glass and Tim Hume, "The 'Hallelujah Moment' behind the Invention of the Post-it Note," CNN, April 4, 2013, https://www .cnn.com/2013/04/04/tech/post-it-note-history.

81   *in 3,000 varieties:* "History Timeline: Post-it Notes."

81   *More than half a century:* Author interviews with Art Fry, March 2 and May 25, 2021.

83   *Film director James Cameron:* Rebecca Keegan, *The Futurist: The Life and Films of James Cameron* (New York: Crown, 2010), 34–35.

83   *J. K. Rowling has claimed:* Doreen Carvajal, "Children's Book Casts a Spell over Adults; Young Wizard Is Best Seller and a Copyright Challenge," *New York Times,* April 1, 1999, https://www.nytimes.com/1999/04/01/books/children-s -book-casts-spell-over-adults-young-wizard-best-seller-copyright.html.

83   *Louise Glück was working:* Alexandra Alter, "'I Was Unprepared': Louise Glück on Poetry, Aging, and a Surprise Nobel Prize," *New York Times,* October 8, 2020, https://www.nytimes.com/2020/10/08/books/louise-gluck-nobel-prize -literature.html?searchResultPosition=1.

83   *Carole King said:* Althea Legaspi, "Carole King, James Taylor Perform 'You've Got a Friend,' 'It's Too Late,' 'Sweet Baby James' in New Concert Doc Trailer," *Rolling Stone,* December 21, 2021, https://www.rollingstone.com/music/music-news /carole-king-james-taylor-just-call-out-my-name-trailer-premiere-date-1274383/.

83   *For centuries afterward:* Vlad Petre Glăveanu and James C. Kaufman, "Creativity: A Historical Perspective," in *The Cambridge Handbook of Creativity,* edited by James C. Kaufman and Robert J. Sternberg (New York: Cambridge University Press, 2019), 11–26.

83   *Stowe supposedly claimed:* Thompson Eldridge Ashby and Louise R. Helmreich, *A History of the First Parish Church in Brunswick, Maine* (Hamilton, Ontario: J. H. French, 1969), 229.

84   *The word "creativity":* Steven Meyer, "Introduction," *Configurations* 3, no. 1 (2005): 1–33, https://muse.jhu.edu/article/213703.

84   *A few years ago:* Author interview with Erik Dane, November 30, 2021.

84   *Olin Business School's Erik Dane:* Erik Dane, "Suddenly Everything Became Clear: How People Make Sense of Epiphanies Surrounding Their Work and Careers," *Academy of Management Discoveries* 6, no. 1 (2020), https://journals.aom .org/doi/abs/10.5465/amd.2018.0033.

85   *"They go from zero":* Author interview with Erik Dane, November 30, 2021.

85   *"my dad had just":* Dane, "Suddenly Everything Became Clear."

86   *"bestowed as gifts":* Author interview with Erik Dane, November 30, 2021.

86   *"kind of weird":* Dane, "Suddenly Everything Became Clear."

86   *In 1939:* James Webb Young, *A Technique for Producing Ideas* [1939] (New York: McGraw-Hill, 2003), 43, 45–46, 48.

87   *The nineteenth-century mathematician:* Henri Poincaré, "Mathematical Creation," *Resonance* 5, no. 2 (2000): 85–94, http://vigeland.caltech.edu/ist4/lectures/Poincare %20Reflections.pdf.

88   *In brain scans:* John Kounios and Mark Beeman, *The Eureka Factor: Aha Moments, Creative Insight, and the Brain* (New York: Random House, 2015), 71.

89   *In a series of studies:* John Kounios and Mark Beeman, "The *Aha!* Moment: The Cognitive Neuroscience of Insight," *Current Directions in Psychological Science* 18, no. 4 (2009), https://www.jstor.org/stable/20696033?pq-origsite=summon&seq=2.

89 *In some cases:* Edward M. Bowden and Mark Jung-Beeman, "Normative Data for 144 Compound Remote Associate Problems," *Behavior Research Methods, Instruments, and Computers* 35, no. 4 (2003): 634–39, https://link.springer.com/content/pdf/10.3758/BF03195543.pdf.

89 *"It seems to integrate":* Author interviews with John Kounios, January 22 and 27, 2020.

91 *Legendary advertising executive:* Author's email correspondence with Keith Reinhard, February 18, 2021.

92 *Years later, Reinhard was named:* "Keith Reinhard, Chairman Emeritus, DDB Worldwide," Advertising Hall of Fame, http://advertisinghall.org/members/member_bio.php?memid=2712 (accessed May 10, 2022).

92 *she spent five years:* Marie Kondo, *The Life-Changing Magic of Tidying Up: The Japanese Act of Decluttering and Organizing* (New York: Clarkson Potter, 2014), 160.

92 *When people asked her about her:* Kondo, *The Life-Changing Magic of Tidying Up,* 175.

92 *At one point, she said, she fainted:* Richard Lloyd Parry, "Marie Kondo Is the Maiden of Mess," *The Australian,* April 19, 2014, https://archive.ph/lkEXf.

93 *In fact, trying too hard:* Andreas Fink, Roland H. Grabner, Mathias Benedek, Gernot Reishofer, Verena Hauswirth, Maria Fally, Christa Neuper, Franz Ebner, and Aljoscha C. Neubauer, "The Creative Brain: Investigation of Brain Activity during Creative Problem Solving by Means of EEG and fMRI," *Human Brain Mapping* 30 (2009): 734–48, https://onlinelibrary.wiley.com/doi/epdf/10.1002/hbm.20538.

93 *But research has shown that this is exactly:* Fink et al., "The Creative Brain."

94 *mind wandering:* Author's phone interview with Jonathan Schooler, February 2, 2021.

94 *In a study that Schooler led:* Benjamin Baird, Jonathan Smallwood, Michael D. Mrazek, Julia W. Y. Kam, Michael S. Franklin, and Jonathan W. Schooler, "Inspired by Distraction: Mind Wandering Facilitates Creative Incubation," *Psychological Science* 23, no. 10 (2012): 1117–22, https://journals.sagepub.com/doi/10.1177/0956797612446024.

95 *"That wandering mind":* Author interviews with John Kounios, January 22 and 27, 2020.

95 *There's a reason why:* "Aaron Sorkin: Maybe I'd Write Better on Coke," Bloomberg Television, November 6, 2014, https://www.youtube.com/watch?v=EOF-AB5c-ko.

95 *Alec Baldwin's blowhard boss:* "The Shower Principle," *30 Rock,* broadcast March 29, 2012, https://www.imdb.com/title/tt2306893/ (accessed May 10, 2022).

96 *For financial executive Sallie Krawcheck:* Author interview with Sallie Krawcheck, November 13, 2020.

96 *Neuroscientists have documented:* David S. Rosen, Yongtaek Oh, Brian Erickson, Fengqing (Zoe) Zhang, Youngmoo E. Kim, and John Kounios, "Dual Process Contributions to Creativity in Jazz Improvisations: An SPM-EEG Study,"

Neuroimage 213 (June 2020), https://www.sciencedirect.com/science/article/pii/S1053811920301191.

97 *Researchers who used brain imaging:* Siyuan Liu, Michael G. Erkkinen, Meghan L. Healey, Yisheng Xu, Katherine E. Swett, Ho Ming Chow, and Allen R. Braun, "Brain Activity and Connectivity during Poetry Composition: Toward a Multidimensional Model of the Creative Process," *Human Brain Mapping* 36, no. 9 (2015): 3351–72, https://onlinelibrary.wiley.com/doi/full/10.1002/hbm.22849.

97 *illustrators while creating book covers:* Melissa Ellamil, Charles Dobson, Mark Beeman, and Kalina Christoff, "Evaluative and Generative Modes of Thought during the Creative Process," *Neuroimage* 59, no. 1 (2012): 1783–94.

97 *rappers improvising freestyle verses:* Siyuan Liu, Ho Ming Chow, Yisheng Xu, Michael G. Erkkinen, Katherine E. Swett, Michael W. Eagle, Daniel A. Rizik-Baer, and Allen R. Braun, "Neural Correlates of Lyrical Improvisation: An fMRI Study of Freestyle Rap," *Scientific Reports* 2 (2012), https://www.nature.com/articles/srep00834.

97 *Famed jazz trumpeter:* Rosen et al., "Dual Process Contributions to Creativity in Jazz Improvisations."

97 *he once said:* "Miles Davis Honda Scooter Commercial," YouTube, December 29, 2013, https://www.youtube.com/watch?v=_ZrbtKUZFqQ.

98 *One morning, as he recalled:* Barry Miles, *Paul McCartney: Many Years from Now* (New York: Henry Holt, 1998), 202.

98 *"And people would say":* Kenneth Womack, *Long and Winding Roads: The Evolving Artistry of the Beatles* (New York: Bloomsbury, 2014), 112.

99 *Similarly, Steve Jobs famously said:* Gary Wolf, "Steve Jobs: The Next Insanely Great Thing," *Wired*, February 1, 1996, https://www.wired.com/1996/02/jobs-2/.

99 *In a 2009 study:* Karuna Subramaniam, John Kounios, Todd B. Parrish, and Mark Jung-Beeman, "A Brain Mechanism for Facilitation of Insight by Positive Affect," *Journal of Cognitive Neuroscience* 21, no. 3 (2009): 415–32, https://direct.mit.edu/jocn/article/21/3/415/4666/A-Brain-Mechanism-for-Facilitation-of-Insight-by.

99 *"expands the scope":* Author interviews with John Kounios, January 22 and 27, 2020.

100 *as he calls it:* Author interview, Erik Dane, November 30, 2021.

100 *She told me how a new business idea:* Author interview with Sheena Allen, April 6, 2021.

102 *In a 2016 study:* Carola Salvi, Emanuela Bricolo, John Kounios, Edward Bowden, and Mark Beeman, "Insight Solutions Are Correct More Often than Analytic Solutions," *Thinking and Reasoning* 22, no. 4 (2016): 443–60, https://www.tandfonline.com/doi/full/10.1080/13546783.2016.1141798.

103 *As Salvi put it:* Author interview with Carola Salvi, August 11, 2020.

103 *"In order to have insight":* Author interview with Carola Salvi, August 11, 2020.

103 *"At times I feel certain":* Albert Einstein, *Einstein on Cosmic Religion and Other Opinions and Aphorisms* [1931] (Meneola, NY: Dover, 2012), 97.

103 *Einstein was a clerk:* Michio Kaku, *Einstein's Cosmos: How Albert Einstein's Vision Transformed Our Understanding of Space and Time* (New York: W. W. Norton, 2005), 52.

103 *"in fruitless considerations":* Abraham Pais, *Subtle Is the Lord: The Science and the Life of Albert Einstein* (New York: Oxford University Press, 1982), 139.

104 *"A storm broke loose in my mind":* Kaku, *Einstein's Cosmos*, 61.

104 *as he put it:* William B. Irvine, *Aha! The Moments of Insight That Shape Our World* (New York: Oxford University Press, 2015), 129.

104 *without even a hello:* Kaku, *Einstein's Cosmos*, 63.

104 *"I thought of it on my bicycle":* Christopher Bergland, "Could Seeing Oneself as Einstein Boost Problem-Solving?" *Psychology Today*, July 11, 2018, https://www .psychologytoday.com/us/blog/the-athletes-way/201807/could-seeing-oneself -einstein-boost-problem-solving.

104 *"Every step":* Pais, *Subtle Is the Lord*, 210.

104 *"He goes to his study":* Pais, *Subtle Is the Lord*, 301.

104 *"returns to his study":* Mitch Waldrop, "Inside Einstein's Love Affair with 'Lina'— His Cherished Violin," *National Geographic*, February 3, 2017, https://www .nationalgeographic.com/adventure/article/einstein-genius-violin-music-physics -science.

104 *"a great speculative leap":* Salvi et al., "Insight Solutions Are Correct More Often than Analytic Solutions."

105 *He was using springs:* Kounios and Beeman, *The Eureka Factor*, 105.

105 *James watched in wonder:* Jonathan Schifman, "The Remarkable, War-Torn, Space-faring History of the Slinky," *Popular Mechanics*, August 8, 2017, https://www .popularmechanics.com/technology/a27657/slinky-toy-history/; Michele Alice, "Collectors Corner: Slinky," eCommerceBytes, November 14, 2020, https://www .ecommercebytes.com/2020/11/14/collectors-corner-slinky/.

105 *a $3 billion business:* Annie Nova, "10 Unlikely Products That Made Millions of Dollars," CNBC, December 11, 2017, https://www.cnbc.com/2017/12/11/10 -unlikely-products-that-made-millions-of-dollars.html.

105 *"Curiosity has always been":* Author interview with Art Fry, March 2, 2021.

106 *the chance to spend 15 percent:* "Life with 3M," 3M, https://www.3m.com/3M/e n_US/careers-us/working-at-3m/life-with-3m/#:~:text=For%20more%20 than%2070%20years,innovative%20ideas%20that%20excite%20them (accessed May 10, 2022).

106 *He attended the technical presentations:* Riham Feshir, "3M Sells Tartan Park Golf Course; New Owner Will Redesign, Make it public," *MPR News*, March 15, 2016, https://www.mprnews.org/story/2016/03/15/3m-sells-tartan-park-golf -course.

107 *Today the sale of sticky notes:* LP Information, "Post-it & Sticky Notes Market to Witness Robust Expansion by 2025," OpenPR, September 8, 2020, https:// www.openpr.com/news/2129666/post-it-sticky-notes-market-to-witness-robust -expansion-by-2025.

Chapter 4: Bouncing Forward

113 *"I was thinking":* Author interview with Kay Wilson, November 16, 2021.

115 *"I love color":* Author interview with Kay Wilson, November 16, 2021.

115 *She plays piano:* Brian London, "Kay Wilson: The Rage Less Traveled at AIPAC and Her Arrangement 'Somewhere over the Rainbow,'" YouTube, March 27, 2019, https://www.youtube.com/watch?v=4vjHTKvCgGI&t=430s.

116 *Mesopotamian cuneiform:* Walid Khalid Abdul-Hamid and Jamie Hacker Hughes, "Nothing New under the Sun: Post-Traumatic Stress Disorders in the Ancient World," *Early Science and Medicine* 19, no. 6 (2014): 549–57, https://pubmed .ncbi.nlm.nih.gov/25577928/.

116 *Herodotus in 440 BCE:* Marc-Antoine Crocq and Louis Crocq, "From Shell Shock and War Neurosis to Posttraumatic Stress Disorder: A History of Psychotraumatology," *Dialogues in Clinical Neuroscience* 2, no. 1 (2000): 47–55, https://www.ncbi.nlm.nih.gov/pmc/articles/PMC3181586/.

117 *More than 1 million:* Erin Blakemore, "How PTSD Went from 'Shell-Shock' to a Recognized Medical Diagnosis," *National Geographic,* June 16, 2020, https:// www.nationalgeographic.com/history/article/ptsd-shell-shock-to-recognized -medical-diagnosis.

117 *Clinical PTSD symptoms:* "Post-Traumatic Stress Disorder (PTSD)," Mayo Clinic, https://www.mayoclinic.org/diseases-conditions/post-traumatic-stress-disorder /symptoms-causes/syc-20355967 (accessed June 16, 2022).

118 *And indeed:* "How Common Is PTSD in Veterans?," U.S. Department of Veterans Affairs, https://www.ptsd.va.gov/understand/common/common_veterans .asp (accessed June 16, 2022).

118 *By that measure:* Amy Paturel, "PTSD from Covid-19? What You Should Know," Cedars-Sinai, June 25, 2021, https://www.cedars-sinai.org/blog/ptsd-covid-19.html.

118 *By some accounts:* "Covid-19: Pandemic Increases PTSD, Suicidal Ideation in Health Care Workers," Psychiatry Advisor, May 5, 2021, https://www .psychiatryadvisor.com/home/conference-highlights/apa-2021/health-care -workers-reported-increased-rates-of-depression-anxiety-and-stress-during-the -covid-19-pandemic/; Delfina Janiri, Angelo Carfi, and Georgios D. Kotzalidis, "Posttraumatic Stress Disorder in Patients after Severe Covid-19 Infection," *JAMA Psychiatry* 78, no. 5 (2021), https://jamanetwork.com/journals/jamapsy chiatry/fullarticle/2776722.

118 *they've found that PTSD:* Bessel van der Kolk, *The Body Keeps the Score: Brain, Mind, and Body in the Healing of Trauma* (New York: Penguin, 2015).

121 *"This was the one thing":* Richard G. Tedeschi and Lawrence G. Calhoun, *Trauma and Transformation: Growing in the Aftermath of Suffering* (Thousand Oaks, CA: SAGE Publications, 1995), 1.

121 *Tedeschi told me:* Author interview with Richard Tedeschi, January 21, 2021.

122 *Over the next few years:* Cheryl H. Cryder, Ryan P. Kilmer, Richard G. Tedeschi, and Lawrence G. Calhoun, "An Exploratory Study of Posttraumatic

Growth in Children Following Natural Disaster," *American Journal of Orthopsychiatry* 76, no. 1 (2006): 65–69, https://ptgi.charlotte.edu/wp-content/uploads/sites/9/2015/01/An-exploratory-study-of-posttraumatic-growth-in-children-following-a-natural-disaster.pdf; Steve Powell, Rita Rosner, Willi Butollo, Richard G. Tedeschi, and Lawrence G. Calhoun, "Posttraumatic Growth after War: A Study with Former Refugees and Displaced People in Sarajevo," *Journal of Clinical Psychology* 59, no. 1 (2002): 71–83, https://onlinelibrary.wiley.com/doi/abs/10.1002/jclp.10117; Amanda R. Cobb, Richard G. Tedeschi, Lawrence G. Calhoun, and Arnie Cann, "Correlates of Posttraumatic Growth in Survivors of Intimate Partner Violence," *Journal of Traumatic Stress* 19, no. 6 (2006): 895–903, https://onlinelibrary.wiley.com/doi/abs/10.1002/jts.20171; Richard G. Tedeschi and Lawrence G. Calhoun, "Beyond the Concept of Recovery: Growth and the Experience of Loss," *Death Studies* 32, no. 1 (2007): 27–39, https://www.tandfonline.com/doi/abs/10.1080/07481180701741251.

122 *They had a sense:* Richard G. Tedeschi and Lawrence G. Calhoun, "The Posttraumatic Growth Inventory: Measuring the Positive Legacy of Trauma," *Journal of Traumatic Stress* 9, no. 3 (1996): 455–71, https://ptgi.charlotte.edu/wp-content/uploads/sites/9/2015/01/The-Posttraumatic-Growth-Inventory-Measuring-the-positive-legacy-of-trauma.pdf.

122 *for the phenomenon:* Tedeschi and Calhoun, "The Posttraumatic Growth Inventory"; Jim Rendon, "How Trauma Can Change You—for the Better," *Time*, July 22, 2015, https://time.com/3967885/how-trauma-can-change-you-for-the-better/?utm_source=pocket_mylist.

122 *Marie J. C. Forgeard:* Marie J. C. Forgeard, "Perceiving Benefits after Adversity: The Relationship between Self-Reported Posttraumatic Growth and Creativity," *Psychology of Aesthetics, Creativity, and the Arts* 7, no. 3 (2013): 245–64, https://doi.apa.org/doiLanding?doi=10.1037%2Fa0031223.

123 *Survivors of a New Zealand:* Robin Achterhof, Martin J. Dorahy, Amy Rowlands, Charlotte Renouf, Eileen Britt, and Janet D. Carter, "Predictors of Posttraumatic Growth 10–11 Months after a Fatal Earthquake," *Psychological Trauma: Theory, Research, Practice, and Policy* 10, no. 2 (2018): 208–15, https://doi.apa.org/doiLanding?doi=10.1037%2Ftra0000286; Manuel Cárdenas-Castro, Ximena Faúndez-Abarca, Héctor Arancibia-Martini, and Cristián Ceruti-Mahn, "The Relationship between Posttraumatic Growth and Psychosocial Variables in Survivors of State Terrorism and Their Relatives," *Journal of Interpersonal Violence* 36, nos. 1/2 (2017): 428–47, https://journals.sagepub.com/doi/10.1177/0886260517727494; Carmelo Vázquez, "Perceived Benefits after Terrorist Attacks: The Role of Positive and Negative Emotions," *Journal of Positive Psychology* 5, no. 2 (2010): 154–63, https://www.tandfonline.com/doi/abs/10.1080/17439761003630060?mobileUi=0&journalCode=rpos20.

123 *Hundreds of studies:* Avital Kaye-Tzadok and Bilha Davidson-Arad, "Posttraumatic Growth among Women Survivors of Childhood Sexual Abuse," *Psychological Trauma: Theory, Research, Practice, and Policy* 8, no. 5 (2016): 550–58, https://psycnet.apa.org/record/2016-15313-001; Patricia Frazier, Amy Conlon, and

Theresa Glaser, "Positive and Negative Changes Following Sexual Assault," *Journal of Consulting and Clinical Psychology* 69, no. 6 (2002): 1048–55, https://www.researchgate.net/publication/11581126_Positive_and_negative_changes_following_sexual_assault; Cobb et al., "Correlates of Posttraumatic Growth in Survivors of Intimate Partner Violence"; Jack Tsai, Renée El-Gabalawy, William Hurt Sledge, Steven M. Southwick, and Robert H. Pietrzak, "Post-Traumatic Growth among Veterans in the USA: Results from the National Health and Resilience in Veterans Study," *Psychological Medicine* 45, no. 1 (2014): 165–79, https://www.cambridge.org/core/journals/psychological-medicine/article/abs/posttraumatic-growth-among-veterans-in-the-usa-results-from-the-national-health-and-resilience-in-veterans-study/F277B55F1975DA6E378E4D71CC207AED; Michelle R. Widows, Paul B. Jacobsen, Margaret Booth-Jones, and Karen K. Fields, "Predictors of Posttraumatic Growth Following Bone Marrow Transplantation for Cancer," *Health Psychology* 24, no. 3 (2005): 266–73, http://www.cas.usf.edu/~jacobsen/ptgibmt.pdf; Yvonne W. Leung, Shannon Gravely-Witte, Alison Macpherson, Jane Irvine, Donna E. Stewart, and Sherry L. Grace, "Post-Traumatic Growth among Cardiac Outpatients," *Journal of Health Psychology* 15, no. 7 (2010): 1049–63, https://pubmed.ncbi.nlm.nih.gov/20472608/; Irit Bluvstein, Liat Moravchick, David Sheps, Shaul Schreiber, and Miki Bloch, "Posttraumatic Growth, Posttraumatic Stress Symptoms and Mental Health among Coronary Heart Disease Survivors," *Journal of Clinical Psychology in Medical Settings* 20, no. 2 (2013): 164–72, https://pubmed.ncbi.nlm.nih.gov/22886704/.

123 *almost half:* Xiaoli Wu, Atipatsa C. Kaminga, Wenjie Dai, Jing Deng, Zhipeng Wang, Xiongfeng Pan, and Aizhong Liu, "The Prevalence of Moderate-to-High Posttraumatic Growth," *Journal of Affective Disorders* 243 (2019): 408–15, https://www.sciencedirect.com/science/article/pii/S0165032717326009?via%3Dihub.

123 *One of the earliest:* Stephen Joseph, "Lessons from Disaster at Sea," *Psychology Today*, January 23, 2012, https://www.psychologytoday.com/us/blog/what-doesnt-kill-us/201201/lessons-disaster-sea.

123 *Yet when Joseph:* Aruna Sankaranarayanan, "Can There Be a Bright Side to Trauma?," *Mint*, August 4, 2014, https://www.livemint.com/Leisure/NvHbQX5O0AtDmJohd2YGHI/Can-there-be-a-bright-side-to-trauma.html.

123 *What's more:* Darshit Parikh, Paolo De Ieso, Gail Garvey, Thanuja Thachil, Ramya Ramamoorthi, Michael Penniment, and Rama Jayaraj, "Post-Traumatic Stress Disorder and Post-Traumatic Growth in Breast Cancer Patients," *Asian Pacific Journal of Cancer Prevention* 16, no. 2 (2015): 641–46, http://journal.waocp.org/article_30483_464ce15f36ce5755982f83f09a658833.pdf.

123 *In one study:* Suzanne C. Danhauer, L. Douglas Case, Richard Tedeschi, Greg Russell, Tanya Vishnevsky, Kelli Triplett, Edward H. Ip, and Nancy E. Avis, "Predictors of Posttraumatic Growth in Women with Breast Cancer," *Psycho-Oncology* 22 (2013): 2676–83, https://www.researchgate.net/publication/258056421_Predictors_of_posttraumatic_growth_in_women_with_breast_cancer.

124 *"I think I was":* Jonathan Kandell, "Sumner Redstone Dies at 97; Built Media Empire and Long Reigned over It," *New York Times*, August 12, 2020, https://

www.nytimes.com/2020/08/12/obituaries/sumner-redstone-dead.html?search ResultPosition=1.

124 *In Christianity:* John 16:20–21, New International Version.

124 *Literature is filled:* Lynn Gumb, "Trauma and Recovery: Finding the Ordinary Hero in Fictional Recovery Narratives," *Journal of Humanistic Psychology* 58, no. 4 (2017): 460–74, https://journals.sagepub.com/doi/abs/10.1177/002216781774 9703?journalCode=jhpa.

125 *In recounting:* Victor E. Frankl, *Man's Search for Meaning* (Boston: Beacon Press, 2014), 64, 129.

125 *Astonishingly, research to date:* Mariusz Zięba, Katarzyna Wiecheć, and Wiktoria Mieleszczenko-Kowszewicz, "Coexistence of Post-Traumatic Growth and Post-Traumatic Depreciation in the Aftermath of Trauma: Qualitative and Quantitative Narrative Analysis," *Frontiers in Psychology* 10, no. 687 (2019), https://www .frontiersin.org/articles/10.3389/fpsyg.2019.00687/full.

125 *That phase is followed:* Author interview with Richard Tedeschi, January 21, 2021.

126 *Intriguingly, survivors:* Author interview with Richard Tedeschi, January 27, 2022.

127 *Yet today:* Damian Cristodero, "Turning an Injury into an Opportunity," *Mason Sprit,* September 7, 2021, https://spirit.gmu.edu/2021/09/turning-an-injury-into -an-opportunity/.

127 *The key, he realized:* Michael Murphy, "So, How Was Your Decade? Growth after Trauma and Views of Future You," Michael Murphy Speaks, December 29, 2019, http://www.michaelmurphyspeaks.com/blog/2019/12/29/so-how-was-your-decade-growth-after-trauma-and-views-of-future-you.

127 *"I'm blessed to have":* Author interview with Kay Wilson, November 16, 2021.

128 *In 1993:* Darrin R. Lehman, Christopher G. Davis, and Anita Delongis, "Positive and Negative Life Changes Following Bereavement and Their Relations to Adjustment," *Journal of Social and Clinical Psychology* 12, no. 1 (1993): 90–112; "The Top 5 Most Stressful Life Events and How to Handle Them," University Hospitals, July 2, 2015, https://www.uhhospitals.org/Healthy-at-UH/articles/2015/07/the-top-5-most-stressful-life-events.

128 *Researchers have found:* Yibo Peng, Jinghua Tang, and Hanzhou Li, "Good Deeds Could Come From Frustrated Individuals," *Frontiers in Psychology* 12 (2021), https://www.ncbi.nlm.nih.gov/pmc/articles/PMC8129031/.

128 *One study of Scottish:* "Cancer 'Changes Outlook on Life,'" BBC, December 31, 2012, https://www.bbc.com/news/uk-scotland-20879212.

128 *She hopes to:* Lorna Collier, "Growth after Trauma," *American Psychological Association Monitor on Psychology* 47, no. 10 (2016), https://www.apa.org/monitor /2016/11/growth-trauma.

128 *Her charitable work:* Author interview with Kay Wilson, January 16, 2022.

129 *More than two thousand:* Nancy Cutler, "Deaths from 9/11 Diseases Will Soon Outnumber Those Lost on That Fateful Day," *Journal News,* September 6, 2018, https://www.usatoday.com/story/news/nation-now/2018/09/06/9-11-deaths -aftermath-soon-outnumber-killed-sept-11/1209605002/.

131 *Unwittingly we were:* Madhuleena Roy Chowdhury, "What Is Post-Traumatic Growth (+ Inventory & Scale)," Positive Psychology, August 31, 2019, https://positivepsychology.com/post-traumatic-growth/.

131 *had a sample of 1,505:* Lisa D. Butler, Christine M. Blasey, Robert W. Garlan, Shannon E. McCaslin, Jay Azarow, Xin-Hua Chen, Juliette C. Desjardins, Sue DiMiceli, David A. Seagraves, T. Andrew Hastings, Helena C. Kraemer, and David Spiegel, "Posttraumatic Growth Following the Terrorist Attacks of September 11, 2001: Cognitive, Coping, and Trauma Symptom Predictors in an Internet Convenience Sample," *Traumatology* 11, no. 4 (2005): 247–67, https://journals.sagepub.com/doi/abs/10.1177/153476560501100405?journalCode=tmta.

131 *Another study that followed:* Michael J. Poulin, Roxane Cohen Silver, Virginia Gil-Rivas, E. Alison Holman, and Daniel N. McIntosh, "Finding Social Benefits after a Collective Trauma: Perceiving Societal Changes and Well-being Following 9/11," *Journal of Traumatic Stress* 22, no. 2 (2009): 81–90, https://onlinelibrary.wiley.com/doi/epdf/10.1002/jts.20391.

131 *Shortly before:* Christopher Peterson and Martin E. P. Seligman, "Character Strengths before and after September 11," *Psychological Science* 14, no. 4 (2003): 381–84, https://journals.sagepub.com/doi/abs/10.1111/1467-9280.24482.

132 *"My least favorite":* Author interview with Josh Goldberg, January 12, 2022.

133 *"When we struggle":* Author interview with Josh Goldberg, August 25, 2021.

133 *Despite all the evidence:* Author interview with Richard Tedeschi, August 18, 2020.

134 *"What is my identity":* Sally Maitlis, "Making Sense of the Future after Losing a Job You Love," *Harvard Business Review*, April 30, 2020, https://hbr.org/2020/04/making-sense-of-the-future-after-losing-a-job-you-love.

134 *Yet after spending:* Author interview with Sally Maitlis, September 3, 2020.

135 *When researchers followed:* Sharon Dekel, Christine Mandl, and Zahava Solomon, "Shared and Unique Predictors of Post-Traumatic Growth and Distress," *Journal of Clinical Psychology* 67, no. 3 (2011): 241–52, https://onlinelibrary.wiley.com/doi/10.1002/jclp.20747.

135 *"I've never been able":* Author interview with Kay Wilson, January 16, 2022.

136 *"This helplessness":* Author interview with Kay Wilson, November 16, 2021.

Chapter 5: The "Necessity Entrepreneur"

137 *"It was twelve":* Author interview with Jane Veron, March 21, 2022.

140 *Black employees:* Bryan Hancock, James Manyika, Monne Williams, and Lareina Yee, "The Black Experience at Work in Charts," *McKinsey Quarterly*, April 15, 2021, https://www.mckinsey.com/featured-insights/diversity-and-inclusion/the-black-experience-at-work-in-charts.

140 *And while Hispanics:* Mark Hugo Lopez, Jens Manuel Krogstad, and Jeffrey S. Passel, "Who Is Hispanic?," Pew Research Center, September 23, 2021, https://www.pewresearch.org/fact-tank/2021/09/23/who-is-hispanic/; Hancock et al., "The Black Experience at Work in Charts."

140 *In a study:* Michelle K. Ryan and S. Alexander Haslam, "The Glass Cliff: Exploring the Dynamics Surrounding the Appointment of Women to Precarious Leadership Positions," *Academy of Management Review* 32, no. 2 (2007): 549–72, https://www.jstor.org/stable/20159315?seq=1; Michelle K. Ryan and S. Alexander Haslam, "The Glass Cliff: Evidence That Women Are Over-Represented in Precarious Leadership Positions," *British Journal of Management* 16, no. 2 (2005): 81–90, https://psycnet.apa.org/record/2005-06147-001.

140 *These coaches are given:* Alison Cook and Christy Glass, "Glass Cliffs and Organizational Saviors: Barriers to Minority Leadership in Work Organizations?," *Social Problems* 60, no. 2 (2013): 168–87, https://academic.oup.com/socpro/article-abstract/60/2/168/1610869.

140 *Across industries:* Jennifer L. Knight, Michelle R. Hebl, Jessica B. Foster, and Laura M. Mannix, "Out of Role? Out of Luck: The Influence of Race and Leadership Status on Performance Appraisals," *Journal of Leadership and Organizational Studies* 9, no. 3 (2003): 85–93, https://journals.sagepub.com/doi/10.1177/107179190300900308; Ashleigh Shelby Rosette and Robert W. Livingston, "Failure Is Not an Option for Black Women: Effects of Organizational Performance on Leaders with Single versus Dual-Subordinate Identities," *Journal of Experimental Social Psychology* 48, no. 5 (2012): 1162–67, https://www.sciencedirect.com/science/article/abs/pii/S0022103112000832?via%3Dihub.

140 *A recent survey:* Tristan Bove, "Baby Boomers Are Killing the Idea of Retirement and Want to Work Forever," *Fortune*, January 12, 2022, https://fortune.com/2022/01/12/baby-boomers-retirement-flexible-hours-savings-covid/.

141 *In another survey:* Rebecca Perron, "Age Discrimination Continues to Hold Older Workers Back," *AARP*, May 2021, https://www.aarp.org/research/topics/economics/info-2021/older-workers-new-skills-covid-19-pandemic.html.

141 *Meanwhile, multiple studies:* Sophia Ahn and Amelia Costigan, "Trend Brief: Gendered Ageism," Catalyst, October 17, 2019, https://www.catalyst.org/research/gendered-ageism-trend-brief/.

141 *The firing was so beyond:* Author interview with Paul Tasner, September 25, 2020.

142 *As he told the audience:* Paul Tasner, "How I Became an Entrepreneur at 66," TED Conferences, https://www.ted.com/talks/paul_tasner_how_i_became_an_entrepreneur_at_66/.

142 *Multiple studies:* Lesley Evans Ogden, "Working Mothers Face a 'Wall' of Bias—but There Are Ways to Push Back," *Science*, April 10, 2019, https://www.science.org/content/article/working-mothers-face-wall-bias-there-are-ways-push-back.

142 *An analysis of labor data:* Caitlin Mullen, "Amid Pandemic, Mothers Far More Likely to Be Laid Off than Fathers," *Bizwomen*, September 16, 2020, https://www.bizjournals.com/bizwomen/news/latest-news/2020/09/amid-pandemic-mothers-far-more-likely-to-be-laid.html?page=all#:~:text=In%20reviewing%20U.S.%20employment%20data,and%20other%20factors%20were%20considered.

142 *What's more, while ageism:* Ahn and Costigan, "Gendered Ageism."

143 *The problem starts early:* "Women in the Workplace 2021," McKinsey and Company, September 27, 2021, https://www.mckinsey.com/featured-insights /diversity-and-inclusion/women-in-the-workplace.

143 *Just 8.8 percent:* Emma Hinchliffe, "The Number of Women Running Fortune 500 Companies Reaches a Record High," *Fortune*, May 23, 2022, https://fortune .com/2022/05/23/female-ceos-fortune-500-2022-women-record-high-karen -lynch-sarah-nash/?utm_source=email&utm_medium=newsletter&utm _campaign=broadsheet&utm_content=2022052313pm&tpcc=nlbroadsheet.

143 *Lauren Hobart:* Sarah Nassauer, "Dick's Sporting Goods' New CEO: Being a Female Leader Is a Huge Asset," *Wall Street Journal*, September 24, 2021, https://www.wsj .com/articles/dicks-sporting-goods-ceo-lauren-hobart-11632330592?mod=h p_listc_pos1&tpcc=nlbroadsheet.

143 *The phenomenon:* "'The Tiara Syndrome': Cited in Sheryl Sandberg's Lean In," Negotiating Women, Inc., https://negotiatingwomen.com/the-tiara-syndrome -in-sheryl-sandbergs-lean-in/ (accessed June 15, 2022).

144 *Companies with more women:* Chloe Taylor, "Firms with a Female CEO Have a Better Stock Price Performance, New Research Says," CNBC, October 18, 2019, https://www.cnbc.com/2019/10/18/firms-with-a-female-ceo-have-a-better -stock-price-performance-sp.html.

144 *Those firms:* Corinne Post, Boris Lokshin, and Christophe Boone, "Research: Adding Women to the C-Suite Changes How Companies Think," *Harvard Business Review*, April 6, 2021, https://hbr.org/2021/04/research-adding-women-to-the-c-suite -changes-how-companies-think?utm_medium=email&utm_source=newsletter _daily&utm_campaign=dailyalert_notactsubs&deliveryName=DM126621.

144 *A Rockefeller Foundation study:* "Does the Media Influence How We Perceive Women in Leadership?," Rockefeller Foundation, 2016, https://www.rockefeller foundation.org/wp-content/uploads/100x25_MediaLanguage_report1.pdf.

144 *Women's mistakes:* Sarah Green Carmichael, "Jill Abramson's Ouster: Why Aren't Standards This High for Male Leaders?," Conference Board, July 24, 2014, https://www.conference-board.org/blog/postdetail.cfm?post=3122.

144 *In a revealing exercise:* Therese Huston, "Research: We Are Way Harder on Female Leaders Who Make Bad Calls," *Harvard Business Review*, April 21, 2016, https://hbr.org/2016/04/research-we-are-way-harder-on-female-leaders-who -make-bad-calls; Victoria L. Brescoll, Erica Dawson, and Eric Luis Uhlmann, "Hard Won and Easily Lost: The Fragile Status of Leaders in Gender-Stereotype- Incongruent Occupations," *Psychological Science* 21, no. 11 (2010): 1640–42, https://www.jstor.org/stable/41062426?seq=1.

144 *What's worse:* Heather Sarsons, "Interpreting Signals in the Labor Market: Evidence from Medical Referrals," November 28, 2017, working paper, Harvard University, https://scholar.harvard.edu/files/sarsons/files/sarsons_jmp.pdf.

144 *From an early age:* Vanessa Fuhrmans, "Even among Entrepreneurs, There's a Gender Pay Gap," *Wall Street Journal*, October 21, 2018, https://www.wsj.com /articles/even-among-entrepreneurs-theres-a-gender-pay-gap-1540127024.

145 *When the experiment:* Charlene M. Callahan-Levy and Lawrence A. Messé, "Sex Differences in the Allocation of Pay," *Journal of Personality and Social Psychology* 37, no. 3 (1979): 433–46, https://psycnet.apa.org/fulltext/1980-23329-001.pdf?auth_token=dac1302e130e5f457e61357f8b7d09be364c9b10.

145 *Perhaps, then:* Healy Jones, "What Salaries Did Startup CEOs Earn in 2022?," Kruze Consulting, May 9, 2022, https://kruzeconsulting.com/blog/startup-ceo-salary-report/?tpcc=nlbroadsheet.

145 *Female CEOs:* Vishal K. Gupta, Sandra C. Mortal, Sabatino Silveri, Minxing Sun, and Daniel B. Turban, "You're Fired! Gender Disparities in CEO Dismissal," *Journal of Management* 46, no. 4 (2018): 560–82, https://journals.sage pub.com/doi/abs/10.1177/0149206318810415?journalCode=joma&journalCode=joma.

145 *Yet when Fortune:* Jennifer Reingold, "Why Top Women Are Disappearing from Corporate America," *Fortune*, November 9, 2016, https://fortune.com/longform/women-corporate-america/.

146 *An American Express report:* "The 2019 State of Women-Owned Businesses Report," American Express, 2019, https://s1.q4cdn.com/692158879/files/doc_library/file/2019-state-of-women-owned-businesses-report.pdf.

146 *Globally, one-third:* Daniel Halim, "Women Entrepreneurs Needed—Stat!," World Bank, March 5, 2020, https://blogs.worldbank.org/opendata/women-entrepreneurs-needed-stat; "MSME Finance Gap: Assessment of the Shortfalls and Opportunities in Financing Micro, Small, and Medium Enterprises in Emerging Markets," International Finance Corporation, 2017, https://www.ifc.org/wps/wcm/connect/03522e90-a13d-4a02-87cd-9ee9a297b311/121264-WP-PUBLIC-MSMEReportFINAL.pdf?MOD=AJPERES&CVID=m5SwAQA.

146 *In a study of professional:* Deborah A. O'Neil and Diana Bilimoria, "Women's Career Development Phases: Idealism, Endurance, and Reinvention," *Career Development International* 10, no. 3 (2005), https://www.researchgate.net/publication/235267738_Women's_career_development_phases_Idealism_endurance_and_reinvention.

147 *Women she studied:* Author interview with Deborah O'Neil, November 12, 2020.

147 *A Catalyst survey:* Nancy M. Carter and Christine Silva, "The Myth of the Ideal Worker: Does Doing All the Right Things Really Get Women Ahead?," Catalyst, October 1, 2011, https://www.catalyst.org/wp-content/uploads/2019/02/The_Myth_of_the_Ideal_Worker_Does_Doing_All_the_Right_Things_Really_Get_Women_Ahead.pdf.

146 *And a global study:* Lauren Noël and Christie Hunter Arscott, "Millennial Women: What Executives Need to Know about Millennial Women," International Consortium for Executive Development Research, Special Report, 2016, https://www.icedr.org/research/documents/15_millennial_women.pdf; Christie Hunter Arscott, "Why So Many Thirtysomething Women Are Leaving Your Company," *Harvard Business Review*, March 15, 2016, https://hbr.org/2016/03/why-so-many-thirtysomething-women-are-leaving-your-company.

149 *But after the kids:* Sallie Krawcheck, "The Power of the 'Third Act' in Women's Careers," *Ellevest* November 14, 2018, https://www.ellevest.com/magazine/career /power-third-act-career.

149 *When psychologists surveyed:* Lea E. Waters and Kathleen A. Moore, "Predicting Self-Esteem during Unemployment: The Effect of Gender, Financial Deprivation, Alternate Roles, and Social Support," *Journal of Employment Counseling* 39, no. 4 (2011): 171–89, https://onlinelibrary.wiley.com/doi/10.1002/j.2161-1920.2002 .tb00848.x.

151 *"It was comforting":* Julia Boorstin, *When Women Lead: What They Achieve, Why They Succeed, and How We Can Learn from Them* (New York: Simon & Schuster/ Avid Reader Press, 2022), 8.

152 *"I wouldn't call":* Author interview with Kathryn Finney, April 7, 2021.

152 *The potential investor:* "Kathryn Finney: Author & Entrepreneur," Lean In, https:// leanin.org/stories/kathryn-finney (accessed June 15, 2022).

152 *Even positive:* Ashley McDonough, "Meet Kathryn Finney: The Fairy Godmother of Tech Start-ups," *Essence*, October 23, 2020, https://www.essence.com/news /money-career/meet-kathryn-finney-the-fairy-godmother-of-tech-start-ups/.

152 *Female founders:* Lizette Chapman, "Female Founders Raised Just 2% of Venture Capital Money in 2021," *Bloomberg*, January 11, 2022, https://www .bloomberg.com/news/articles/2022-01-11/women-founders-raised-just-2-of -venture-capital-money-last-year#:~:text=Female%20founders%20secured%20 only%202,report%20by%20research%20firm%20PitchBook; Emma Hinchliffe, "The Number of Black Female Founders Who Have Raised More than $1 Million Has Nearly Tripled since 2018," *Fortune*, December 2, 2020, https://fortune .com/2020/12/02/black-women-female-founders-venture-capital-funding-vc -2020-project-diane/.

152 *Venture capital firms:* Nick Frost, "How VC Bias in Viewing Pitch Decks Can Affect Fundraising Success," Dropbox DocSend, August 14, 2020, https://www.docsend .com/blog/how-vc-bias-in-viewing-pitch-decks-can-affect-fundraising-success/.

152 *Across the board:* Solange Lopes, "5 Challenges Faced by Women Entrepreneurs of Color," Ellevate, https://www.ellevatenetwork.com/articles/9061-5-challenges -faced-by-women-entrepreneurs-of-color (accessed June 15, 2022).

153 *"It was difficult":* Author interview with Kathryn Finney, April 7, 2021.

155 *When she speaks:* Author interview with Jane Veron, March 21, 2022.

156 *"There were so many":* Author interview with Mika Brzezinski, May 10, 2022.

157 *according to Pew:* "Nearly Half of Post-Millennials Are Racial or Ethnic Minorities," Pew Research Center, November 13, 2018, https://www.pewresearch.org /social-trends/2018/11/15/early-benchmarks-show-post-millennials-on-track -to-be-most-diverse-best-educated-generation-yet/psdt-11-15-18_postmillennials -00-00/.

157 *Ruzwana spoke only:* "Icons Aren't Born, They're Made" (advertorial for Audemars Piguet), *New York Times*, https://www.nytimes.com/paidpost/audemars-piguet /icons-arent-born-theyre-made.html.

157 *Ruzwana herself:* Ruzwana Bashir, "The Untold Story of How a Culture of Shame Perpetuates Abuse. I Know, I Was a Victim," *Guardian*, August 29, 2014, https://www.theguardian.com/society/2014/aug/29/-sp-untold-story-culture-of-shame-ruzwana-bashir.

157 *"It sparked":* Author interview with Ruzwana Bashir, March 30, 2022.

160 *In 2021:* "2021 Review of Funding for Female Founders," Female Founders Fund, April 11, 2022, https://blog.femalefoundersfund.com/2021-review-of-funding-for-female-founders-b3008c13d390.

Chapter 6: Move before You Move

167 *"We never would":* Author interview with William Brown, May 27, 2021.

168 *Google cofounder:* Miguel Helft, "How Music Education Influenced Larry Page," *Fortune*, November 18, 2014, https://fortune.com/2014/11/18/larry-page-music-education/.

169 *Whitney Wolfe Herd:* Amelia Tait, "Swipe Right for Equality: How Bumble Is Taking on Sexism," *Wired* (UK), August 3, 2017, https://www.wired.co.uk/article/bumble-whitney-wolfe-sexism-tinder-app.

169 *She successfully experimented:* Charlotte Alter, "How Whitney Wolfe Herd Turned a Vision of a Better Internet into a Billion-Dollar Brand," *Time*, March 19, 2021, https://time.com/5947727/whitney-wolfe-herd-bumble/.

170 *"At my lowest point":* Whitney Wolfe Herd, "You Reported Sexual Harassment, Now What? Bumble's Whitney Wolfe Herd Offers Advice," *Harper's Bazaar*, November 30, 2017, https://www.harpersbazaar.com/culture/features/a13395335/reporting-sexual-harassment-advice-whitney-wolfe-bumble/#:~:text=I%20was%20only%2024%2C%20and,and%20turns%20women%20into%20targets.%22.

170 *The stock price:* Katy Mousinho and Giles Lury, "How Whitney Wolfe Herd Became the World's Youngest Female Self-Made Billionaire," *Management Today*, https://www.managementtoday.co.uk/whitney-wolfe-herd-became-worlds-youngest-female-self-made-billionaire/women-in-business/article/1707471.

171 *Millennials spend an average:* "Millennials or Gen Z: Who's Doing the Most Job-Hopping," Career Builder, October 5, 2021, https://www.careerbuilder.com/advice/how-long-should-you-stay-in-a-job.

171 *Gen Zers—those born:* Sawdah Bhaimiya, "Gen Z Workers Change Jobs More Often than Any Other Generation Because They're Prioritizing Happiness, High Expectations, and Raises," *Business Insider*, January 6, 2022, https://www.businessinsider.com/gen-z-spends-less-time-in-jobs-than-earlier-generations-2021-11.

171 *One study:* Kate Beckman, "Will Gen Z Be the Next Generation of Job Hoppers?," RippleMatch, December 6, 2018, https://ripplematch.com/insights/will-gen-z-be-the-next-generation-of-job-hoppers-b04feb4e/.

171 *What's more, while financial security:* Rachel Pelta, "Generation Z in the Workplace: A Changing Workforce," FlexJobs, https://www.flexjobs.com/employer-blog/generation-z-workforce/.

171 *They would even:* Robin Madell, "What's Most Important to Job Seekers in 2019?," FlexJobs, https://www.flexjobs.com/employer-blog/whats-most-important-to-job-seekers-in-2019/.

171 *On the career front:* Shafin Tejani, "What I've Learned from Working with Gen Z Entrepreneurs," Worth, April 16, 2021, https://www.worth.com/gen-z-entrepreneurs.

171 *Some 80 percent:* Valerie J. Calderon, "US Students' Entrepreneurial Energy Waiting to Be Tapped," *Gallup News*, October 13, 2011, https://news.gallup.com/poll/150077/Students-Entrepreneurial-Energy-Waiting-Tapped.aspx.

173 *"Entrepreneurship never":* Author interview with Lauren Strayhorn, February 22, 2022.

173 *"I was now":* Ryan Buxton, "How They Quit: 3 Personal Stories from the Great Resignation," Katie Couric Media, January 30, 2022, https://katiecouric.com/lifestyle/workplace/great-resignation-personal-stories/?utm_source=Sailthru&utm_medium=email&utm_campaign=WUC_Thurday&utm_term=all_users.

175 *In his book:* Adam Grant, *Originals: How Non-Conformists Move the World* (New York: Penguin, 2017), 17–18.

175 *"Intelligent planning":* Oliver Napoleon Hill, *Think and Grow Rich* (Meneola, NY: Dover, 2018), 19, 97.

176 *They are the living embodiment:* "'You've Got to Find What You Love,' Jobs Says," *Stanford News*, June 14, 2005, https://news.stanford.edu/2005/06/12/youve-got-find-love-jobs-says/.

176 *"I wasn't on board":* Author interview with Joanne Lee Molinaro, June 9, 2022.

177 *Her real job:* "Humans of HOKA: Joanne Molinaro," Hoka, January 4, 2022, https://www.hoka.com/en/us/blog-post/?id=humans-hoka-joanne-molinaro-aka-korean-vegan; Bradley P. Moss and Joanne Molinaro, "The Sanctioning of Trump's Lawyers Is Exactly What Is Supposed to Happen," *Atlantic*, August 28, 2021, https://www.theatlantic.com/ideas/archive/2021/08/trumps-lawyers-kraken/619915/; Bradley P. Moss and Joanne Molinaro, "No Self-Respecting Lawyer Should Touch Trump's Election-Fraud Claims," *Atlantic*, November 11, 2020, https://www.theatlantic.com/ideas/archive/2020/11/trumps-lawyers-election/617064/.

177 *After Covid-19:* "Meet Joanne Lee Molinaro," The Korean Vegan, https://thekoreanvegan.com/about (accessed June 23, 2022).

177 *"It was this internal fear":* https://www.facebook.com/watch/?v=2796899077217365&ref=sharing.

178 *"I think just":* Monica Eng, "How a High-Powered Lawyer Became a TikTok Superstar: Meet the Korean Vegan," *Washington Post*, October 4, 2021, https://www.washingtonpost.com/food/2021/10/04/korean-vegan-joanne-molinaro/.

178 *Transformations like Joanne Lee Molinaro's:* Author interview with Adam Grant, April 20, 2022.

180 *He and Jihae Shin:* Jihae Shin and Adam M. Grant, "When Putting Work Off Pays Off: The Curvilinear Relationship between Procrastination and Creativity,"

Academy of Management Journal 64, no. 3 (2021), https://journals.aom.org/doi/full/10.5465/amj.2018.1471.

181 *The average NBA player's:* Luke Zhang, "What Is the Average Career Length of an NBA Player?," Dunk or Three, October 11, 2021, https://dunkorthree.com/nba-player-career-length/.

181 *Even the top salaries:* Author interview with Len Elmore, October 13, 2020.

181 *A 2009* Sports Illustrated: Pablo S. Torre, "How (and Why) Athletes Go Broke," *Sports Illustrated*, March 23, 2009, https://vault.si.com/vault/2009/03/23/how-and-why-athletes-go-broke.

181 *He was mesmerized:* Author interview with Len Elmore, April 15, 2022.

185 *"Warwick was left":* Author interview with William Brown, May 27, 2021.

186 *"Do whatever":* Author interview with Barbara Felton, June 29, 2021.

Chapter 7: Stop What You're Doing

192 *In fact, a study:* Melanie S. Brucks and Jonathan Levav, "Virtual Communication Curbs Creative Idea Generation," *Nature* 605 (2022): 108–12.

193 *Americans leave one-third:* "National Plan for Vacation Day," US Travel Association, 2021, https://www.ustravel.org/sites/default/files/media_root/document/NPVD_FactSheet-2021.pdf.

193 *During the pandemic:* Roy Maurer, "Remote Employees Are Working Longer than Before," December 16, 2020, SHRM, https://www.shrm.org/hr-today/news/hr-news/pages/remote-employees-are-working-longer-than-before.aspx#:~:text=Nearly%2070%20percent%20of%20professionals,based%20staffing%20firm%20Robert%20Half.

193 *We venerate the executives:* Vauhini Vara, "Why Aren't There More Indra Nooyis?," *Atlantic*, August 7, 2018, https://www.theatlantic.com/business/archive/2018/08/pepsi-indra-nooyi/566936/; "Tom Ford, Fashion Designer," *Dolce*, May 26, 2010, https://dolcemag.com/fashion/tom-ford-fashion-designer/5310; Vanna Le, "Donald Trump's Workday Starts at 11 a.m.—Here's How His Morning Routine Stacks Up against 7 Other Millionaires," CNBC, February 13, 2019, https://www.cnbc.com/2019/02/13/donald-trumps-workday-starts-at-11-am-heres-how-it-compares-to-other-millionaires.html.

193 *All of this makes us:* Vijay Bharath, Deepika Chamoli, R. Kumar, and R. Shankar, "The Effect of Busyness on Productivity of an Individual," *International Journal of Indian Psychology* 4, no. 4 (2017), https://ijip.in/articles/the-effect-of-busyness-on-productivity-of-an-individual/.

194 *A North Dakota State:* Ann Hodgman, "The History of Our Love-Hate Relationship with the Christmas Letter," *Smithsonian*, December 2018, https://www.smithsonianmag.com/history/history-love-hate-relationship-christmas-letter-180970725/.

194 *And when 112:* Silvia Bellezza, Neeru Paharia, and Anat Keinan, "Conspicuous Consumption of Time: When Busyness and Lack of Leisure Time Become a

Status Symbol," *Journal of Consumer Research* 44 (2017): 118–38, https://www0
.gsb.columbia.edu/mygsb/faculty/research/pubfiles/19293/Conspicuous%20
Consumption%20of%20Time.pdf.

195   *Microsoft cofounder Paul Allen:* Author interview with Paul Allen, September 24,
2013; Joanne Lipman, "Is Music the Key to Success?" *New York Times*, October 12,
2013, https://www.nytimes.com/2013/10/13/opinion/sunday/is-music-the
-key-to-success.html.

195   *Even in the best of times:* Claire Zedelius, "Daydreaming Might Make You More
Creative—but It Depends on What You Daydream About," *Behavorial Scientist*,
November 2, 2020, https://behavioralscientist.org/daydreaming-might-make
-you-more-creative-but-it-depends-on-what-you-daydream-about/; Matthew A.
Killingsworth and Daniel T. Gilbert, "A Wandering Mind Is an Unhappy Mind,"
Science 330, no. 6006 (2010): 932, https://www.science.org/doi/10.1126
/science.1192439; Jennifer Windt, "Our Minds May Be Wandering More during
the Pandemic—and This Can Be a Good Thing," *The Conversation*, October 30,
2020, https://www.weforum.org/agenda/2020/10/day-dreaming-mind-wandering
-pandemic-covid19-coronavirus/.

196   *A few years ago:* Shelly L. Gable, Elizabeth A. Hopper, and Jonathan W. Schooler,
"When the Muses Strike: Creative Ideas of Physicists and Writers Routinely
Occur during Mind Wandering," *Psychological Science* 30, no. 3 (2019): 396–
404, https://labs.psych.ucsb.edu/schooler/jonathan/sites/labs.psych.ucsb.edu
.schooler.jonathan/files/pubs/0956797618820626.pdf.

196   *Other research:* Marily Oppezzo and Daniel L. Schwartz, "Give Your Ideas Some
Legs: The Positive Effect of Walking on Creative Thinking," *Journal of Experimental Psychology: Learning, Memory, and Cognition* 40, no. 4 (2014): 1142–52,
https://www.apa.org/pubs/journals/releases/xlm-a0036577.pdf; Ruth Ann Atchley, David L. Strayer, and Paul Atchley, "Creativity in the Wild: Improving Creative Reasoning through Immersion in Natural Settings," *PLoS ONE* 7, no. 12
(2012): e51474, https://journals.plos.org/plosone/article/file?id=10.1371/journal
.pone.0051474&type=printable; Po Bronson and Ashley Merryman, "Forget
Brainstorming," *Newsweek*, July 12, 2010, https://www.newsweek.com/forget
-brainstorming-74223; Célia Lacaux, Thomas Andrillon, and Delphine Oudi-
ette, "Sleep Onset Is a Creative Sweet Spot," *Science Advances* 7, no. 50 (2021),
https://www.science.org/doi/10.1126/sciadv.abj5866; Sumathi Reddy, "The
Perfect Nap: Sleeping Is a Mix of Art and Science," *Wall Street Journal*, September 2, 2013, https://www.wsj.com/articles/the-perfect-nap-sleeping-is-a-mix-of
-art-and-science-1378155665?tesla=y; Xiaoqian Ding, Y-Yuan Tang, Rongxiang
Tang, and Michael Posner, "Improving Creativity Performance by Short-Term
Meditation," *Behavorial and Brain Functions* 10, no. 9 (2014), https://behavior
alandbrainfunctions.biomedcentral.com/articles/10.1186/1744-9081-10-9;
Jacquelyn Smith, "72% of People Get Their Best Ideas in the Shower—Here's
Why," *Business Insider*, January 14, 2016, https://www.businessinsider.com/why
-people-get-their-best-ideas-in-the-shower-2016-1.

196 *A third said:* Linda A. Ovington, Anthony J. Saliba, Carmen C. Moran, Jeremy Goldring, and Jasmine B. MacDonald, "Do People Really Have Insights in the Shower?," *Journal of Creative Behavior* 52, no. 1 (2015): 21–34, https://online library.wiley.com/doi/full/10.1002/jocb.126.

197 *In one study:* Oppezzo and Schwartz, "Give Your Ideas Some Legs."

197 *helps explain:* Minda Zeitlin, "Steve Jobs Loved Walking Meetings: New Research Shows Why He Was Right," *Inc.*, February 24, 2020, https://www.inc.com /minda-zetlin/steve-jobs-walking-meetings-effectiveness-university-hong-kong-experiment-miao-cheng.html; Maureen Dowd, "Reed Hastings Had Us All Staying Home before We Had To," *New York Times*, September 4, 2020, https:// www.nytimes.com/2020/09/04/style/reed-hastings-netflix-interview.html.

197 *Composers Beethoven:* Mason Currey, "Tchaikovsky, Beethoven, Mahler: They All Loved Taking Long Daily Walks," *Slate*, April 25, 2013, https://slate.com/culture /2013/04/tchaikovsky-beethoven-mahler-they-all-loved-taking-long-daily-walks .html.

197 *So did writers:* Christopher Bergland, "Eureka! Deconstructing the Brain Mechanics of 'Aha!' Moments," *Psychology Today*, March 18, 2016, https://www .psychologytoday.com/us/blog/the-athletes-way/201603/eureka-deconstructing -the-brain-mechanics-aha-moments.

197 *"All truly great thoughts":* Charlotte Bates and Alex Rhys-Taylor, eds., *Walking through Social Research* (New York: Taylor & Francis, 2017), 189.

197 *A 2012 study:* Atchley, Strayer, and Atchley, "Creativity in the Wild."

197 *a Scottish study:* Peter Aspinall, Panagiotis Mavros, Richard Coyne, and Jenny Roe, "The Urban Brain: Analysing Outdoor Physical Activity with Mobile EEG," *British Journal of Sports Medicine* 49, no. 4 (2013): 272–76, https://bjsm .bmj.com/content/49/4/272.

197 *Canada even instituted:* Tik Root, "Doctors in Canada Can Now Prescribe National Park Passes to Patients," *Washington Post*, February 7, 2022, https://www .washingtonpost.com/climate-solutions/2022/02/07/national-park-prescription s-mental-health/.

198 *The woods:* "The Institute Woods: Protection against the Noise and the Bustle," Institute for Advanced Study, 2007, https://www.ias.edu/ideas/2007/institute -woods.

198 *But a British study:* Paul Knytl and Bertram Opitz, "Meditation Experience Predicts Negative Reinforcement Learning and Is Associated with Attenuated FRN Amplitude," *Cognitive, Affective, and Behavioral Neuroscience* 19 (2019): 268–82, https://link.springer.com/article/10.3758/s13415-018-00665-0.

198 *"Nonthinking is":* Seth Mydans, "Thich Nhat Hanh, Monk, Zen Master and Activist, Dies at 95," *New York Times*, January 21, 2022, https://www.nytimes .com/2022/01/21/world/asia/thich-nhat-hanh-dead.html?referringSource=article Share.

199 *Recent research:* Mary Helen Immordino-Yang, Joanna A. Christodoulou, and Vanessa Singh, "Rest Is Not Idleness: Implications of the Brain's Default Mode for Human

Development and Education," *Perspectives on Psychological Science* 7, no. 4 (2012): 352–64, https://journals.sagepub.com/doi/abs/10.1177/1745691612447308.

199 *The* Harvard Business Review: David Rock, "Your Brain on Facebook," *Harvard Business Review*, May 18, 2012, https://hbr.org/2012/05/your-brain-on -facebook.

199 *Mary Shelley wrote:* "Frankenstein Chronology," The Shelley-Godwin Archive, http://shelleygodwinarchive.org/contents/frankenstein/frankenstein-chronology/ (accessed June 20, 2022).

199 *The writer John Steinbeck:* Deirdre Barrett, "The 'Committee of Sleep': A Study of Dream Incubation for Problem Solving," *Dreaming* 3, no. 2 (1993): https:// www.asdreams.org/journal/articles/barrett3-2.htm.

199 *Rock and Roll Hall of Famer:* Author interview with Todd Rundgren, July 26, 2022.

200 *About 20 percent:* Deirdre Barrett, "When the Answer Comes in a Dream," *American Scientist* 108, no. 4 (2020): 200, https://www.americanscientist.org/article /when-the-answer-comes-in-a-dream.

200 *Two decades later:* Barrett, "The 'Committee of Sleep.'"

200 *In a particularly devious:* Michael Hopkin, "Sleep Boosts Lateral Thinking," *Nature*, January 22, 2004, https://www.nature.com/articles/news040119-10.

201 *"It was like a gift":* John Cleese, *Creativity: A Short and Cheerful Guide* (New York: Crown, 2020), 14–15.

202 *More than a third:* "A Good Night's Sleep Is Critical for Good Health," Centers for Disease Control and Prevention, February 18, 2016, https://www.cdc.gov /media/releases/2016/p0215-enough-sleep.html.

202 *Yet researchers have found:* Marie Söderström, Kerstin Jeding, Mirjam Ekstedt, and Aleksander Perski, "Insufficient Sleep Predicts Clinical Burnout," *Journal of Occupational Health Psychology* 17, no. 2 (2012): 175–83, https://content.sph.harvard .edu/ecpe/CourseMats/IPHM/2012_09_27_1350_VELABUENO_02.pdf.

202 *More rest:* "Road Trip! Health Net Points Out the Health Benefits of Vacations," Health Net, https://www.healthnet.com/portal/home/content/iwc/home/articles /health_benefits_of_vacations.action.

202 *An analysis by:* Eric Klinger, "Goal Commitments and the Content of Thoughts and Dreams: Basic Principles," *Frontiers in Psychology* 4 (2013): 1, https://www .frontiersin.org/articles/10.3389/fpsyg.2013.00415/full.

203 *Harvard Medical School:* Erin J. Wamsley, Matthew Tucker, Jessica D. Payne, Joseph Benavides, and Robert Stickgold, "Dreaming of a Learning Task is Associated with Enhanced Sleep-Dependent Memory Consolidation," *Current Biology* 20, no 9 (2010), 850–55, https://www.ncbi.nlm.nih.gov/pmc/articles/PMC2869395/; Denise Mann, "Naps Boost Memory, but Only if You Dream," CNN, April 23, 2010, https://www.cnn.com/2010/HEALTH/04/22/naps.memory.dream.brain /?hpt=Sbin.

203 *Scientists have long theorized:* Andrew G. Haldane, "The Dog and the Frisbee," speech delivered at the Federal Reserve Bank of Kansas City's 366th economic policy symposium "The Changing Policy Landscape," Jackson Hole, Wyoming, August 31, 2012, https://www.bis.org/review/r120905a.pdf.

203 *What's more, when the:* Steve Calechman, "Sleep to Solve a Problem," Harvard Health Publishing, May 24, 2021, https://www.health.harvard.edu/blog/sleep-to-solve-a-problem-202105242463.

203 *There's evidence that our:* B. J. Shannon, R. A. Dosenbach, A. G. Vlassenko, L. J. Larson-Prior, T. S. Nolan, and M. E. Raichle, "Morning-Evening Variation in Human Brain Metabolism and Memory Circuits," *Journal of Neurophysiology* 109, no. 5 (2013): 1444–56, https://journals.physiology.org/doi/full/10.1152/jn.00651.2012.

203 *Thomas Edison:* Jeffrey Kluger, "The Spark of Invention," *Time*, November 14, 2013, https://techland.time.com/2013/11/14/the-spark-of-invention/.

203 *Winston Churchill:* Jeremy Campbell, *Winston Churchill's Afternoon Nap: A Wide-Awake Inquiry into the Human Nature of Time* (London: Aurum Press, 1988).

204 *Nintendo video game:* Eric Mack, "5 Strange Places Famous Creators Do Their Best Thinking," *Inc.*, October 24, 2016, https://www.inc.com/eric-mack/5-strange-places-famous-creators-do-their-best-thinking.html.

204 *Director Ingmar Bergman:* "Famous People Who Worked Less than You," Captain Time, https://captaintime.com/famous-people-who-worked-less-than-you/.

204 *Stephen King:* Lane Florsheim, "Stephen King's Daily Routine Involves Four Hours of Writing and a Nap in the Afternoon," *Wall Street Journal*, June 7, 2021, https://www.wsj.com/articles/stephen-kings-daily-routine-involves-four-hours-of-writing-and-a-nap-in-the-afternoon-11623068593.

204 *People who use their vacation days:* Shawn Achor and Michelle Gielan, "The Data-Driven Case for Vacation," *Harvard Business Review*, July 13, 2016, https://hbr.org/2016/07/the-data-driven-case-for-vacation.

204 *Deborah S. Linnell:* Deborah S. Linnell and Tim Wolfred, "Creative Disruption: Sabbaticals for Capacity Building and Leadership Development in the Nonprofit Sector," NCFP, 2009, https://www.ncfp.org/wp-content/uploads/2007/02/Creative-Disruption-Sabbatical-Durfee-2016.pdf.

204 *He likens the:* Author interview with Jonathan Schooler, February 2, 2020.

205 *George Spencer-Brown:* George Spencer-Brown, *Laws of Form* (New York: Julian Press, 1972), 110.

206 *That incubation period:* Rachel Mucha, "Employees Are Ready to Quit—with or without a New Job Secured," *HR Morning*, October 11, 2021, https://www.hrmorning.com/news/employees-quitting/?utm_source=Charter&utm_campaign=8c3be037fd-EMAIL_CAMPAIGN_2021_09_27_11_40_COPY_01&utm_medium=email&utm_term=0_8de2b7fe0d-8c3be037fd-1339922772.

206 *The initial shutdown:* Author interview with Lucy Chang Evans, May 17, 2021.

207 *"That clean break":* Author interview with Lucy Chang Evans, April 27, 2022.

207 *"I feel like I'm not":* Author interview with Lucy Chang Evans, May 17, 2021.

207 *When the* New York Times: Jonathan Malesic, "The Pandemic Reminded Us: We Exist To Do More than Just Work," *New York Times*, September 23, 2021,

https://www.nytimes.com/interactive/2021/09/23/opinion/covid-return-to
-work-rto.html?referringSource=articleShare.

207 *"Think back":* Celeste Headlee, *Do Nothing: How to Break Away from Overworking, Overdoing, and Overliving* (New York: Random House/Harmony Books, 2020), 126, 128.

209 *Six decades ago:* Nathaniel Kleitman, "The Basic Rest-Activity Cycle and Physiological Correlates of Dreaming," *Experimental Neurology* 19 (suppl., 1967): 2–4, https://www.sciencedirect.com/science/article/pii/0014488667901513.

209 *Nineteenth-century:* Alex Soojung-Kim Pang, "Darwin Was a Slacker and You Should Be Too," *Nautilus*, March 28, 2017, https://nautil.us/darwin-was-a-slacker -and-you-should-be-too-6001/.

209 *K. Anders Ericsson:* K. Anders Ericsson, Ralf Th. Krampe, and Clemens Tesch-Romer, "The Role of Deliberate Practice in the Acquisition of Expert Performance," *Psychological Review* 100, no. 3 (1993): 363–406, https://graphics8 .nytimes.com/images/blogs/freakonomics/pdf/DeliberatePractice(Psychological Review).pdf.

210 *Aristotle was a big booster:* David Charles, "Aristotle on Well-being and Intellectual Contemplation," *Aristotelian Society Supplementary* 73, no. 1 (1999): 205–23, https://academic.oup.com/aristoteliansupp/article-abstract/73/1/205/17780 15?redirectedFrom=fulltext.

210 *After Captain John Smith:* John Smith, *The Generall Historie of Virginia* (Chapel Hill: University of North Carolina Library, 2006).

211 *It's no coincidence:* Benjamin Franklin, *The Way to Wealth* [1757], edited by Richard A. Catalina (Princeton, NJ: Princeton Cambridge Publishing Group, 2010).

211 *Schoolmarms taught:* Roger B. Hill, "The Work Ethic and the Industrial Revolution," History of Work Ethic, 1996, http://workethic.coe.uga.edu/hir.html.

211 *Economists estimate:* Robert Whaples, "Hours of Work in US History," EH.net Encyclopedia, August 14, 2001, https://eh.net/encyclopedia/hours-of-work-in -u-s-history/.

211 *He bemoaned:* William James, "The Gospel of Relaxation."

212 *Economist Thorstein Veblen:* Thorstein Veblen, *The Theory of the Leisure Class* (New York: Macmillan, 1899).

212 *"careless people":* F. Scott Fitzgerald, *The Great Gatsby* (New York: Scribner's, 1925), 105.

213 *Indeed, economist:* John Maynard Keynes, "Economic Possibilities for Our Grandchildren," in Keynes, *Essays in Persuasion* (W. W. Norton & Co., 1963), 358–73.

213 *Nikola Tesla:* Andrew Schwedel, James Root, James Allen, John Hazan, Eric Almquist, Thomas Devlin, and Karen Harris, "The Working Future: More Human, Not Less," Bain & Company, 2022, https://www.bain.com/insights/the -working-future-more-human-not-less-future-of-work-report/.

213 *Fully one-quarter:* "Work and Workplace," *Gallup News*, https://news.gallup .com/poll/1720/work-work-place.aspx (accessed June 24, 2022).

213 *global study of workers:* Pega et al., "Global, regional, and national burdens of ischemic heart disease and stroke attributable to exposure to long working hours for 194 countries, 2000–2016: A systematic analysis from the WHO/ILO Joint Estimates of the Work-related Burden of Disease and Injury," Environmental International, Vol. 154, September 2021, https://www.sciencedirect.com/science/article/pii/S0160412021002208

214 *a trial in Iceland:* "Four-Day Week 'an Overwhelming Success' in Iceland," BBC, July 6, 2021, https://www.bbc.com/news/business-57724779.

214 *Meanwhile, Salesforce:* Kyle Hagerty, "Six Lease Terminations Driven by Remote Work," Propmodo, January 24, 2022, https://www.propmodo.com/six-lease-terminations-driven-by-remote-work/?utm_source=Charter&utm_campaign=ebde254b63-EMAIL_CAMPAIGN_2022_01_29_11_51&utm_medium=email&utm_term=0_8de2b7fe0d-ebde254b63-1339922772.

215 *Americans in 2019:* "Census Bureau Estimates Show Average One-Way Travel Time to Work Rises to All-Time High," US Census Bureau, March 18, 2021, https://www.census.gov/newsroom/press-releases/2021/one-way-travel-time-to-work-rises.html#:~:text=In%202019%2C%20the%20average%20one,about%2010%25%20over%2014%20years; Max Knoblauch, "Americans Spend 19 Full Work Days a Year Stuck in Traffic on Their Commutes," *New York Post*, April 19, 2019, https://nypost.com/2019/04/19/americans-spend-19-full-work-days-a-year-stuck-in-traffic-on-their-commute/.

216 *"I did some soul":* Author interview with Britt and Kari Altizer, May 18, 2021.

216 *"Covid was a cue":* Author interview with Britt and Kari Altizer, May 13, 2022.

Chapter 8: Find Your "Expert Companion"

218 *"I was sitting":* Tess Bonn, "Ina Garten on How She Went from Being a Nuclear Budget Analyst to an Iconic Chef," Katie Couric Media, December 21, 2021, https://katiecouric.com/podcast/next-question/ina-garten-going-there/.

219 *"A grocery store!":* Enid Nemy, "Exchanging Standard Careers for Dreams," *New York Times*, August 7, 1981, https://www.nytimes.com/1981/08/07/style/exchanging-standard-careers-for-dreams.html.

219 *"This is the stupidest":* Anneta Konstantinides, "Ina Garten Says She Quit Her White House Job to Buy a Grocery Shop at the Age of 30 Thanks to Advice from Her Husband," *Insider*, October 21, 2020, https://www.insider.com/ina-garten-left-white-house-job-became-famous-cook-2020-10.

219 *"I forced myself":* Ina Garten, *Cooking for Jeffrey: A Barefoot Contessa Cookbook* (New York: Clarkson Potter, 2016), 14–15.

220 *"Those early days":* Garten, *Cooking for Jeffrey*, 16.

220 *"It just takes one person":* Tess Bonn, "Ina Garten on How She Went from a Nuclear Budget Analyst to an Iconic Chef," Katie Couric Media, December 21, 2021, https://katiecouric.com/podcast/next-question/ina-garten-going-there/

222 *Jim VandeHei:* Jim VandeHei, "Find Your Tough-Love Life Coach," *Axios*, April 14, 2022, https://www.axios.com/2022/04/15/find-your-tough-love-life

-coach?utm_source=newsletter&utm_medium=email&utm_campaign=newsletter
_axiosfinishline&stream=top.

223 *It was there that:* Author interview with Christopher and Amy Handy, March 31, 2022.

224 *"As a lead flight":* Debra Spark, "Career Pivots," *Yale Alumni Magazine*, January/February 2022, https://yalealumnimagazine.org/articles/5422-career-pivots.

224 *His entire knowledge:* Jessica Fecteau, "Ina Garten's Husband 'Chef Jeffrey' Adorably Shows How to Make 'the Perfect Cup of Coffee,'" *People*, December 21, 2018, https://people.com/food/ina-garten-husband-jeffrey-making-perfect-cup-of-coffee-instagram/.

225 *"Since you were a child":* Danny Meyer, *Setting the Table: The Transforming Power of Hospitality in Business* (New York: HarperCollins, 2006), 29–30.

226 *"I knew":* Author interview with Danny Meyer, January 15, 2021.

226 *"We can only imagine":* Grant, *Originals*, 13.

227 *Yes, she was highly:* Author interview with Cyndi Stivers, November 9, 2020.

227 *Boston Consulting Group:* Roselinde Torres, Martin Reeves, Peter Tollman, and Christian Veith, "The Rewards of CEO Reflection," Boston Consulting Group, June 29, 2017, https://www.bcg.com/publications/2017/leadership-talent-people-organization-rewards-ceo-reflection.

228 *She instructs the women:* Author interview with Jane Veron, February 7, 2022.

228 *Fifty years:* Mark S. Granovetter, "The Strength of Weak Ties," *American Journal of Sociology* 78, no. 6 (1973): 1360–80, https://snap.stanford.edu/class/cs224w-readings/granovetter73weakties.pdf.

229 *"It is remarkable":* Granovetter, "The Strength of Weak Ties," 1372.

229 *About a decade ago:* Daniel Z. Levin, Jorge Walter, and J. Keith Murnighan, "Dormant Ties: The Value of Reconnecting," *Organization Science* 22, no. 4 (2011): 923–39, https://www.jstor.org/stable/20868904?refreqid=excelsior%3Aa20ffceb7a6bb092f9282d012887e85e&ab_segments=&origin=.

230 *"Before contacting them":* Daniel Z. Levin, Jorge Walter, and J. Keith Murnighan, "The Power of *Reconnection*—How Dormant Ties Can Surprise You," *MIT Sloan Management Review*, March 23, 2011, https://sloanreview.mit.edu/article/the-power-of-reconnection-how-dormant-ties-can-surprise-you/.

230 *As a side benefit:* Ian Leslie, "Why Your 'Weak-Tie' Friendships May Mean More than You Think," The Life Project, BBC, July 2, 2020, https://www.bbc.com/worklife/article/20200701-why-your-weak-tie-friendships-may-mean-more-than-you-think.

230 *Gillian Sandstrom:* Gillian M. Sandstrom and Elizabeth W. Dunn, "Social Interactions and Well-being: The Surprising Power of Weak Ties," *Personality and Social Psychology Bulletin* 40, no. 7 (2014): 910–22, https://journals.sagepub.com/doi/pdf/10.1177/0146167214529799.

231 *Over your lifetime:* "Dunbar's Number: Why We Can Only Maintain 150 Relationships," BBC Future, BBC, 2019, https://www.bbc.com/future/article/20191001-dunbars-number-why-we-can-only-maintain-150-relationships.

231 *The expert companion:* Richard G. Tedeschi and Bret A. Moore, *The Posttraumatic Growth Workbook* (Oakland, CA: New Harbinger Publications, 2016).

232 *In a series of studies:* Alison Wood Brooks, Francesca Gino, and Maurice E. Schweitzer, "Smart People Ask for (My) Advice: Seeking Advice Boosts Perceptions of Competence," *Management Science* 61, no. 6 (2015): 1421–35, https://static1.squarespace.com/static/55dcde36e4b0df55a96ab220/t/55e74acce4b0c94c8afb6b97/1441221324825/smart+advice.pdf.

233 *In a separate study:* Karen Huang, Michael Yeomans, Alison Wood Brooks, Julia Minson, and Francesca Gino, "It Doesn't Hurt to Ask: Question-Asking Increases Liking," *Journal of Personality and Social Psychology* 113, no. 3 (2018): 430–52, https://static1.squarespace.com/static/55dcde36e4b0df55a96ab220/t/59aeffd0a803bbdf2bc1bbee/1504640999506/1+Huang+et+al+2017.pdf.

233 *A 2015 study:* Sarah Gardner and Dave Albee, "Study Focuses on Strategies for Achieving Goals, Resolutions," Dominican University of California, February 1, 2015, https://scholar.dominican.edu/cgi/viewcontent.cgi?article=1265&context=news-releases.

234 *It's important:* Herminia Ibarra, *Working Identity: Unconventional Strategies for Reinventing Your Career* (Boston: Harvard Business Review Press, 2004), xii.

235 *Her encouragement was:* Author interview with Glen Mazzara, March 3, 2021.

235 *The expert companion:* Tedeschi and Moore, *The Posttraumatic Growth Workbook.*

236 *Yet while he liked:* Author interview with Khemaridh Hy, November 23, 2020.

237 *As the newsletter:* Heather Long, "Meet Khe Hy, the Oprah for Millennials," CNN Business, December 31, 2016, https://money.cnn.com/2016/12/30/news/economy/khemaridh-hy-rad-reads-oprah-for-millennials/.

239 *We hadn't seen:* Joanne Lipman, "And the Orchestra Played On," *New York Times*, February 27, 2010, https://www.nytimes.com/2010/02/28/opinion/28lipman.html.

Chapter 9: Lessons from Play-Doh

242 *At a time:* "How Long Do Firms Live? Finding Patterns of Company Mortality in Market Data," *Science Daily*, April 1, 2015, https://www.sciencedaily.com/releases/2015/04/150401132856.htm.

243 *In fact:* Brian Merchant, *The One Device: The Secret History of the iPhone* (Boston: Little, Brown & Co., 2017).

244 *Other companies:* Adam Robinson, "Want to Boost Your Bottom Line? Encourage Your Employees to Work on Side Projects," *Inc.*, March 12, 2018, https://www.inc.com/adam-robinson/google-employees-dedicate-20-percent-of-their-time-to-side-projects-heres-how-it-works.html.

244 *One of the unlikeliest:* Kat Eschner, "The Surprising Origins of Kotex Pads," *Smithsonian*, August 11, 2017, https://www.smithsonianmag.com/innovation/surprising-origins-kotex-pads-180964466/. See also Thomas Heinrich and Bob Batchelor, *Kotex, Kleenex, Huggies: Kimberly-Clark and the Consumer Revolution in American Business* (Columbus: Ohio State University Press, 2004).

245 *"In the past":* Ben M. Bensaou, *Built to Innovate: Essential Practices to Wire Innovation into Your Company's DNA* (New York: McGraw-Hill Education, 2021), 30.

246 *"fail to recognize":* Bensaou, *Built to Innovate*, 12.

247 *According to lore:* "History of America's Favorite Sandwiches," What's Cooking America, https://whatscookingamerica.net/history/sandwichhistory.htm (accessed June 29, 2022).

247 *He was just being:* Ian Osterloh, "How I Discovered Viagra," *Cosmos*, April 27, 2015, https://cosmosmagazine.com/science/biology/how-i-discovered-viagra/.

247 *"I wasn't thinking":* Author interview with Ian Osterloh, December 11, 2020.

248 *The male participants:* Author interview with Ian Osterloh, December 11, 2020.

248 *While the medication:* Author interview with Ian Osterloh, May 17, 2022.

248 *"The drug had":* Author interview with Ian Osterloh, December 11, 2020.

249 *"In Sandwich":* Author interview with Ian Osterloh, May 17, 2022.

249 *"There were people":* Author interview with Ian Osterloh, December 11, 2020.

249 *Still, resistance was:* Author interview with Ian Osterloh, December 11, 2020.

250 *"I think if":* Author interview with Ian Osterloh, May 17, 2022.

250 *"I was like a man":* Author interview with Ian Osterloh, December 11, 2020.

250 *"Impotence is":* Author interview with Janice Lipsky, December 10, 2020.

251 *with former senator:* "Bob Dole ED Commercial," YouTube, August 24, 2017, https://www.youtube.com/watch?v=Kjhc0-6eSiw.

253 *The company is famous:* Nancy Hass, "And the Award for the Next HBO Goes to . . . ," *GQ*, January 29, 2013, https://www.gq.com/story/netflix-founder-reed-hastings-house-of-cards-arrested-development?mobify=0.

253 *"Volunteering to":* Robert Kyncl, "The Inside Story of How Netflix Transitioned to Digital Video after Seeing the Power of YouTube," *Vox*, September 13, 2017, https://www.vox.com/2017/9/13/16288364/streampunks-book-excerpt-youtube-netflix-pivot-video.

254 *"I saw grainy videos":* Kyncl, "The Inside Story of How Netflix Transitioned to Digital Video."

255 *"Let me be clear":* Reed Hastings and Erin Meyer, *No Rules Rules: Netflix and the Culture of Reinvention* (New York: Penguin, 2020), 148.

255 *"Mr. Lutz doesn't do":* Paul Ingrassia, "Can Bob Lutz Shake GM Out of Its Stupor?," *Wall Street Journal*, August 7, 2001. https://www.wsj.com/articles/SB99714198046556057.

256 *"Chrysler products":* Author interview with Robert Lutz, December 4, 2020.

256 *It was:* Craig Jamieson, "Top Gear's Guilty Pleasures: The Original Dodge Viper," BBC TopGear, December 30, 2021, https://www.topgear.com/car-news/opinion/top-gears-guilty-pleasures-original-dodge-viper.

256 *Corporate finance:* Alden M. Hayashi, "When to Trust Your Gut," *Harvard Business Review*, February 2001, https://hbr.org/2001/02/when-to-trust-your-gut.

256 *"with its head-turning":* Ingrassia, "Can Bob Lutz Shake GM Out of Its Stupor?," *Wall Street Journal*, August 7, 2001.

257 *He and his team:* Bob Lutz, "How the 1993 Jeep Grand Cherokee Changed Car-Show Debuts Forever," *Road and Track*, November 27, 2019, https://www.road andtrack.com/car-culture/a29356030/bob-lutz-grand-cherokee-debut/.

257 *"You do something":* Author interview with Robert Lutz, December 4, 2020.

257 *When University of Chicago:* Lingfei Wu, Dashun Wang, and James A. Evans, "Large Teams Develop and Small Teams Disrupt Science and Technology," *Nature* 566 (2019): 378–82, https://www.nature.com/articles/s41586-019 -0941-9.

258 *Bruce D. Fischer:* Bruce D. Fischer and Matthew Rohde, "Feedback and Follow-through: Cornerstones of Innovation," *American Journal of Management* 13, no. 3 (2013): 39–45, http://www.na-businesspress.com/AJM/FischerBD_Web13_3 _.pdf.

259 *It had been a big hit:* Davin Hiskey, "The Shocking Story behind Playdoh's Original Purpose," *Business Insider*, September 20, 2015, https://www.businessinsider .com/the-shocking-story-behind-playdohs-original-purpose-2015-9.

260 *forty-six years old:* "Local Manufacturer Killed in Plane Crash after Battling Fog over Eastern Airports," *Cincinnati Enquirer*, November 5, 1949, https://www .newspapers.com/clip/15283448/1944-president-cleophus-mcvicker-plane/.

261 *in the decades afterward:* Zoë Chafe, Michael Brauer, Marie-Eve Héroux, Zbigniew Klimont, Timo Lanki, Raimo O. Salonen, and Kirk R. Smith "Residential Heating with Wood and Coal: Health Impacts and Policy Options in Europe and North America," World Health Organization, 2015, https://www.euro .who.int/__data/assets/pdf_file/0009/271836/ResidentialHeatingWoodCoal HealthImpacts.pdf.

262 *"Kutol was":* Author interview with Juliet McVicker, October 12, 2020.

262 *"The brassy":* Author interview with David Zufall, October 3, 2020.

263 *"She was difficult":* Author interview with Margaret Zufall Roberts, December 17, 2020.

263 *Dr. Zufall:* Author interview with Robert Zufall, December 15, 2020.

264 *Play-Doh aroma:* Tim Walsh, *Timeless Toys: Classic Toys and the Playmakers Who Created Them* (Kansas City, MO: Andrews McMeel Publishing, 2005), 118.

264 *"Today, in this digital":* Author interview with Mary Noyes, October 9, 2020.

265 *"it was a big":* Author interview with Juliet McVicker, December 14, 2020.

265 *"Captain Kangaroo":* Author interview with Juliet McVicker, October 12, 2020.

266 *More than two thousand:* Whitney Joiner, Alexa McMahon, and Richard Just, eds., "Local News Deserts Are Expanding: Here's What We'll Lose," *Washington Post Magazine*, November 30, 2021, https://www.washingtonpost.com/magazine /interactive/2021/local-news-deserts-expanding/.

266 *"People who have":* Dean A. Shepherd, Vinit Parida, and Joakim Wincent, "The Surprising Duality of Jugaad: Low Firm Growth and High Inclusive Growth," *Journal of Management Studies* 57, no. 1 (2017): 87–128, https://www.diva -portal.org/smash/get/diva2:1340790/FULLTEXT01.pdf.

267 *The payday:* "Millionaires: How They Do It," *Time,* December 3, 1965, http://content.time.com/time/subscriber/article/0,33009,842283,00.html.

268 *recalled years later:* "Playmakers Part II: Play-Doh," Parents' Choice: Children's Media & Toy Reviews, 2009, http://archive.parentschoice.org/print_article.cfm?art_id=237&the_page=editorials (site discontinued).

Epilogue: Next! A Tool Kit

274 *Psychologists Hazel Markus and Paula Nurius:* Hazel Markus and Paula Nurius, "Possible Selves," *American Psychologist* 41, no. 9 (September 1986), https://web.stanford.edu/~hazelm/publications/1986_Markus%20&%20Nurius_Possible Selves.pdf.

276 *Reams of research:* Vivian Giang, "What LinkedIn Data Reveals about Who Will Help You Get Your Next Job," *Fast Company,* June 14, 2016, https://www.fastcompany.com/3060887/what-linkedin-data-reveals-about-who-will-help-you-get-your-next-job.

276 *What's more, when researchers:* Daniel Z. Levin, Jorge Walter, and J. Keith Murnighan, "Dormant Ties: The Value of Reconnecting," *Organization Science* 22, no. 4 (2011): 923–39, https://www.jstor.org/stable/20868904?refreqid=excelsior%3Aa20ffceb7a6bb092f9282d012887e85e&ab_segments=&origin=.

276 *"Do something differently":* Isaac Fitzgerald, "It's Never Too Late to Publish a Debut Book and Score a Netflix Deal," *New York Times,* September 28, 2021, https://www.nytimes.com/2021/09/28/style/jocelyn-nicole-johnson-my-monticello-debut-book.html?tpcc=nlbroadsheet.

276 *A 2015 study:* Sarah Gardner and Dave Albee, "Study Focuses on Strategies for Achieving Goals, Resolutions," Dominican University of California, press release 266 February 1, 2015, https://scholar.dominican.edu/cgi/viewcontent.cgi?article=1265&context=news-releases.

277 *In a 2015 survey:* Linda A. Ovington, Anthony J. Saliba, Carmen C. Moran, Jeremy Goldring, and Jasmine B. MacDonald, "Do People Really Have Insights in the Shower?," *Journal of Creative Behavior* 52, no. 1 (2015): 21–34, https://onlinelibrary.wiley.com/doi/full/10.1002/jocb.126.

277 *Nonprofit leaders:* Deborah S. Linnell and Tim Wolfred, "Creative Disruption: Sabbaticals for Capacity Building and Leadership Development in the Nonprofit Sector," NCFP, 2009, https://www.ncfp.org/wp-content/uploads/2007/02/Creative-Disruption-Sabbatical-Durfee-2016.pdf.

277 *Even in the best of times:* Claire Zedelius, "Daydreaming Might Make You More Creative—but It Depends on What You Daydream About," *Behavioral Scientist,* November 2, 2020, https://behavioralscientist.org/daydreaming-might-make-you-more-creative-but-it-depends-on-what-you-daydream-about/; Matthew A. Killingsworth and Daniel T. Gilbert, "A Wandering Mind Is an Unhappy Mind," *Science* 330, no. 6006 (2010): 932, https://www.science.org/doi/10.1126/science.1192439; Jennifer Windt, "Our Minds May Be Wandering More

during the Pandemic—and This Can Be a Good Thing," *The Conversation*, October 30, 2020, https://www.weforum.org/agenda/2020/10/day-dreaming-mind-wandering-pandemic-covid19-coronavirus/.

277 *Psychologist K. Anders Ericsson:* K. Anders Ericsson, Ralf Th. Krampe, and Clemens Tesch-Romer, "The Role of Deliberate Practice in the Acquisition of Expert Performance," *Psychological Review* 100, no. 3 (1993): 363–406, https://graphics8.nytimes.com/images/blogs/freakonomics/pdf/DeliberatePractice(Psychological Review).pdf.

279 *When management professor:* Erik Dane, "Suddenly Everything Became Clear: How People Make Sense of Epiphanies Surrounding Their Work and Careers," *Academy of Management Discoveries* 6, no. 1 (2020): https://journals.aom.org/doi/abs/10.5465/amd.2018.0033.

Index